Aftermath of War in Europe
The West VS. the Global South?

Len Ishmael, Editor

Aftermath of War in Europe
The West VS. the Global South?

Copyright © 2022 by Policy Center for the New South. All rights reserved. No part of this work may be reproduced, stored in a retrieval system, or transmitted in any form or by any means, mechanical, electronic, photocopying, recording, or otherwise, without the prior written permission of the publisher.

Editor
Len Ishmael, Senior Fellow, Policy Center for the New South

General Coordination
Nabil El Qamçaoui, Program Officer, Policy Center for the New South

Editing
Septhen Gardner

Graphic Composition
Youssef Ait El Kadi, Senior Graphic Designer, Policy Center for the New South

Policy Center for the New South

Complexe Suncity, Immeuble C, Albortokal Street, Hay Riad, Rabat - Maroc
Email : contact@policycenter.ma
Phone : +212 5 37 54 04 04 / Fax : +212 5 37 71 31 54
Website : www.policycenter.ma

ISBN : 978-9920-633-27-7

Table of Contents

List of Contributors V

List of Acronyms VI

About the Policy Center for the New South X

Preface XI

Chapter I: A World Divided: A Multilayered, Multipolar World 1
Len Ishmael

Chapter II: Southeast Asia: A Tapestry of Economic and Security Ties in a Neighborhood of Superpower Competition 27
Christian Bachheimer

Chapter III: China and a New World Order After Ukraine 59
Marcus Vinicius De Freitas

Chapter IV: Turkey's Policy Response to War-Induced Economic Downturn and Geopolitical Shifts 81
Serhat S. Çubukçuoğlu

Chapter V: India's Rise to Global Stature: The Challenges of Strategic Autonomy 101
Rahul Sharma

Chapter VI: Latin America in the Aftermath of Europe's War 119
Otaviano Canuto

Chapter VII: Global Powers in North and West Africa 137
Rida Lyammouri & Amine Ghoulidi

Chapter VIII: African Debt Management in a Time of Pandemic and War .. 157
Abdelaaziz Aït Ali & Badr Mandri

Chapter IX: A World on the Brink: Implications for Global Supply Chains and Food Security for the Global South 181
Isabelle Tsakok

Chapter X: Sanctions and Energy Supplies: Challenges and Opportunities for the Global South 203
Rim Berahab

Chapter XI: The EU Carbon Border Adjustment Mechanism Amid Global Tensions: A Recipe for Disaster 225
Kevin Verbelen

Biographies 247

List of Contributors

- **Abdelaaziz Aït Ali**, Manager – Economics, Policy Center for the New South
- **Christian Bachheimer**, Doctoral Researcher, SOAS University
- **Rim Berahab**, Senior Economist, Policy Center for the New South
- **Otaviano Canuto**, Senior Fellow, Policy Center for the New South
- **Serhat S. Çubukçuoğlu**, Independent Senior Consultant
- **Marcus Vinicius De Freitas**, Senior Fellow, Policy Center for the New South
- **Amine Ghoulidi**, Researcher, King's College London
- **Len Ishmael**, Senior Fellow, Policy Center for the New South
- **Rida Lyammouri**, Senior Fellow, Policy Center for the New South
- **Badr Mandri**, Economist, Policy Center for the New South
- **Rahul Sharma,** Senior Public Affairs Consultant
- **Isabelle Tsakok**, Senior Fellow, Policy Center for the New South
- **Kevin Verbelen**, Expert International Trade & Company Lawyer, Agoria

List of Acronyms

ADMM	ASEAN Defense Minister Meeting
AfCFTA	African Continental Free Trade Area
AfDB	African Development Bank
ADFC	African Diaspora Finance Corporation
AKP	Justice and Development Party's
AFPM	American Fuel and Petrochemical Manufacturers
AFSM	African Financial Stability Mechanism
AFRICOM	Special Operations at Africa Command
AIIB	Asia Infrastructure Investment Bank
AOIP	ASEAN Outlook for Indo Pacific
ASEAN	Association of Southeast Asian Nations
AUKUS	Australia, United Kingdom, and United States' alliance
BIS	Bureau of Industry and Security
BJP	Bharatiya Janata Party
BNDES	National Economic and Social Development Bank
BRI	Belt and Road Initiative
BRICS	Brazil, Russia, India, China, and South Africa
CAATSA	Countering America's Adversaries Through Sanctions Act
CAF	Development Bank of Latin America
CARI	China-Africa Research Initiative
CBAM	Carbon Border Adjustment Mechanism
CBJ	Congressional Budget Justification for Foreign Operations
CCP	Chinese Communist Party
CEO	Chief Executive Officer
CH4	Methane
CICDA	China International Cooperation Development Agency
CIPS	Cross Border Interbank Payment System
CMR	Conflict Minerals Regulation
CO2	Carbon Dioxide
CoC	Code of Conduct
CPC	Chinese Communist Party
CPEC	China-Pakistan Economic Corridor
CS3D	Corporate Sustainability Due Diligence Directive
CSP	Comprehensive Strategic Partnership
DSSI	Debt Service Suspension Initiative
DSA	Debt Sustainability Analysis
EAC	East African Community
EAS	East Asia Summit
EFTA	European Free Trade Area
ELI	Export-Led Industrialization
EMDEs	Emerging Markets and Developing Economies

EPC	European Political Community
ETS	Emission Trading System
EU	European Union
EUCAP	European Union Capacity Building Mission
EV	Electrical Vehicle
FDI	Foreign Direct Investment
FIF	Financial Intermediary Fund
FLR	Forced Labour Regulation
FSH	Food Security
FSS	Food Self-Sufficiency
FSY	Food Sovereignty
FTA	Free Trade Agreement
GATT	General Agreement on Tariffs and Trade
GDP	Gross Domestic Product
GHG	Green House Gas
GPS	Global Positioning System
GVCs	Global Value Chains
HFCs	Hydrofluorocarbons
HIPC	Heavily Indebted Poor Countries
ICT	Information and Communications Technology
IDA	International Development Association
ICJ	International Court of Justice
IFFs	Illicit Financial Flows
IIRSA	South American Regional Infrastructure Integration
IMF	International Monetary Fund
IOCs	International Oil Companies
IPCEI	Important Project of Common European Interest
ISI	Import-Substitution Industrialization
IDB	Inter-American Development Bank
IPEF	Indo-Pacific Economic Framework for Prosperity
ISIS	Islamic State of Irak and Syria
LAC	Latin American and Caribbean
LDC	Least Developed Countries
LMC	Lancang Mekong Cooperation
LNG	Liquefied Natural Gas
LPG	Liquefied Petroleum Gas
LULUCF	Land Use and Land Use Change and Forestry
MBS	Mohammed Bin Salman
MDBs	Multilateral Development Banks
MDRI	Multilateral Debt Relief Initiative
MERCOSUR	Southern Common Market
MFN	Most Favored Nation
MTS	Multilateral Trading System

MINUSMA	United Nations Multidimensional Integrated Stabilization Mission in Mali
N20	Nitrous Oxide
NAFTA	North American Free Trade Agreement
NAM	Non-Aligned Movement
NATO	North Atlantic Treaty Organization
NF3	Nitrogen Trifluoride
NDB	New Development Bank
NSS	National Security Strategy
NOx	Nitrogen Oxide
ODI	Outbound Direct Investment
OECD	Organization for Economic Co-operation and Development
OPEC	Organization of the Petroleum Exporting Countries
PFCs	Perfluorocarbons
PPP	Purchasing Power Parity
PPR	Pandemic Prevention, Preparedness, and Response
PPRFIF	Pandemic Prevention, Preparedness, and Response Financial Intermediary Fund
PRC	People's Republic of China
PRGT	Poverty Reduction and Growth Trust
QUAD	Quadrilateral Security Dialogue
RCEP	Regional Comprehensive Economic Partnership
RECs	Regional Economic Communities
RIC	Russia-India-China
RUW	Russia-Ukraine War
SCO	Shanghai Cooperation Organization
SCS	South China Sea
SDR	Special Drawings Rights
SDT	Special and Differential Treatment
SF6	Sulphur Hexafluoride
SOEs	State-owned enterprises
SPFS	Financial Messaging System of the Bank of Russia
SSA	Sub-Saharan Africa
SWIFT	Society for Worldwide Interbank Financial Telecommunication
UAE	United Arab Emirates
UAV	Unmanned Aerial Vehicle
UN	United Nations
UNASUR	Union of South American Nations
UNCLOS	United Nations Convention on the Law of the Sea
UNCTAD	United Nations Conference on Trade and Development
UNFCCC	United Nations Framework Convention on Climate Change
UNGA	United Nations General Assembly
UNSC	United Nations Security Council
UK	United Kingdom

USA	United States of America
USAID	US Agency for International Development
USD	United States Dollar
USMCA	United States Mexico Canada Agreement
USSR	Union of Soviet Socialist Republics
VEOs	Violent Extremist Organizations
WHO	World Health Organization
WFP	World Food Programme
WTI	West Texas Intermediate
WTO	World Trade Organization

About the Policy Center for the New South

The Policy Center for the New South (PCNS) is a Moroccan think tank aiming to contribute to the improvement of economic and social public policies that challenge Morocco and the rest of Africa as integral parts of the global South.

The PCNS pleads for an open, accountable and enterprising "new South" that defines its own narratives and mental maps around the Mediterranean and South Atlantic basins, as part of a forward-looking relationship with the rest of the world. Through its analytical endeavours, the think tank aims to support the development of public policies in Africa and to give the floor to experts from the South. This stance is focused on dialogue and partnership, and aims to cultivate African expertise and excellence needed for the accurate analysis of African and global challenges and the suggestion of appropriate solutions.

As such, the PCNS brings together researchers, publishes their work and capitalizes on a network of renowned partners, representative of different regions of the world. The PCNS hosts a series of gatherings of different formats and scales throughout the year, the most important being the annual international conferences "The Atlantic Dialogues" and "African Peace and Security Annual Conference" (APSACO).

Finally, the think tank is developing a community of young leaders through the Atlantic Dialogues Emerging Leaders program(ADEL) a space for cooperation and networking between a new generation of decision-makers from the government, business and civil society sectors. Through this initiative, which already counts more than 300 members, the Policy Center for the New South contributes to intergenerational dialogue and the emergence of tomorrow's leaders.

www.policycenter.ma

Preface

This publication provides an insight into the lens through which countries of the Global South view the current period of successive crises, brought about by an ongoing global pandemic and a war in Europe. It highlights how the combined weight of history, culture, and geography has shaped the Global South's interests and is influencing its foreign policy stance during one of the most dangerous periods of Great-Power competition in recent times—one that could see the fracturing of the world into different blocs.

Russia's invasion of Ukraine on February 24, 2022, and the Western sanctions imposed in retaliation, have unleashed a domino-like sequencing of effects and consequences, not only for the two countries at war, but for the world. The war has come on the heels of more than two years of a pandemic that has affected global supply chains and output, and has impacted the world's poorest countries even more severely. The World Bank estimates that developing countries added at least 45% of new debt to already unsustainable burdens, in an effort to manage the health crisis and deal with its most egregious economic and social effects. Millions have been pushed back into poverty. Debt repayments, suspended for a short period at the height of the pandemic, resumed in 2022 with stark warnings from the International Monetary Fund (IMF) about the debt-distressed situation of several countries. Zambia and Mali have defaulted on their sovereign debts, so has Sri Lanka, for the first time in its history. Others are on the brink.

The consequences of default are significant. Default affects a country's ability to access capital markets. It increases the cost of borrowing, undermines investor confidence, exerts downward pressure on the local currency and can lead to the roll back of years of working towards gains in the delivery of social goods and services. Egypt has devalued its currency as a precursor to its recent request for standby facilities from the IMF. This will impact prices, inflaming already heightened social tensions. Tunisia has reached preliminary agreement with the IMF for a $1.9 billion loan. Inflationary pressures, and soaring food and energy prices associated with the effects of the war, have exacerbated an ongoing crisis first precipitated by the COVID-19 pandemic. These two crises and their combined effects have dimmed, even further, prospects for global economic recovery, with no end in sight.

Russia's invasion of Ukraine has united the western world more swiftly and robustly than expected, and has strengthened the resolve of the transatlantic partners to stay the course in a relationship that, even under the Biden Administration has proven to be challenging. There is a sense of fierce reaffirmation of the ideals that bind Atlantic partners to each other, to NATO, and to their allies. Yet there is also a sense that the world order in place since the Second World War is being upended, and trends that were emerging at the beginning of the pandemic have now coalesced and are accelerating.

Countries of the Global South and some others have mostly declined to implement Western sanctions against Russia. They represent more than half of the world's population and their shares of global economic resources and output are significant, and growing. In this conflict they have adopted a neutral stance. Interests are intertwined and too complex. They seek an end to the war and yearn for conditions of stability to allow global economic recovery to take place, and issues of global governance to be addressed. The level of sanctions deployed against Russia is unprecedented in modern history, and many of these countries ponder a future in which seats at the table of global governance and rule-making shrink, rather than expand, reducing the options available to them. Such a world does not promote their interests and they are pursuing various modalities to secure the future they need and want. Deepening and enlarging distinctly non-Western alliances is one such option. This only enhances the view that a two-bloc world is in the making.

At the same time, the European Union's (EU) drive to wean itself from Russian oil and gas, while promoting opportunities for greater exports from Africa and other countries of the Global South, raises awkward and vexing questions. So too does the EU's renewed efforts to enact carbon taxes on the border of the single market—with significant implications for countries of the Global South. This not only raises new issues at the World Trade Organization (WTO), but its timing comes at the very moment when these countries need to trade their way out of poverty and relieve the burden of significant debt, which has accrued during the pandemic and the war. This publication frames the voices of the Global South and their pronouncement on the multiplicity of issues arising from this period of disruption and Great-Power rivalry. The very act of their neutrality and the deepening of alliances with 'like-minded' others is accelerating a period of change in the international structure. For all countries, for the West and the rest of the world, the stakes are high.

We thank the many colleagues whose efforts were instrumental in supporting the final product, and wish also to acknowledge the assistance of Avantika Singha in compiling the background research that contributed to the chapter on India. Finally, I wish to specially recognize the superb efforts of my PCNS colleague Nabil El Qamçaoui, who provided invaluable support to me over the course of an entire year in moving an early idea for this publication through all the stages and across the finish line. His unflagging dedication, enthusiasm, and skill in navigating the logistics and countless details along the way, have been priceless.

Dr. Len Ishmael
Editor & Senior Fellow, Policy Center for the New South
Horta, Faial, Azores
November 2022

CHAPTER I

A World Divided: A Multilayered, Multipolar World

Len Ishmael

These are extraordinary times, punctuated by two historic shocks in rapid succession. A global pandemic and a war in Europe caused by Russia's invasion of Ukraine on February 24, 2022, have ushered in a period of profound change on the geopolitical landscape. The decade of the 2020's might well rank among the most consequential in recent times, as geography, history, and Great Power competition threaten fragmentation of the world into a two-bloc configuration, except that today's configuration is balanced by other factors. The international structure with two superpowers - one declining (the United States), openly pursuing a strategy of containment, the other rising (China), increasingly asserting its 'rightful place' is accompanied by increasing multipolarity, as a number of countries, mainly from the Global South, transform their increasing economic *heft* into soft power, deepening and expanding their reach through an array of bilateral and non-western multilateral arrangements. A multilayered, multipolarity is being seeded across the international structure, adding new dimensions to the world order, in a process that has deepened and accelerated during this period of crises.

A bipolar world of increasing complexity has widened the menu of choice available to the Global South. In a girdle extending across Latin America, Africa, and Asia, countries are choosing not to pick a side in the Ukraine war. There is no desire to be trapped between the two superpowers. Many countries seek to do business with both sides as their own interests dictate. The current landscape is not a re-emergence of the Non-Aligned Movement of the 1950's and 1960's. Times have changed and the agenda is different.

One member of the group is a *"superpower in the making,"*[1] and others have attained Great Power status. The group represents significant shares of the world's global output and the bulk of the world's population.[2] The majority of those who have abstained from adhering to Western sanctions levied on Russia belong to this group. They are deepening alliances, repairing regional arrangements, and attempting to shore-up areas of vulnerability to protect against the worst effects of Great Power rivalry and war, and the disruptions posed by other exogenous shocks, such as global pandemics. Indeed, they are hedging their bets by seeking accommodation in other groupings bound by region, identity, and ideals, just not the West's. The days of assuming that Western interests are those of the rest of the world, are ending.

1. Rolling Back Globalization and Multilateralism

After decades of relative global prosperity, peace, and stability, thanks largely to the United States and allied-led Western liberal world order, with its principles of free trade and open markets, disruption, disequilibrium and disquiet are the order of the day. New concepts and words such as de-globalization, friend-shoring, de-swifting, attempt to describe the various trends as the world retreats from processes of globalization which have resulted not only in shared prosperity, but also deeper economic interdependence. There is a sense that the world as we know it has been upended. What replaces it will be shaped not only by Great Power competition, but increasingly by new actors asserting their presence on the world stage as multipolarity hedges against the excesses of hegemonic power.

After two years of a global pandemic, 2022 was to have been the year of global recovery. Instead, the pandemic continues. Up to a third of the world's population have yet to receive a single Covid-19 vaccination, though most westerners have had "at least two, some as many as five."[3] An untimely war in Europe which commenced with Russia's invasion of Ukraine on February 24, 2022, has further disrupted global supply chains and deepened the human misery occasioned by the pandemic. Prices are soaring, debt

---

1 . Len Ishmael. The Rise of China. Soft Power & Global Ambition. The Case of China's Growing Reach in Europe. The Fletcher Forum World Affairs. Publication. Winter (January) 2019 VOL 43:1.
2 . Len Ishmael. (August 2021) Beyond Aid. Making the EU Partnership with Africa, work for Africa. Hanns Seidel Stiftung Foundation. Germany/Brussels. https://www.hss.de/publikationen/ueber-entwicklungshilfe-hinaus-beyond-aid-pub1954/.
3 . Edward Luce. The World is Starting to Hate the Fed. Financial Times. Europe Edition. October 12, 2022. https://www.ft.com/content/2f5af583-2250-4908-9dc7-7edf458c8996

is increasing, and inflation stands at record levels. For the Global South, not only are these exceptionally difficult times economically, but they are politically unstable as well, as the example of Sri Lanka shows. And there is no end in sight. The war, which was forecast to be over in a matter of days, grinds on. Objectives have changed, positions deepened; escalatory actions are in play. If anything, the war has morphed into a conflict between Russia and NATO and its Western allies, in all but name. *"The frightening gap between global challenges and the world's responses, the increased prospects for major-power wars in Europe and the Indo-Pacific-have come together to produce the most dangerous moment since World War 11. Call it a perfect -or, more accurately, an imperfect – storm."*[4] Russian President Vladimir Putin has pointed to this as *"the most dangerous period in world history since the Second World War."*[5]

The Western alliance, which seemed fractured and discordant after the messy pullout of American forces from Afghanistan on August 31, 2021, and the surprise announcement of the launch of the Australia-UK-US (AUKUS) security arrangement in the Indo-Pacific fourteen days later,[6] is back. Its members have engaged with laser-like focus on punishing and isolating Russia and damaging the country's economic structures, in retaliation for its invasion of Ukraine. But while the members of the Western alliance remain among the most powerful of states, they are in the minority, and have failed to bring the rest of the world along in isolating Russia. And while the alliance is preoccupied with Russia in Europe, it seems united - at least for the time being - in pushing against threats posed by an increasingly assertive China. Despite a slowing economy, China's trajectory towards superpower status remains and, for the first time, the Biden Administration has been explicit in its identification of China as the most significant threat to US hegemony.[7]

While united against external threats, the world's most mature democracies face internal political chaos and distractions at home. The U.S., at the helm of providing global stability and world order since the Second World War, is struggling to uphold democratic values and ideals

---

[4]. Richard Haas. The Dangerous Decade. A Foreign Policy for a World in Crisis. Foreign Affairs. September/October 2022

[5]. Steve Rosenberg. Putin Pins Ukraine Hopes on Winter and Divisive US Politics. Vladimir Putin: Valdai Discussion Club. Russia Editor. BBC News. Europe. October 29, 2022.

[6]. Len Ishmael. (June 2021) The Trans-Atlantic Relationship: The Grand Alliance for the Western Led Liberal World Order. Important but no longer Enough to Shape the World. In L. Ishmael (Ed). After the COVID-19 Pandemic. How Does the World Change? Brussels. ASP EDITIONS

[7]. Edward Luce. Containing China is Biden's Explicit Goal. Financial Times. Europe Edition. October 20, 2022.

at home. On October 29, 2022, the Biden administration sounded the alarm amidst threats of domestic extremism around the country's mid-term elections in mid-November 2022. Government officials and electoral officers received deadly threats and armed Republican supporters stood guard at mail-in ballot boxes and stations, intimidating fellow citizens. Images of the January 6, 2021 insurrection at the U.S. Capitol remain seared in public memory. Across the Atlantic, the United Kingdom (UK) is gripped in its own internal chaos as it struggles to manage the effects of Brexit, the imperatives of the ongoing war and pandemic, and a political leadership crisis that has shaken market confidence and led to the sterling's worst performance in decades. in Europe, populist forces rise on all sides, as recent elections in Italy, Denmark, and elsewhere show, making issues of migration, for example, one of the continuing flashpoints between countries of the North and South. In this context, all countries, rich and poor, are trying to secure and protect their interests. Alliances are increasingly transactional, interest driven, and overlapping. In turbulent times, having more options matters more, not less, especially for the Global South.

2. Polycrises: Effects on the Global South

The war in Europe, coming on the heels of a pandemic which disproportionately affected countries of the Global South, has unleashed inflationary forces globally. Rising costs have crippled economies and are causing political instability as citizens take to the street in protest, as shown by recent events in Sri Lanka. Sovereign debt, already an issue of concern for developing countries, has attained crisis proportions. The International Monetary Fund (IMF) and World Bank have identified at least 18 countries in debt distress, with more to follow.[8] These are all countries of the Global South in which 70 million more people were pushed into poverty in the first three months of the war.[9] As many as 685 million people are in danger of being pushed into extreme poverty by the end of 2022 as gains in poverty reduction stall.[10] Heavily-indebted Tunisia is a case in point: thought to be on the brink of default by some analysts, the country recently reached

---

8 . IMF and World Bank Report. Poverty and Shared Prosperity 2022. Correcting Course. https://www.worldbank.org/en/publication/poverty-and-shared-prosperity?cid=ECR_TT_worldbank_EN_EXT
9 . IMF Managing Director Kristina Georgieva and World Bank President David Malpass. Conversation during the Fall Meetings 2022. The Way Forward: Addressing Multiple Crises in an Era of Volatility. October 10, 2022. https://live.worldbank.org/events/annual-meetings-2022-the-way-forward
10 . World Bank. Poverty and Shared Prosperity 2022. https://www.worldbank.org/en/publication/poverty-and-shared-prosperity?cid=ECR_TT_worldbank_EN_EXT

a preliminary agreement with the IMF on a $1.9 billion loan to assist it in the face of crises linked to both energy and food shortages.[11] A recent Organization for Economic Co-operation and Development (OECD) report warned that the world *"will pay the price of the Ukraine war in 2023."*[12] The IMF warns of the *"darkest hour"* for the global economy. In its revised forecasts, 93% of countries received a downgraded economic outlook.[13] Both Bretton Woods institutions (the IMF and World Bank) have pronounced as bleak, outlooks for the world's three largest economies, the US, China and the euro-area. The IMF has downgraded global output from 3.2% in 2022 to 2.7% in 2023, the lowest in any year since 2001, apart for the years of the COVID-19 pandemic and the subprime crisis of 2008. *"In few periods have so many growth engines stalled at the same time."*[14]

During the subprime crisis of 2008, China fueled the world economy. Chinese demand for commodities and raw materials pulled Latin America and countries in Africa and Asia, along, as well as the world economy.[15] Today, China's property market is in a slump, while curbs on the growth of high-tech growth sectors and firms such as Alibaba, coupled with a Zero-COVID policy, have crippled production and slowed growth, causing ripple effects across the world. A declining labor force, constraints on the internal financial system, President Xi's 'people first' and 'common prosperity' agendas, and the implications of deliberate attempts at constraining the country's movement up the value chain, have all provided a brake on growth.[16] US trade sanctions have not helped. For the first time in decades, China's economy failed to meet growth targets set by the Chinese Communist Party (CCP), coming in at 3.9% from a projected 5.5% target.[17] Global inflation now stands at the highest rate in forty years. This, coupled with higher interest rates and a strong dollar[18] is exporting inflation to the

---

11 . Part of this loan is aimed at cash transfers targeted at the most poor and social safety net support for vulnerable families most affected by higher prices.
12 . OECD Economic Outlook. Paying the Price of War. Interim Report. September 2022. https://www.oecd.org/economic-outlook/september-2022/
13 . IMF and World Bank Report. Poverty and Shared Prosperity 2022. Correcting Course. https://www.worldbank.org/en/publication/poverty-and-shared-prosperity?cid=ECR_TT_worldbank_EN_EXT
14 . Ibid.
15 . Len Ishmael. The Rise of China. Soft Power & Global Ambition. The Case of China's Growing Reach in Europe. The Fletcher Forum World Affairs. Publication. Winter (January) 2019 VOL 43:1.
16 . Financial Times Op Ed. Xi Consolidates Hold on China's Levers of Power. Financial Times. Europe Edition. October 26, 2022
17 . Ibid.
18 . There is a tendency for investment capital to seek safe haven in the US capital markets in times of uncertainty and the US currency to appreciate in times of turmoil. This is the case today as the greenback has appreciated against all currencies driving both the euro and

rest of the world, with many fearing a repeat of the period in the 1970's when higher US interest rates triggered deep recession in the Global South, with both Africa and Latin America suffering a *"decade of lost growth"* made worse by IMF structural adjustment plans.[19]

Important reforms undertaken since the subprime crisis of 2008 are, however, blunting some of the worst effects of volatility for many Latin American countries which are weathering this storm in better shape than they might have otherwise. Countries like Brazil, Chile, Peru, and Colombia, among others, were the first to start tightening interest rates in March 2021, a year before fiscal tightening became the go-to policy of Western countries to rein in inflation. But fiscal tightening has to be balanced against tipping economies into recession. The fact that OECD central banks are purchasing each other's bonds is making capital both scarce and more expensive for the countries of the Global South. Higher capital costs have implications for both investment and consumption in a region that cannot afford another lost decade, having grown more slowly than much of the rest of the world, has been worse hit by the pandemic than any other region, and is today having to manage the effects of war.[20] The IMF has lowered its growth forecast for Latin America from 2.5% to 1.7% in 2023.[21] Recovery will take time. Fiscal and monetary conditions have converged to create new tensions which have increased volatility in emerging markets as capital outflows seek safe havens and dollar-denominated debt becomes more burdensome. A debt servicing crisis may be unavoidable. It is against these realities that the reluctance of some of the biggest actors in the Global South to implement western sanctions against Russia needs to be understood. Simply put, this war, on multiple levels, is not in their interest. It is a source of great harm to their economies, citizens and the political stability on which they depend.

3. The Rise of the Global West

So successful has the Ukraine war been in unifying the Western alliance that there is now talk of a 'Global West'. Much like the Global South, this is a concept, dictated not by geography, but by *"ideas, liberal democracy, [and]*

---

sterling to historic lows against the dollar, now at its strongest levels since the early 2000's.
19 . Edward Luce. The World is Starting to Hate the Fed. Financial Times. Europe Edition. October 12, 2022. https://www.ft.com/content/2f5af583-2250-4908-9dc7-7edf458c8996
20 . Ibid.
21 . IMF and World Bank Report. Poverty and Shared Prosperity 2022. Correcting Course. https://www.worldbank.org/en/publication/poverty-and-shared-prosperity?cid=ECR_TT_worldbank_EN_EXT

strong security ties to the USA."[22] The defense of 'universal values' is a rallying call, as is the threat posed by China's global ambitions and its competitive edge in future technologies.[23] Included in this like-minded group are not only the USA and Europe, but also allies in the Pacific, Japan and Australia, and Canada, all countries at the core of executing sanctions against Russia.

The establishment of AUKUS, the invitations extended to Australia, Japan, New Zealand and South Korea to attend the June 2022 NATO summit in Madrid for the first time, as observers, and the-post summit communique' explicitly referencing China as its main adversary, point to a West keen to shore up its traditional alliances against common threats.[24] The G7, previously supplanted by the G20 in matters of global financial governance, has been revitalized, proclaiming itself as *"the steering committee of the free world."*[25] On its agenda is the need to build supply chain resilience in order to decrease dependencies on China through trade with friendly countries, in the process of "friend-shoring,"[26] and the launching, rather late, of a counter to China's Belt and Road Initiative (BRI) via a $600 billion fund to finance infrastructure.[27]

Across the Atlantic, the war in Ukraine has provided additional impetus to the creation of the European Political Community (EPC) launched in Prague on October 6, 2022. Forty-four European nations, with the exceptions of Russia and Belarus, attended this first gathering. The EPC aims to provide an informal forum for all European nations to discuss common threats and prosperity via *"an inclusive approach to solutions, faster responses to problems and a place for mediating dialogues between nations-regardless of their membership in different, sometimes overlapping, clubs; a platform capable of accommodating different interests across Europe - the EPC is a space to do just that."*[28] The forum's first agenda included energy security and interconnections in the North Sea and Balkans, increasing fossil fuel production in both Norway and Azerbaijan, and beefing up security and

---

22 . Gideon Rachman. Xi's China and the Rise of the 'Global West'. Financial times. Europe Edition. October 25, 2022.
23 . Ibid.
24 . Ibid.
25 . Ibid.
26 . The term 'friend-shoring' is said to have been coined by US Treasury Secretary, Janet Yellen
27 . Gideon Rachman makes the point that the fund may be quite late, given the fact of the almost $4 trillion expended by China since 2013 on infrastructure investments.
28 . Petr Fiala. PM of the Czech Republic, President of the European Union Council. The European Political Community is built for challenging times. Financial Times. Europe Edition. Monday 17 October,2022.

peace monitoring activities in different areas.[29] The war in Ukraine and the relationship between Russia and China, seemed to have provided a rationale for the withdrawal of both Latvia and Estonia from the 17+1 grouping[30] comprising China and a number of Central and Eastern European countries, twelve of which are European Union (EU) members, through which China has been able to deepen and widen the scope of its soft power in Europe.[31]

Other platforms and mechanisms for dialogue and consensus building are taking on heightened significance. The EU-U.S. Trade and Technology Council established in 2021 as a pillar in the transatlantic relationship, is one such mechanism, given the central role of the partners in addressing Russia's threat to peace and stability in Europe, and the need to coordinate actions and interests around control of future technologies: *"Russian aggression against Ukraine has further underlined the key importance of our cooperation with the US on economic and technology issues – when we act together we can set the standards for tomorrow's economy."*[32]

In the Pacific, the Quadrilateral Security Dialogue (QUAD), comprising members Australia, the USA, India, and Japan (plus trade spokespersons for Canada and the EU), has taken steps to deepen its cooperation arrangements, augmented by AUKUS. Japan and Australia have taken bilateral steps to strengthen intelligence co-operation by upgrading an agreement signed in 2017, and are expanding cooperation via another instrument which allows mutual use of each other's military bases.[33] They are widening cooperation beyond just that of security and defense in another bid to counter the threat from China. Indeed, Japan, whose oil and gas imports derive mainly from the contested South China Sea, has changed its long-standing policy of spending 1% of GDP and relying on U.S. leadership for its security arrangements. It will double defense spending over the next five years.[34] Japan is also strengthening cooperation with the Five Eyes Countries -Canada, US, UK, Australia, New Zealand[35]- and has taken steps to

---

29 . Ibid.
30 . China-CEEC. This is an organization for cooperation between China and Central and Eastern European Countries, which includes both EU and non-EU members.
31 . Len Ishmael. The Making of a Superpower. China's Use of Crises to Deepen and Extend Power and Influence in Europe and the World. Horizons ISSG. April 09, 2020, Vol. 3, Issue 1.
32 . European Commission. EU-US Trade and Technology Council: Strengthening our Renewed Partnership in Turbulent Times. Press Release. May 16, 2022. https://ec.europa.eu/commission/presscorner/detail/en/IP_22_3034
33 . Kana Inagaki and Nic Fildes. Japan and Australia Strengthen Intelligence Cooperation. Financial Times. Europe Edition. October 22, 2022.
34 . Ibid.
35 . Ibid.

significantly increase cooperation in South East Asia and with ASEAN.[36] In the meantime, members of the QUAD continue to recalibrate their relations with China. While defrosting, somewhat, as a result of the new government in Canberra, Australia is nonetheless concerned by the challenge posed by China in the Pacific, especially given new security agreements with the Solomon Islands as of April 2022. India, sharing a long border with China, the site of recent skirmishes, continues to view China as a neighbor that must be both accommodated and balanced.

4. The US and China: Superpowers in the Era of Strategic Competition

As the week-long events associated with the Chinese Communist Party's (CCP) Congress came to an end, on October 23, 2022, Xi Jinping announced an unprecedented third term in power, cementing his place as the most powerful ruler since Mao. While the first period of Xi's presidency seemed to be one of a 'peaceful rise,' policies and actions since underline a more assertive stance on China's 'rightful' place in the world and his bid to achieve a *"great rejuvenation of the Chinese nation"* by 2049, the year of the country's centennial celebration of rule by the CCP.[37] President Xi has pointed to this as a "critical time" for China. Russia and China have declared theirs to be a relationship of *"unlimited friendship."*[38] The war in Ukraine, while cementing Western resolve aimed at punishing and isolating Russia, has among other things, brought China and Russia closer. Both hold the longstanding belief that the Western led liberal world order is inimical to their interests. Despite this, China seems weary of being ensnared in confrontation with the West as a result of the Russian invasion of Ukraine. While various agreements, including the settlement of trade purchases in local currency, are viewed as moves to bypass SWIFT[39] (the Society for Worldwide Interbank Financial Telecommunication), China is carefully seeking lessons from Russia's altercations with the West as an opportunity to shore up areas in which it might be vulnerable to future Western sanctions: not just in trade, but also with respects to the global financial architecture.

---

36 . The Association of South East Asian Nations (ASEAN) was established on August 8, 1967 in Bangkok by the five Founding Fathers: Indonesia, Philippines, Singapore, Malaysia, and Thailand.
37 . Financial Times Op Ed. Xi Consolidates Hold on China's Levers of Power. Financial times. Europe Edition. 26 October 2022.
38 . Ibid.
39 . SWIFT is a Belgian cooperative society which supports the execution of interbank financial transactions and payments worldwide.

While China's cross-border payment mechanism represents a fraction of currency payments globally, it is growing, and the platform is being used by some countries involved in the Chinese funded BRI as a means of paying off debts related to Chinese loans.

In the CCP's most recent Congress, President Xi underscored the fact that *"the Taiwan issue is a matter for the Chinese people themselves,"* and that the CCP would *"combat protectionism and bullying"* by other nations, and would not retreat from the use of force over Taiwan if necessary.[40] Indeed, the visit by United States House of Representatives Speaker Nancy Pelosi to Taipei in August 2022, brought a show of might from China in the skies and seas around Taiwan by the People's Liberation Army, with warships, fighter jets, and military drones engaged in daily drills. The 2022 CCP Congress has been viewed by some as signaling many things for the rest of the world including *"more engagement with the Global South - and more divergence from the West - the US in particular."*[41]

a. China: An Explicit Threat

The announcement by the US Department of Commerce's Bureau of Industry and Security (BIS), on October 7, 2022, of sweeping export controls on the semiconductor sector signaled an admission that China is the single biggest threat to U.S. hegemony. It signals, too, the end of the process of globalization as we have known it. The new restrictions are far-reaching. They cover advanced chips made with U.S. technology *"regardless of where these are made."*[42] The move is viewed as a *"full blown economic war on China – all but committing the US to stopping its rise."*[43] Since many of the chips are dual purpose and are used in both military and civilian technologies, the U.S. is seen as *"committed to blocking China in all kinds of civilian technologies that make up a modern economy,"* which will *"hobble China's economy so it can never compete on equal terms."*[44] Indeed, the U.S. *National Security Strategy*, unveiled a few days later on October 12, 2022, is clear-eyed regarding both the challenge and threat posed by China to American hegemony and the current world order. It places a primary focus on strengthening U.S. deterrence against China: *"China harbors the*

---

40 . Financial Times Op Ed. Xi Consolidates Hold on China's Levers of Power. Financial Times. Europe Edition. 26 October 2022.
41 . Ibid.
42 . Robert Harding. Slowing Chinese Growth is a Recipe for Global Instability. Financial Times. Europe Edition. October 14, 2022.
43 . Edward Luce. Containing China is Biden's Explicit Goal. Financial Times. Europe Edition. October 20, 2022.
44 . Ibid.

intention and increasingly the capacity, to reshape the international order in favor of one that tilts the global playing field to its benefit."[45] The U.S. is resolute in its intention to ensure that its military "*is equipped for the era of strategic competition with major powers.*"[46] Both the administration's new *National Defense Strategy* and its *Nuclear Posture Review* aim to further elaborate the posture to be adopted by the US in response to these strategic threats. Critics note that "*the US is once again giving notice that the only lens through which it sees the world is through that of national security in a zero-sum game in which China's rise is at the expense of American hegemony.*"[47] Is the era of PAX Americana over?

b.   Friend-Shoring: Bringing it Home

The deepening alliances of the Global West are not limited to security and defense. In *Bringing it Home*, a recent publication that speaks to the mood of these times, the author Rana Foroohar argued that free trade has enriched "*plutocrats*" and not ordinary people, and that change is needed. The charge resonates. After all, at the height of the pandemic, financial markets were bullish; the world's richest one percent saw their wealth quadruple.[48] But, while the author acknowledged the contribution of free trade to prosperity and the decline in poverty across the world, the wider point being made is that in the absence of cooperation around western values, the liberal model has fueled inequality between and within societies by concentrating immense wealth and power in the hands of a few. Foroohar claims that "*the idea that trade was primarily a pathway to global peace and unity, rather than a necessary way of balancing both domestic and global concerns,*" and the idea of swapping "*cheap capital (from the USA) for cheap labor (China),*" is over.[49] There has been a growing sense in Western societies that free trade, coupled with the movement of capital and labor, have taken away domestic jobs. These sentiments have fed the backlash against globalization and the swing towards populism in several Western countries, including the USA, France, Italy, the United Kingdom and Hungary. Disruptions to global supply chains at the height of the pandemic made worse by the war, have

---

45   . Demetri Sevastopulo. US Security Strategy Warns of Decisive Decade for China Links. Financial Times. Europe Edition. October 13, 2022.
46   . Ibid.
47   . Ibid.
48   . Len Ishmael. (June 2021) The Trans-Atlantic Relationship: The Grand Alliance for the Western Led Liberal World Order. Important but no longer Enough to Shape the World. In L. Ishmael (Ed). After the COVID-19 Pandemic. How Does the World Change? Brussels. ASP EDITIONS
49   . Rana Foroohar. Free Trade Has Not Made Us Free. Financial Times. Europe edition. October 17, 2022

fueled calls to 'make local for local,' and sentiments against globalization have hardened. Western countries point to national security as a decisive factor in bringing production on-shore, or to friendly countries. Foroohar's take on the state of the world reflects a growing call in the Global West for states to cooperate more, not only in security and defense domains, but also economically.

This line of thinking is echoed by multinational companies, among which, interestingly, are those that have benefited most from globalization. Rio Tinto, an Australian/Anglo mineral conglomerate, warned recently of *"excesses of globalization hitting supply chains for critical metals,"* in the wake of the group's announcement with the Canadian government that it would invest $537 million in Quebec, in an attempt to 'loosen' China's grip on metals critical to the defense and aerospace sectors.[50] China currently produces more than 75% of finished titanium products globally, and this investment is seen as an important boost to North America's production capacity of this metal. This is the latest in recent investments in Canada's mining and battery sectors, which have seen investors from Germany, Belgium, and South Korea exploring an array of opportunities, including essential minerals, nickel, and cobalt, for use in electric car production.[51] These have been made all the more attractive by U.S. climate change tax credits to buyers of electric cars, batteries for which are sourced either domestically or from allies, in a move to further incentivize the push to decouple from China.

Re-shoring effectively neutralizes the reason why comparative advantage moved production lines of some goods to countries with abundant labor and lower costs. Countries with abundant labor, such as Bangladesh, Vietnam and countless others, have benefited, but so too have consumers in capital-rich countries, given the variety of goods available to them, at cheaper prices. On-shoring or friend-shoring will not be painless; it will come at a cost both for the West and the rest of the world, and will put a spoke in the rising prosperity that has accompanied free trade over much of the last thirty years.

---

50 . Harry Dempsey. Rio Tinto Warns of Excessive Globalization in Supply Chains for Critical Metals. Financial Times. October 11, 2022.
51 . Ibid.

5. Alliance of the Global South: The Global West Fails to Convince the Rest

The need to diversify alliances and spheres of influence in a world moving away from a one-pole structure, is an important objective at the core of the growing impulse to greater multilateralism on the part of the rest of the non-Western world. Western initiatives towards de-coupling from China and Russia, and the processes of 'de-swifting' and 'on-shoring' are not in their interests. Neither is the ongoing war in Europe. As the Global West moves to consolidate and protect its interests, the rest of the world is doing much the same via a number of distinctly non-Western configurations, resulting in a multilayered, multipolar world. This, albeit informal, alliance of the Global South, comprises multiple groupings with agendas and memberships that increasingly overlap, and whose purpose is to elaborate frameworks for deepening cooperation in a bid not only to marshal mutual benefits using the weight of their collective economic clout, but also to hedge against the isolation and bankruptcy Western sanctions can bring.

The Alliance of the Global South seeks cooperation guided by principles of sovereignty and non-interference in the internal affairs of others. Countries are multiplying their non-Western bilateral and multilateral cooperation relations. Most have refused to publicly take a position on the matter of Russia's invasion of Ukraine, and have distanced themselves from enacting sanctions. Together they represent more than half of the world's population and global output at a time when shares of global output and wealth in the USA and the EU, are declining.[52] The U.S., which represented 40% of global output in 1960, though still the world's largest economy, has declined to 25% in 2021. China's share is rising. At 18% of global output, China is the world's second largest economy. It is projected to become the world's largest by 2030, and surpassed the EU in February 2022.[53] The EU's share of global output at 25% in the 1990's is projected to decline to 11% by 2040.[54] At this rate, the EU's global output will be equal to that of India, below the U.S.'s share of 14%, and less than half that of China's.[55]

---

52 . Len Ishmael, (August 2021) Beyond Aid. Making the EU Partnership with Africa, work for Africa. Hanns Seidel Stiftung Foundation. Germany/Brussels. : https://www.hss.de/publikationen/ueber-entwicklungshilfe-hinaus-beyond-aid-pub1954/.
53 . Dorothy Neufeld, Sabrina Fortin and Harrison Schell. Visualizing the $94 trillion World Economy in One Chart. The Global GDP 2022. Money. December 22, 2021. https://www.visualcapitalist.com/visualizing-the-94-trillion-world-economy-in-one-chart.
54 . Len Ishmael, (August 2021) Beyond Aid. Making the EU Partnership with Africa, work for Africa. Hanns Seidel Stiftung Foundation. Germany/Brussels. : https://www.hss.de/publikationen/ueber-entwicklungshilfe-hinaus-beyond-aid-pub1954/.
55 . Len Ishmael. Global Governance in a Post- American World order: The End of Hubris.

Countries in the alliance have also grown weary of rules of the game in international governance which do not seem to apply to the rule makers. They point to the wars in Afghanistan and Syria, and the second Gulf war, and regime changes in Iraq and Libya, which were not backed by UN resolutions. Countries are alarmed by the crippling nature of the Global West's approach to those who violate certain codes of conduct. Sanctions on central banks, the freezing of reserves, the seizing of personal assets, and the cutting of access to the global financial infrastructure are alarming, and are shaking their confidence in the use of the dollar as the world's reserve currency. Countries are hedging their bets by seeking accommodation with other groupings bound by region, identity, and ideals – just not the West's. While not explicit, the building of resilience against the consequences of Western sanctions should they be deployed, is an objective.

This is not to say that other peoples in the world are not attracted by the ideals of liberty, or freedom, but they view such ideals through a different lens. They witness failures in Western democracies which no longer convey or convince of the 'dream' of such a world, and are increasingly seeking a paradigm that allows culture and traditions to determine organically the rules they wish to live by, with non-interference in internal affairs being an abiding principle. This period is being seen as a fundamental shift in global equilibrium with consequences for the international order and structure, though the West might seem to be in denial.[56]

a. India: Sovereignty Expressed through Neutrality

In March and April 2022, during the early days of the Russian invasion of Ukraine, ministers of foreign affairs from several Western countries descended on Delhi in a flurry of diplomatic traffic, in an effort to get the world's largest democracy, and increasingly important global actor, to throw its weight behind Western efforts to isolate and punish Russia.[57] Envoys from both Russia and China also visited. While India has been clear about its stance concerning the inviolability of territorial integrity, and President Modi, at the most recent summit of the Shanghai Cooperation Organization (SCO), suggested that President Putin bring the war to an end,[58] India has

---

In: Atlantic Currents, 8th ED. The South in Times of Turmoil. Policy Center for the New South. Pages 23-39. December 2019.
56 . Jacques Sapir. Le Nouveau "Grand-Sud" fait-il secession? Le Spectacle Du Monde – Trimestriel No 10: Automme 2022
57 . Bhaswar Kumar. Why Foreign Diplomats are Rushing to New Delhi? Business Standard. April 4, 2022. https://wap.business-standard.com/amp/podcast/current-affairs/why-foreign-diplomats-are-rushing-to-new-delhi-122040400038_1.html
58 . SCO comprises India, Russia, China, Kazakhstan, Kyrgyzstan, Pakistan, Tajikistan, Uzbekistan

refused to publicly take a side in this war affirming, instead, that the country "*is on the side of peace.*" In this tug of war, India is a prize. While it is a member of the Quad in the Indo-Pacific configuration, and is cooperating closely with the USA and the EU (and is currently negotiating a free trade agreement (FTA) with the latter), it also has defense and economic ties with Russia, and formed strong economic, military, and diplomatic relations with the Soviet Union during the Cold War. It is party to the Russia-India-China (RIC) trilateral, as well as the Brazil, Russia, India, China, and South Africa configuration (BRICS). India's trade with Russia has grown significantly in the last few months and, with China, represented the major destinations for Russian crude in October 2022, with 58% of all seaborne shipments. Bilateral trade between India and Russia hit a new high of $18.2 billion by value, from April through August 2022, versus $13.1 billion reported for the whole fiscal year 2021-2022.[59] India is also considering a ruble-rupee trade payment scheme which would skirt SWIFT using Russia's messaging system SPFS.[60] Indeed, on November 8, 2022, the agenda for India's foreign minister's talks in Moscow with his counterpart, included the use of national currencies in mutual settlements. India has ambitions as a global actor. Like other actors in the Global South, India is aware of evolving shifts in global power and is calibrating its stance, carefully balancing a number of diverging interests in a bid to secure its own. The desire to cooperate more closely with Western allies in the Indo Pacific, while increasing visibility as a global actor, requires that it tread carefully in a volatile neighborhood, in which both China and Pakistan are nuclear-equipped neighbors.

b. Turkey: Geography and History Enables Balancing of East and West

While assuming an important mediator role in this war, Turkey, like India, has not aligned with Western sanctions on Russia. Pushing back against the appearance of aiding Russia's attempts at sanctions evasion, Turkey refers to the economic ties between the two as nothing more than "*good neighborly relations.*"[61] Turkey has become adept at balancing its interests in both East and West, optimizing its geography, history, and position in

---

59 . Sam Chambers. India's Foreign Minister touches down in Moscow for key trade talks. Splash247.com November 8th, 2022. https://splash247.com/indias-foreign-minister-touches-down-in-moscow-for-key-trade-talks/
60 . Bhaswar Kumar. Why Foreign Diplomats are Rushing to New Delhi. Business Standard. New Delhi. April 04, 2022. https://wap.business-standard.com/amp/podcast/current-affairs/why-foreign-diplomats-are-rushing-to-new-delhi-122040400038_1.html
61 . Laura Pitel and Adam Samson. Turkey Finance Chief Defends Kremlin Ties. Financial Times. Europe Edition. October 26, 2022.

NATO to leverage and secure its interests, especially given the realization that its long drawn out application to join the EU may never materialize. Averting pressure on the lira and the need to avoid a balance of payment crisis are priorities, especially given important presidential elections next summer. Turkey purchases significant quantities of gas from Gazprom at discounted rates, has received funds from Russia's nuclear agency for the construction of an atomic power plant, and collaborates with Russia on the TurkStream natural gas pipeline.[62] Russians were the second largest group of visitors to Turkey in 2022. Despite NATO pressure, the country procured the S-400 missile defense system from Russia. And while Turkey has supported the UN vote on condemning the invasion, ensured security in the strategically located Bosporus and Black Sea, and has brokered prisoner swaps and shipments of Ukraine grain, by not endorsing Western sanctions, it is carefully balancing both sides. In so doing, Turkey acts as a bridge between East and West in keeping with its own geography, and, in the process, is expanding its sphere of influence and power as a global actor.

Turkey is conscious of the wider role it plays in a volatile environment, as conflicts in Syria, Iraq, Ukraine, Azerbaijan, and Armenia attest. In recent times it has rebranded its image *"as a free agent"* and "*world power in its own right.*"[63] After the Arab Spring events of 2011, Turkey's ties to the Quartet, an informal grouping including Bahrain, Egypt, Saudi Arabia, and the United Arab Emirates ruptured as a result of its support for Egypt's Muslim Brotherhood and Qatar.[64] The relationship deteriorated even further after the Khashoggi murder on Turkish soil in 2018 but has since been reset in a redoubling of efforts to secure regional ties. But tensions with the West - including recurrent issues with Greece in the maritime sphere and the EU on the matter of migration - have spurred Turkey to move beyond resetting relations in its immediate neighborhood, and to also expand these more deeply with Russia and China principally, but also with others, as a counter measure.

At the September 2022 SCO Summit in Uzbekistan, Turkey announced plans to apply for full membership of the organization. China, Russia, and India are important members. Turkey is already a Dialogue Member, and, should its full membership bid be successful, it will be the first NATO member to have this status, a move widely interpreted to be Turkey's response to

---

62 . Ibid.
63 . Kali Robinson. Turkey's Growing Foreign Policy Ambitions. Council on Foreign Relations. August 24, 2022. https://www.cfr.org/backgrounder/turkeys-growing-foreign-policy-ambitions?amp
64 . Ibid.

tensions with the West via an alternate, non-Western grouping.[65] Turkey has also expressed an interest in pursuing membership of the BRICS. The Organization of Turkic States provides another layer of cooperation among independent Turkic countries. Azerbaijan, Kazakhstan, Kyrgyzstan, Turkey, and Uzbekistan are full members. Hungary, an EU member state, obtained observer status in 2014.

c. Saudis: Widening Non-Western Alliances to Secure Influence in a Changing World

The deliberate move away from support for Western interests is evident in other quarters. The U.S., for example, was blindsided by Israel and Saudi Arabia's initial abstention from voting on the United Nations General Assembly (UNGA) resolution on the matter of Russia's invasion of Ukraine. As America signed off on a $3 billion package of missiles sales to Riyadh in August 2022, the Saudis raised oil output by 100,000 b/d *"one of the smallest increases ever, only to put in place steps to reduce output by September."*[66] By October, as part of OPEC+,[67] the Saudis decreased output by 2m b/d, an action supportive of Moscow, but especially humiliating for the Biden Administration given the President's visit to the Kingdom in July and the missiles sales agreed in August. And while the Saudis say this decision was purely economic, there is nonetheless the perception that several factors, including Biden's previous denouncement of the Kingdom as a pariah state, his early unwillingness to meet de-facto leader Crown Prince Mohammed bin Salman (MBS), tensions over Saudi attacks on Houthi in Yemen using American hardware, the Kingdom's relations with China and Russia, and the warm relations between the Saudis and the previous Trump Administration, may also have played a role, especially in its timing.

Among MBS's core objectives is to position the Kingdom as a regional actor with global influence no longer sympathetic to Western opinion or interests. Preserving Saudi influence and protecting its interests requires expanding partnerships with different influential powers, both bilaterally and within multilateral groupings. MBS has taken steps to deepen the Kingdom's relations with Russia, visiting Putin at the height of the war

---

65 . Umut Uras. Can the SCO be Turkey's Alternative to the West? Aljazeera. News. September 21, 2022. https://www.aljazeera.com/amp/news/2022/9/21/turkey-shanghai-cooperation-organisation-membership-nato-west-alternative
66 . Andrew England, Samer Al-Atrush. Biden Has Limited Scope to Act over Saudi Oil Cuts. Financial Times. European edition. October 17, 2022.
67 . Opec+1 is an alliance led by Saudi Arabia which also includes Russia. The group took the decision on October 14th 2022 to cut daily output by 2million barrels.

and securing the release of international prisoners, including five British nationals captured in Ukraine. The Kingdom has announced plans to seek Dialogue Partner status with SCO as have other Gulf states. At the time of this writing, the highly publicized 'Davos in the Desert Event' - The Future Investment Initiative - is taking place in Riyadh. In attendance are A-listed American, British, and other western CEOs, sending a clear message of their intent to continue engagement in lucrative business prospects in the region, despite the unfolding geopolitical landscape. Notwithstanding calls by several U.S. Congress and Senate members to curb further weapons sales and security cooperation, Saudi Arabia remains a vital ally on the security front in a neighborhood threatened by Iran and its proxies. The Biden Administration has little room for maneuver. Though pre-scheduled US-Gulf Cooperation Council meetings were delayed, US reaction is also balanced by the reality that the Kingdom is an important buyer of US military hardware, representing almost 25% of US sales in 2017-2021.[68] Riyadh's calculated gamble in following its self-interests seems to be paying off.

Within the Gulf, other states are engaging in the conflict, even though it seems to fall outside of their normal sphere of interest. On October 11, 2022, around the time when the decision was taken to increase oil prices, Sheikh Mohamed bin Zayed al-Nahyan, President of the United Arab Emirates (UAE), met the Russian President in St Petersburg, ostensibly to find a diplomatic solution to the Ukraine crisis through dialogue.[69] The UAE, Saudis, Turkey, Indonesia, and others from the Global South have all presented themselves as interlocutors in the ongoing conflict at a time when trust in Western brokers is at its lowest.

6. Africa, Latin America, and Asia: Widening and Deepening Multilateralism

While the Global West speaks of friend-shoring, the Global South is alert to the idea that there is more that they can - and should be doing together - in this time of turbulence and change. The September 2022, three-day Caribbean-Africa Investment Forum - the first of its kind, which convened in Bridgetown, Barbados - is one of a series of initiatives that are gaining traction. This historic gathering saw 1200 African officials and

---

68 . Andrew England, Samer Al-Atrush. Biden Has Limited Scope to Act over Saudi Oil Cuts. Financial Times. European edition. October 17, 2022.
69 . Chris Devonshire-Ellis. The New Candidate Countries for BRICS Expansion. Silk Road Briefing. November 09, 2022. https://www.silkroadbriefing.com/news/2022/11/09/the-new-candidate-countries-for-brics-expansion/

businesspersons meet Caribbean counterparts. Cooperation agreements were signed between Africa's Export Import Bank and regional entities to establish Caribbean Headquarters and branches, seeded with $700 million to spur investments. Joint Chambers of Commerce and Open Skies Agreements were among the issues discussed. China is an important partner for both Africa and the Caribbean, and neighboring Latin America, engaging in regular summits with the leadership of each of these regions. The return of President Lula - a renowned regionalist - to the helm of Brazilian politics, will add further momentum to initiatives across the South Atlantic and beyond, especially given the importance of Brazil in the BRICS. At the height of the pandemic, while the West was contemplating the outlines of a global strategy (after domestic needs had been met), Africa, Latin America, the Caribbean, and Asia benefitted significantly from Chinese, Russian, and Indian vaccine diplomacy. Caribbean countries also benefited from inclusion in Africa's vaccine procurement effort. For the countries of the Global South, non-Western multilateral organizations that espouse solidarity, respect for sovereignty, and non-interference in the internal affairs of others, are providing forums of increasing importance, within which cooperation around economic and political matters can be cemented. Leaders of these countries meet in a number of overlapping groups and configurations including the BRICS and SCO, which have provided buffers against Western efforts to isolate Russia during the war.

In 2011, South Africa joined Brazil, Russia, India and China as one of the BRICS - the grouping of countries representing the most important emerging economies.[70] Other important regional powers, including Algeria, Argentina, and Iran, have applied for membership. Indonesia was expected to make a formal application at the Bali Summit, while Turkey, Saudi Arabia, Egypt, and Afghanistan have declared an interest. The BRICS agreed to a 'Plus' configuration to include "like minded" new partners earlier this year at the BRICS Expansion Dialogue, held in May 2022 and attended by Kazakhstan, Senegal, Nigeria, Thailand, Nicaragua, and the UAE. The BRICS coordinate on trade matters.[71] The group has its own bank, the New Development Bank (NDB), established in 2014 as an alternative to the Bretton Woods Institutions to support investment in development and commercial enterprises, an idea long championed by Brazil's Lula. China's Asian Infrastructure Investment Bank (AIIB) was also established around

---

70 . The grouping BRIC, entered into force in 2009
71 . Chris Devonshire-Ellis. The New Candidate Countries for BRICS Expansion. Silk Road Briefing. November 09, 2022. https://www.silkroadbriefing.com/news/2022/11/09/the-new-candidate-countries-for-brics-expansion/

the same time. Both banks are triple A rated, with capitalization of $100 billion.[72] In this current configuration, the BRICS are expected to represent 50% of global GDP by 2030, and expansion of the group will accelerate that process. If accepted, the proposed new membership of BRICS *"would create a global entity with GDP 30% larger than the USA, over 50% of the global population and in control of 60% of global gas reserves."*[73]

SCO is a non-Western multilateral political, economic, and security forum which, like the BRICS, is becoming an increasingly important bloc in Central and South Asia, and a global actor. Founded in 2001, with full members China, India, Kazakhstan, Kyrgyzstan, Russia, Tajikistan, Pakistan, and Uzbekistan, SCO has continued to expand in recent times with the accessions of Iran, Belarus, and Mongolia currently underway. Dialogue Partners include Turkey, Turkmenistan, Azerbaijan, Armenia, Cambodia, Nepal, and Sri Lanka, now joined for the first time by Arab countries including Egypt, Saudi Arabia, Qatar, UAE, Bahrain, and Kuwait. In a show of might, Eurasia and Arab countries are joining forces. This bodes well for China's use of soft power as it seeks to expand membership of organizations in which it is a main actor by building strategic partnerships that are inclusive, in keeping with President's Xi's view that *"the West seeks to isolate or punish states on normative grounds for example, failure to adhere to universal values of liberal democracies."*[74] This view resonates with many in the Global South. Turkey's involvement in the group as a NATO member that intends to seek full membership is explained as one which *"moves our ties with these countries to a much different position,"*[75] while providing leverage in light of Western tensions.

Across the ASEAN group, while there is weariness with China, it is balanced by disenchantment with Washington, and the sense that the latter is not sufficiently engaged with regional actors, instead undertaking actions without consultation and acting in its own interest with respect to Great Power competition with China. This group does not wish to be caught in any open confrontation between the two superpowers, since its members have the most to lose. Singapore has repeatedly noted that these countries

---

72 . Ibid.
73 . Ibid.
74 . Jagannath P. Panda and Wooyeal Paik. The Russian-India-China Trilateral After Ukraine: Will Beijing take the lead? China Brief Volume: 22 Issue:16. September 9, 2022. https://jamestown.org/program/the-russia-india-china-trilateral-after-ukraine-will-beijing-take-the-lead/
75 . Kali Robinson. Turkey's Growing Foreign Policy Ambitions. Council on Foreign Relations. August 24, 2022. https://www.cfr.org/backgrounder/turkeys-growing-foreign-policy-ambitions?amp

do not wish to choose between China and the USA; it is not in their interests to do so.⁷⁶ China is the giant in their backyard, and the primary trade and investment partner with which they are engaged in the world's largest trading bloc, which includes India, Japan, South Korea, Australia, and New Zealand. Conversely, the U.S. has not offered an economic alternative, though this region is arguably "*the most trade dependent in the world.*"⁷⁷ Many perceive the failure to engage economically as the weakness of US strategy in the Pacific. Though the U.S. has recently unveiled financing for infrastructure development, this is seen as too little and late, compared to Chinese investments and engagements in the region. The US focus on the QUAD and now AUKUS, is seen to have weakened, and once again, sidelined, ASEAN. Attempts to rekindle the relationship with Pacific Island leaders with a summit in Washington and a pledge of $810 million in July 2022, were largely seen as an attempt to counter growing Chinese influence in the region. In the Pacific Strategy Document, the U.S. warns of "*the heightened geopolitical competition impacts*" for the region, pledging, in addition to the funding mentioned previously, to open a US Agency for International Development (USAID) regional office in Suva, the capital of Fiji, and to reopen embassies on a number of islands.⁷⁸ The US, however, has been criticized for "*being largely absent as a partner for the Pacific in recent decades,*" leaving a vacuum and opportunity for increasing Chinese influence in the region.⁷⁹

India and China both had close relationships with the USSR during the Cold War and, in some respects, Russia has inherited the relationship. The trilateral Russia-India-China (RIC) relationship was established in the early 2000s. Though the trilateral configuration has not developed into one of importance, given, among other things, issues between China and India in which Russia has played a mediating role, there is a sense that the Ukraine crisis has revitalized interest for the parties in the role the RIC configuration can play with India as a bridge to the West. Indeed, there are some who imagine that the RICs are well placed to "*coordinate the goals of a multipolar world order,*" and that this could be the beginning of a re-

---

76 . Len Ishmael. Global Governance in a Post- American World order: The End of Hubris. In: Atlantic Currents, 8th ED. The South in Times of Turmoil. Policy Center for the New South. Pages 23-39. December 2019.
77 . Jonathan Head. The US wants to play in China's Backyard. BBC News. November 10, 2022. https://www.bbc.co.uk/news/world-asia-63565875.amp
78 . Kate Lyons and agencies. US announces aid for the Pacific, as it tries to combat China's influence in the region. The Guardian. September 30, 2022. https://amp.theguardian.com/world/2022/sep/30/us-announces-aid-for-pacific-as-it-tries-to-combat-chinas-influence-in-region
79 . Ibid.

energized relationship.[80]

The G20, representing the world's wealthiest countries, is evenly split along a North - South divide, between those who enforce western sanctions against Russia and those who have declined to do so. Despite a high-ranking tour of US Secretary of State Blinken through Africa and South East Asia, half of the G20 countries have not signed up to the sanction regimes against Russia.[81] These include India, China, Brazil, South Africa, Turkey, Indonesia, Argentina, Saudi Arabia, and Mexico. Indeed, Indonesia's Joko Widodo, in the role of presidency of the G20, withstood pressure to disinvite the Russian president from the Bali Summit on November 15-16, 2022, pushing instead for an end to the war, so that conditions of global stability can be restored and vital issues such as food security and the process of rebuilding battered economies can begin.[82] In June 2022, Germany invited Argentina, Indonesia, South Africa, and India as observers to the G7 summit, also in an unsuccessful bid to encourage a change of stance on the implementation of sanctions. In late July 2022, the South American trade bloc Mercosur declined the request from Ukraine's President Zelenskyy to address their summit.[83] Russia's Foreign Minister Lavrov, on the other hand, was received warmly by African leaders during his two-day visit to the continent in July 2022, and on October 26, 2022, South Africa provided safe haven to the superyacht of a sanctioned Russian oligarch, dismissing the idea that it should act on Western sanctions

The widening divide between Russia and the West has provided avenues for exploitation for countries like Iran. The latter has an interest in trilateral military drills and enhanced military cooperation with China and Russia, in a bid to minimize the continuing effects of U.S. sanctions. Access to Russian investment, military hardware, and trade, support this objective. Tehran recently acknowledged supplying "*a small quantity*" of military drones to Russia in advance of the war. Russia is already engaged in a contract to build the Bushehr nuclear plant in the southern part of Iran. The two countries were supporters of the Assad government in Syria

---

80 . Jagannath P. Panda and Wooyeal Paik. The Russian-India-China Trilateral After Ukraine: Will Beijing take the lead? China Brief Volume: 22 Issue:16. September 9, 2022. https://jamestown.org/program/the-russia-india-china-trilateral-after-ukraine-will-beijing-take-the-lead/

81 . Rahul Shrivastava. As PM Modi unveils G20 logo, India Readies to Display Global Muscle in Elite Grouping. India Today. November 8, 2022.

82 . Alan Crawford, Jenni Marsh and Anthony Squazzin. The US-Led Drive to Isolate Russia and China is falling Short. Bloomberg. Politics. August 5, 2022. https://www.bloomberg.com/news/articles/2022-08-05/the-us-led-drive-to-isolate-russia-and-china-is-falling-short (Presidency of the G20 remains in the Global South as the baton passes to India in 2023)

83 . Ibid.

during the civilian conflict and proxy wars which destroyed much of the country. Russia, with China and the EU, was a party to discussions aimed at restoring the nuclear accord which collapsed under President Trump and, to this date, remains stalled. In 2021, Tehran signed a cooperation agreement with China expanding many areas of mutual interest, including nuclear power, military hardware, technology and energy. On July 19, 2022, in his most recent visit to Tehran, Turkish President Erdogan and his Iranian counterpart pledged closer cooperation through deeper trade and other economic measures, despite the significant policy challenges between the two, and the reality of regional competition. But in this era when both parties experience tensions with the West, common interests provide the push towards more constructive engagement between them. All of these discussions have paved the way for Tehran to join SCO and the Eurasian Economic Union, providing other avenues through which Iran will attempt to secure its interests.

7. No Going Back: A Multilayered Multipolar World

Vladimir Putin could not have expected a fractious West to come together so resolutely against Russian aggression in Ukraine. The war, which was expected to be over within days, is now in its ninth month. Russia is fighting NATO and its allies in everything but name, in a war of attrition with no end in sight. Neither did the Global West expect to receive such clear signaling that Western interests are no longer, de facto, those of the rest of the world. Nor are Western values deemed universal. In many ways, this confluence of crises including this war, coming on the heels of two years of a global pandemic, which underscored the divide between the rich, Western world, and the rest, coupled with earlier attempts by the US and some of its allies to achieve some measure of decoupling from China, has produced a two-block world, the Global West, and a loosely based Alliance of the Rest. A certain disenchantment with a West focused on its own interests during the COVID-19 pandemic, and now determined to secure its interests at any cost during this period of war and Great Power rivalry, regardless of the price being paid by the rest of the world, is pushing many of the world's countries towards a strategy of alliance building with like-minded others. Determined not to choose a side, they believe that one *"can have McDonald's and Burger King on the same street."*[84] Together they demonstrate a *"cherry picking approach to foreign policy and relations building which provides*

---

84. Ibid.

potent grounds for influence peddling, competition," and the exertion of leverage.[85]

Regional actors have also seized this moment. In the contest between two superpowers, they have placed themselves as interlocutors bridging East and West, leveraging their geography, history, and culture adroitly during this war. Indonesia, Turkey, South Africa, and others come to mind. Increasingly, identity and culture have formed the basis for expanding the scope of non-Western multilateral constructs such as the BRICS and SCO, which are growing in stature. Alternative institutions are being established. China's BRI plays a role in this calculus. Loans and debt payments are being negotiated in local currencies. Over time, these initiatives will reduce issues of volatility and dependence on the U.S. dollar and Western interbank structures such as SWIFT. Deepening relations with like-minded non-Western states is a hedge against Western sanctions, should they be deployed. Time is on their side. For many, their populations are increasing, as is their share of global wealth. On both counts, that of the West is declining. Though the West may be in denial, this loosely based Alliance of the Global South is etching new dimensions of multilayered, multipolarity onto the international structure in "*a fundamental shift in global equilibrium with consequences for the international order.*"[86]

But there are reasons for concern. A fragmented two-bloc world undermines the capacity to cooperate on global issues such as climate change and governance. It undermines too, the prospects for shared global prosperity. The fact that President Biden has announced, at the recently concluded Bali Summit, that the US has no intention of pursuing a new Cold War with China, is comforting. But, the new U.S. Security Strategy suggests otherwise. Time will tell. Also, to be seen, is how long the alliance of the Global West will hold. Germany Chancellor Scholz, having offered the U.S. the prize of purchasing F-35 stealth fighters, to the dismay of EU member France, then proceeded to visit China with a business delegation in tow. The EU and U.S. are engaged in a "*growing spat*" over the Inflation Reduction Act which provides subsidies, tax, and other incentives to "*green US businesses.*"[87] Republicans have raised questions about continued support for Ukraine,

---

85 . Rahul Shrivastava. As PM Modi Unveils G20 logo, India Readies to Display Global Muscle in Elite Grouping. India Today. November 8, 2022. The G20 has global muscle. It represents 85% of global GDP, 75% of global trade and 67% of world population.
86 . Jacques Sapir. Le Nouveau "Grand-Sud" fait-il secession? Le Spectacle Du Monde – Trimestriel No 10: Automne 2022
87 . Nicholas Vinocur. Biden Keeps Ignoring Europe. Its time EU Leaders Got the Message. Politico. November 25, 2022. https://www.politico.eu/article/joe-biden-ira-inflation-reduction-us-ignores-eu/

and are now in control of the US House of Representatives following the mid-term elections. Europeans are on the streets in some cities protesting price increases and, in the UK, citizens have seen standards of living rolled back during a period of heightened economic turbulence. Change is afoot. What the future holds is anyone's guess. It would be hard to imagine that there is any going back to the world that was. But a fragmented world is hardly in anyone's best interest.

CHAPTER II

Southeast Asia: A Tapestry of Economic and Security Ties in a Neighborhood of Superpower Competition

Christian Bachheimer

Southeast Asia has been actively hedging since the end of the Cold War. Omni-enmeshment, underpinned by Asian centrality, are the core concepts of this strategy. However, in the decade before the COVID-19 pandemic, ASEAN was under pressure from a rising China coming into collision with the U.S. The pandemic and the Russia-Ukraine war have further entrenched mistrust, undermined multilateralism, and offered opportunistic possibilities for China, while exposing fault lines between the West and the rest. But foreign policy starts at home. Southeast Asian countries must focus on reinforcing their economies and political systems first, while diversifying their partnerships, and making ASEAN more cohesive in the hope of a 'share of the voice' in shaping the agenda.

1. The Pre-COVID-19 Decade: Choppy Waters for ASEAN[1]

The decade before COVID-19 was difficult for Southeast Asia, as the region entered a period of structural uncertainty. In the aftermath of the 2009 financial crisis, China's charm offensive came to an end. U.S. President Obama announced a controversial pivot to Asia that heightened tensions across the region with its security emphasis, while the election of nationalists in Japan, China, India, and the U.S. would prove decisive. During this period, Southeast Asian countries saw their hedging strategies tested and gradually more challenged.

Frontiers in Asia are, and have always been, fluid and mutually enmeshed, with limited and selective sovereignty,[2] pinpointing a subtle idea of international relations. Hedging strategies are a natural fit, and partial alignments are the rule. As a consequence, Southeast Asian countries all display strategic hedging patterns, with idiosyncratic preferences and behaviors.[3]

Strategic hedging is defined as a risk management policy against uncertainty.[4] These strategies are operationalized in various ways by blending cooperation and coercion,[5] mixing "*power acceptance*" and "*power*

---

[1] . Southeast Asia will be used to refer to the geography, the countries of the region acting collectively, or independently; while ASEAN, the political and economic union that includes 10 Southeast Asia countries, will be used when referring to actions that are coordinated by this union. ASEAN members are Indonesia, Cambodia, Thailand, Laos, Vietnam, Malaysia, Singapore, Brunei, Philippines and Myanmar.

[2] . John David Ciorciari, "The Balance of Great-Power Influence in Contemporary Southeast Asia," International Relations of the Asia Pacific 9, no. 1 (2009) 165, https://www.jstor.org/stable/26159461; Amitav Acharya, Rethinking Power, Institutions and Ideas in World Politics: Whose IR?(London: Routledge, 2013), 19.

[3] . Jurgen Haacke, "The concept of hedging and its application to Southeast Asia: a critique and a proposal of a modified conceptual and methodological framework," International Relations of the Asia-Pacific 19, no. 3 (2019), 376,https://doi.org/10.1093/irap/lcz010); Ann Marie Murphy, "Great Power Rivalries, Domestic Politics and Southeast Asian Foreign Policy: Exploring the Linkages," Asian Security 13, no. 3 (2017), 181, DOI: 10.1080/14799855.2017.1354566

[4] . John David Ciorciari & Jurgen Haacke, , "Hedging in international relations: an introduction,"International Relations of the Asia-Pacific19, no. 3 (2019), page 369, https://doi.org/10.1093/irap/lcz017; John D Ciorciari, "The Variable Effectiveness of Hedging Strategies,". International Relations of the Asia-Pacific, 19, no. 3, 2019, 524 https://doi.org/10.1093/irap/lcz007; Haacke, "The Concept of Hedging and its Application to Southeast Asia"; Kuik Cheng-Shwee, "The Essence of Hedging: Malaysia, and Singapore Response to a Rising China," Contemporary Southeast Asia 30, no. 2 (2008), https://www.researchgate.net/publication/265754648_The_Essence_of_Hedging_Malaysia_and_Singapore's_Response_to_a_Rising_China

[5] . Ryan Yu-Lin Liou & Philip Szue-Chin Hsu., "The Effectiveness of Minor Powers' Hedging Strategy: Comparing Singapore and the Philippines", 2016, 8, http://web.isanet.org/Web/Conferences/HKU2017- s/Archive/51e2d842-38c4-4570-b758-e448489d36c0.pdf

rejection",[6] crafting opposite policies that are "*complementary, competing and contradictory*".[7] Hedging does not mean 'fence sitting', as has often been portrayed, but is a means to maintaining a "*dynamic equilibrium*",[8] a conscious decision to stay ambiguous and non-aligned, while refuting the balance-of-power logic.

As strategic hedging is crafted and executed at the country level, how can the Association of Southeast Asian Nations (ASEAN) leverage the power of collective action? ASEAN has historically followed an omni-enmeshment approach to international relations and the management of great powers. Omni-enmeshment calls for attracting all relevant players into a web of engagements, relationships, interactions, and exchanges,[9] hoping that they would "*be unwilling to disrupt the status quo at each other's expense—which would be more costly than if it were at the expense of the small or medium states of the region alone*".[10]

Omni-enmeshment depends on multilateral institutions essential to socialize powerful outsiders to the regional community and its norms. However, the sine qua none condition is also to have alternative partners in the international system, and therefore, ASEAN must remain inclusive, no matter what. It is the cornerstone of the whole approach.

The U.S. neglected Southeast Asia during the Trump Administration. As a result, 67% of Southeast Asia's elite[11] saw a drop in U.S. engagement with ASEAN[12] (except Vietnam where 40% saw U.S. influence increase). China inserted itself into the power vacuum, aiming at dominance within Ming's historical sphere of influence,[13] while other middle powers, including India, Japan, and Australia, jockeyed for a role.

---

6. . Kuik, "The Essence of Hedging," 165.
7. . Cheng-Chwee Kuik (2016) How Do Weaker States Hedge? Unpacking ASEAN states' alignment behavior towards China, Journal of Contemporary China, 25:100, 500-514, DOI: 10.1080/10670564.2015.1132714
8. . Marty Natalegawa, Does ASEAN matter: A View from Inside (Singapore: Yusof Ishak Institute, 2018, 90.
9. . Evelyn Goh, "Great Powers and Southeast Asian Regional Security Strategies: Omni-enmeshment, balancing and hierarchical order," Working Paper, Institute of Defence and Strategic Studies Singapore, no. 84, 2005.
10. . Ibid.
11. . ISEAS survey is an elite survey. Unless mentioned, all poll numbers are elite survey in this chapter
12. . "The State of Southeast Asia," Yusof Ishak Institute, 2019, 16, https://www.iseas.edu.sg/wp-content/uploads/pdfs/TheStateofSEASurveyReport_2019.pdf
13. . Ming Empire lasted from 1368 to 1644. Its influence expended to East and South China Sea, as well as, beyond the Indian Ocean through trading networks. This was spearheaded by Admiral Cheng Ho and his tribute collecting fleet. Ming Dynasty, Chinese History, Britannica, https://www.britannica.com/topic/Ming-dynasty-Chinese-history.

In January 2017, in a dramatic fashion, the U.S. withdrew from the Trans-Pacific Partnership (TPP), the largest global free trade agreement. The TPP excluded China, while ASEAN was only represented by Malaysia, Vietnam, and Singapore. The American decision was taken without consulting regional partners, which had invested domestic political capital and were thrown off guard. The U.S. placed itself entirely out of the regional economic architecture. It chose to criticize China rather than offering any pragmatic alternative beyond small gestures. It then initiated a costly trade war, hoping to counter China. This episode bolstered the perception in the region of the U.S. as a sunset power. By 2019, 59% of Southeast Asians believed its influence has diminished significantly, while trust in the U.S. plunged to a low 27%, with 50% having little confidence that U.S. would "*do the right thing*".[14]

During this period, China fostered parallel institutions such as the Shanghai Cooperation Organization (SCO), the Asia Infrastructure Investment Bank (AIIB), New Development Bank (NDB), the Silk Road Fund, the Boao Forum, and the China International Cooperation Development Agency (CICDA). While sounding the drum beat of Mao's protector of the Third World, the goal was unmistakably to mirror the U.S.-led world order, offering the South an alternative, but on different terms. In September 2013, to accomplish the 'Chinese Dream', President Xi Jinping announced the 'Silk Economic Road Belt'. Southeast Asia was especially highlighted during his October 2013 visit to Jakarta, as the cradle of his initiative. By 2019, the Silk Road had attracted 60 countries and $200 billion in investment,[15] under the new label 'Belt and Road Initiative' (BRI). In many ways, the BRI is China's strategy for containment of U.S. global reach, and has geopolitical aspects.

In 2009, China announced the nine-dash line[16] as new limits to its sovereignty in the South China Sea (SCS). In 2012, ASEAN's first public disagreement over SCS in Cambodia's notorious summit erupted.[17] In 2011, former U.S. Secretary of State Hillary Clinton made an affirmative statement

---

14 . "The State of Southeast Asia 2019", 30.
15 . Andrew Chatzky and James McBride,"China's massive Belt and Road Initiative," Council on Foreign Affairs, January 28, 2020, https://www.cfr.org/backgrounder/chinas-massive-belt-and-road-initiative
16 . The nine-dash line is used by the Chinese Communist Party (CCP) to illustrate claims to South China Sea, that encompasses 90% of the 3 million square kilometre of South China Sea, The Interpreter, 12 April 2022, https://www.lowyinstitute.org/the-interpreter/china-s-nine-dash-line-proves-stranger-fiction
17 . Luke Hunt, "Asean Summit Fall out continues" The Diplomat, July 20, 2012, https://thediplomat.com/2012/07/asean-summit-fallout-continues-on/

on the freedom of navigation in SCS.[18] Breaking its own promises not to militarize the area,[19] China further asserted itself in the SCS. In 2016, China's loss at the International Court of Justice (ICJ) over the Philippines SCS case did not alter what would drift toward a standoff.[20] There were few reactions within ASEAN after all, and support for the Philippines was light. Less publicized, mainland Southeast Asia was subjected to coercion along the Mekong.[21] In 2016, China set-up the Lancang Mekong Cooperation (LMC) to substitute various Mekong mechanisms (arguably inefficient). Its stated goal was to boost *"cooperation...connectivity...sustainable development, and collectively managing the shared water resources of the Mekong river basin"*.[22] However, the LMC grants China both power and influence over the six riparian countries[23]. Despite the lack of push back from ASEAN, the cost of China's misdeeds was further erosion of regional trust, down to 19% by 2019[24].

The China Communist Party's (CCP) 19th Congress in 2017 proved a turning point. It emphasized that China would promote its economic model to developing nations, and lead reform on global governance, a significant shift in foreign policy,[25] which departed from China's own five principles.[26] China would build a limited hierarchy, defined as emphasizing *"unequal*

---

18. U.S Department of State, Press Statement Hillary Rodham Clinton Secretary of State Washington DC, July 22, 2011, https://2009-2017.state.gov/secretary/20092013clinton/rm/2011/07/168989.htm
19. Ankit Panda, "It's Official: Xi Jinping Breaks His Non-Militarization Pledge in the Spratlys," The Diplomat, December 16, 2016,https://thediplomat.com/2016/12/its-official-xi-jinping-breaks-his-non-militarization-pledge-in-the-spratlys/
20. Ankit Panda, "International Court Issues Unanimous Award in Philippines v. China Case on South China Sea," The Diplomat, July 12, 2016, https://thediplomat.com/2016/07/international-court-issues-unanimous-award-in-philippines-v-china-case-on-south-china-sea/
21. Shang Su Wu, "The trouble with the Lancang Mekong Cooperation Forum," The Diplomat, December 19, 2018, https://thediplomat.com/2018/12/the-trouble-with-the-lancang-mekong-cooperation-forum/
22. The Lancang-Mekong Cooperation Mechanism. CSCAP REGIONAL SECURITY OUTLOOK + ARF - The next 25 years 2019. Council for Security Cooperation in the Asia Pacific (2019), 48, http://www.cscap.org/uploads/docs/CRSO/CSCAP%202019%20Regional%20Security%20Outlook.pdf
23. Nguyen K Giang, "The Mekong is caught in a tug of war," East Asia Forum, February 7, 2019,https://www.eastasiaforum.org/2019/02/07/the-mekong-region-is-caught-in-a-tug-of-war/
24. "The State of Southeast Asia 2019", 31.
25. Michael Swaine, "The 19th Party Congress and Chinese Foreign Policy," Carnegie Endowment for International Peace, October 16, 2017, https://carnegieendowment.org/2017/10/16/19th-party-congress-and-chinese-foreign-policy-pub-73432
26. The Five Principles, signed on April 29, 1954, are 1) mutual respect for each other's territorial integrity and sovereignty, 2) mutual non-aggression, 3) mutual non-interference in each other's internal affairs and equality, 4) cooperation for mutual benefit and 5) peaceful co-existence.', The Diplomat, 26 June 2014.

relationships which are nevertheless short of hegemony or empire",[27] in areas uncontested by the U.S., setting up a 'sphere of influence', a bulwark against the Westphalian system's expansion. All the while, China denounced 'sphere of influence' as cold war mentality, a contradiction that did not seems to perturb the CCP.

Japan's 2013 vision statement on 'ASEAN–Japan Friendship and cooperation' was expanded in the field of security under Prime Minister Abe with far reaching consequences. Japan established various infrastructure funds,[28] reaching $116 billion[29] from 2016 to 2020, eclipsing China's BRI.[30] These were also made in cooperation with China to support regional infrastructure needs of $1.7 trillion per year[31] in a radically different approach to the U.S. in the region. Finally, Japan revived the old idea of the Indo Pacific and the Quad, a quadrilateral security dialogue among U.S., Japan, Australia and India, which of late has been elevated by the U.S.[32]

The Crimea crisis of 2014, and the resulting sanctions, accelerated Russia's eastward turn, as she reasserted herself through old Soviet ties with mainland Southeast Asia and engaged in modest strategic partnerships with ASEAN. Lenin's Eurasianism was resuscitated, reiterating "*Let us turn our faces towards Asia….the East will help us conquer the West*", pulling China and India as partners into a 'multi-vector policy',[33] shorthand for hedging against the West. Russia's new anchor would prove useful in the 2022 Ukraine crisis.

---

27. Evelyn Goh, et al., Betwixt and Between: Southeast Asian Strategic Relations with the US and China (Singapore: Institute of Defence and Strategic Studies- Nanyang Technology University, 2005).
28. "Japan Fund for Prosperous and Resilient Asia and the Pacific, ADB, https://www.adb.org/what-we-do/funds/japan-fund-prosperous-resilient-asia-pacific#:~:text=What%20is%20the%20fund%3F,to%20projects%20financed%20by%20ADB.
29. Tobias Harris, "Quality infrastructure: Japan's Robust Challenge to China's Belt and Road," War on the Rocks, April 9, 2019, https://warontherocks.com/2019/04/quality-infrastructure-japans-robust-challenge-to-chinas-belt-and-road/
30. Christian Bachheimer, "China's mercantilist threat to ASEAN is exaggerated," East Asia Forum, September 19, 2021, https://www.eastasiaforum.org/2021/09/18/chinas-mercantilist-threat-to-asean-is-exaggerated/
31. "Meeting Asia infrastructure needs," Asian Development Bank, February 2017 ,http://dx.doi.org/10.22617/FLS168388-2
32. David Brunnstrom, "U.S. seeks meeting soon to revive Asia-Pacific 'Quad' security forum," Reuters, October 28, 2017, https://www.reuters.com/article/us-usa-asia-quad-idUSKBN1CW2O1
33. Neviditac Kapoor, c "Russia Relations in South East Asia since 2014: Continuity and Change," Observer Research Foundation, Occasional Paper 267, August 2020, 7, https://www.orfonline.org/wp-content/uploads/2020/08/ORF_OccasionalPaper_267_Russia-SEA.pdf

India rebooted its 'Act East policy', but with limited success beyond Vietnam and Japan. In a nutshell, Southeast Asia was becoming once more crowded, for better or worse, a reminder of the region's vital importance, and the role of ASEAN as its skipper.

In 2007, the ASEAN charter was adopted, a critical step toward the formalization of the organization and the genesis of a single market. ASEAN signed numerous free trade agreements (FTAs), including with China, South Korea, and Australia.

After the creation of the East Asia Summit (EAS) in 2005, ASEAN expanded its ASEAN Defense Minister Meeting (ADMM) to include most EAS members,[34] an acknowledgement of the challenging security environment. It also admitted the U.S., Russia and China as EAS full members. The ASEAN political security community was incorporated in 2003, but became effective only in 2015. In 2017, it also produced its master plan for connectivity, acknowledging the interdependence of all regional countries.[35] In 2018, an ASEAN–Russia strategic partnership was concluded,[36] covering science and technology, prevention of infectious diseases, water management, and agriculture, among other topics. By 2020, The Treaty of Amity, a non-aggression and cooperation pact among ASEAN members and their partners, was enlarged to 49 contracting parties, including Russia.[37]

Since 2010, despite these initiatives, ASEAN has entered choppy waters stemming from the renewal of power geopolitics, their competing political/economic/security frameworks, and also ASEAN's own weaknesses.

---

34 . The ADMM-Plus is a platform for ASEAN and its eight Dialogue Partners Australia, China, India, Japan, New Zealand, Republic of Korea, Russia and the United States (collectively referred to as the "Plus Countries"), to strengthen security and defence cooperation for peace, stability, and development in the region. The Inaugural ADMM-Plus was convened in Ha Noi, Viet Nam, on 12 October 2010. ASEAN at https://admm.asean.org/index.php/about-admm/about-admm-plus.html

35 . "Master Plan on ASEAN Connectivity 2025," Association of Southeast Asian Nations, December 2017, 8, https://asean.org/wp-content/uploads/2018/01/47.-December-2017-MPAC2025-2nd-Reprint-.pdf

36 . "Joint Statement of the 3rd ASEAN-Russian Federation Summit on Strategic Partnership," Association of Southeast Asian Nations, November 14, 2018, https://asean.org/joint-statement-of-the-3rd-asean-russian-federation-summit-on-strategic-partnership/

37 . "The Treaty of Amity and Cooperation in Southeast Asia (TAC) was established in 1976 and embodies universal principles of peaceful coexistence and friendly cooperation among States in Southeast Asia. It is a legally-binding code for inter-state relations in the region and beyond. The Treaty has been amended three times, in 1987, 1998, and 2010, respectively, to allow for accession by states outside Southeast Asia as well as for regional organisations whose members are sovereign states, among others. As of August 2022, there are 49 High Contracting Parties to the TAC." Treaty of Amity and Cooperation Southeast Asia, Association of Southeast Asian Nations, https://asean.org/our-communities/asean-political-security-community/outward-looking-community/treaty-of-amity-and-cooperation-in-southeast-asia-tac/

Omni-enmeshment remained ASEAN's goal, but the strategy to achieve it needed adjustments yet to be defined. As usual, ASEAN reacted slowly. In 2019, it produced its own ASEAN Outlook for Indo Pacific (AOIP),[38] an Indonesian-inspired aspiration for the regional order that reaffirmed the omni-enmeshment and hedging strategy that has been in place all along. However, as with many other ASEAN initiatives, AOIP lacked the political will for effective execution.

The sustainability of Southeast Asia's countries' hedging strategy was contested. Singapore Prime Minister Lee Hsieng Long's reflection that "*if America–China relations become very difficult, our position becomes tougher because then we will be coerced to choose between being friends with America and friends with China*"[39] resonated in ASEAN capitals. The spirit of the non-alignment movement born in 1955 at the Bandung conference still haunts international relations in the South, well beyond Southeast Asia.

In essence, Southeast Asian countries were worried about China's threat to their autonomy and territory. But, they were also concerned about the U.S.'s threat of regime change in line with its assertive advocacy on human rights and liberal democracy,[40] which collides with the ASEAN states' view of society at large. The region conceded that China's power should be respected, alongside the historical political hierarchy that has always regulated interstate relations.[41] But even as China's influence was acknowledged, trust in China was eroding[42] through its harassment in the SCS, coupled with undiplomatic statements,[43] which revealed how China was thinking. As a result, most ASEAN nations have significantly increased their defense spending in a classical internal balancing act.[44]

---

38 . "AOIP: ASEAN Outlook Indo Pacific," Association of Southeast Asian Nations, June 23, 2019, https://asean.org/speechandstatement/asean-outlook-on-the-indo-pacific/
39 . "Prime Minister's Office Singapore, "PM Lee Hsien Loong's Interview with BBC HARDtalk," February 23, 2017, https://www.pmo.gov.sg/Newsroom/pm-lee-hsien-loongs-interview-bbc-hardtalk
40 . Ann Marie Murphy, "Great Power Rivalries, Domestic Politics and Southeast Asian Foreign Policy: Exploring the Linkages."
41 . David Kang, "International Order in Historical East Asia: Tribute and Hierarchy Beyond Sinocentrism and Eurocentrism," International Organization 74, no. 1 (2019), 65, 65–93. doi:10.1017/S0020818319000274
42 . "The State of Southeast Asia 2019" 31.
43 . See Yang Jeichi in July 2010 where he mocked his hosts, the Vietnamese; at another, he declared, "China is a big country and other countries are small countries, and that's just a fact", https://jamestown.org/program/chinas-missteps-in-southeast-asia-less-charm-more-offensive/ ; or China's use of proxy States voting in its favour within ASEAN; or Wang Yi trying to bully ASEAN state in accepting a draft joint statement in 2016 in D onald K Emmerson, The Deer and the Dragon: Southeast Asia and China in the 21st Century (Shorenstein Asia-Pacific Research Center, 2020), 14 & 15.
44 . ASEAN annual military expenditures were (1) in 2010 30 bn USD, (2) in 2020 43 bn USD

The last pre-COVID-19 Shangri-La dialogue, in 2019 in Singapore, an annual track 1.5 forum attended by all Asia Pacific States, saw only the exchange of barbs between powers. Gone were the years of recognizing differences, bridging gaps, attempting to bring the South to the fore in the U.S.-led world order. Although a weakened ASEAN faces the *"revival of geopolitics and crisis of expectations"*,[45] openly challenged by China-U.S. competition, it nonetheless remains the core institution, staging numerous forums.

2. The COVID-19 pandemic: Opportunism and Mistrust

By early 2022, Southeast Asia had 36 million recorded COVID-19 cases and about 515,000 deaths out of a population of 622 million.[46] Vaccine coverage was only achieved by early 2022, with about 410 million people or 66% of the whole population fully vaccinated.[47] The health impact has not been as devastating as in Europe,[48] but the impact on economic and poverty rates has been more devastating.

As the world scrambled for the few available vaccines, Western countries cornered behind global distribution, appearing again more concerned with themselves than the greater common good. Rising nationalism was certainly a constraint for Western states facing social unrest. Southeast Asian countries had to rely on China as a 'first responder' (Figure 1), content to receive China's COVID-19 vaccine during an emergency.[49] This mirrored China's support to ASEAN in the 1997 financial crisis. Obviously, China did not miss the opportunity to publicize its good deeds, castigating the West as selfish. As such, the term vaccine diplomacy was born.

---

according to the "SIPRI Military Expenditure Database," https://milex.sipri.org/sipri

45 . Amitav Acharya, ASEAN and the Regional Order: Revisiting Security Community in South East Asia (New York: Routledge, 2021), 26.

46 . "Southeast Asia Faces GDP Loss of 8.4% in 2021 as COVID-19 Roils Tourism", Southeast Asia Development Solutions, July 19, 2021, https://seads.adb.org/solutions/southeast-asia-faces-gdp-loss-84-2021-covid-19-roils-tourism

47 . Our World in Data, "Coronavirus (Covid 2019) vaccinations", Our World in Data, https://ourworldindata.org/covid-vaccinations

48 . There is a record of 2 million deaths according to Reuters Covid-19 Tracker,". For more, refer to "Reuters Covid-19 Tracker," Reuters, https://graphics.reuters.com/world-coronavirus-tracker-and-maps/regions/europe/

49 . Dominique Fraser & Richard Maude, "China Won over South East Asia during the Pandemic," The Diplomat, July 20, 2022, https://thediplomat.com/2022/07/china-won-over-southeast-asia-during-the-pandemic/

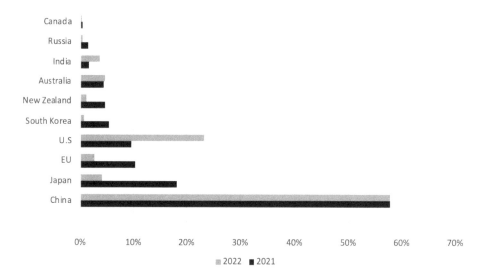

Figure 1: Which ASEAN's Dialogue Partner has provided the most help to the region for COVID-19?
Source : The State of South East Asia in 2021 and in 2022, ISEAS
at https://www.iseas.edu.sg/wp-content/uploads/2022/02/The-State-of-SEA-2022_FA_Digital_FINAL.pdf
at https://www.iseas.edu.sg/wp-content/uploads/2021/01/The-State-of-SEA-2021-v2.pdf

Nevertheless, more than half of Southeast Asians considered China to be a main donor in this time of crisis, and to be well intentioned.[50] If there ever was vaccine diplomacy, it was certainly not perceived as such in ASEAN. In 2022, polling showed that the level of overall trust in China increased from 19% to 26.8%,[51] despite all the security concerns.

Southeast Asia is very trade dependent, with one of the highest trade ratios in the world at 84%.[52] In November 2020, in the midst of the pandemic, the Regional Comprehensive Economic Partnership (RCEP)[53] was signed. Covering 30% of the world GDP and 2.2 billion people, RCEP was expected to underwrite the post-COVID-19 economic recovery in 2022. Oddly, Australia was a signatory too, although the country was in the middle of a trade war with China over COVID-19 investigation comments

---

50 . ISEAS The State of Southeast Asia survey 2022 noted that 58% of the elite saw China as the main partner, 23% considered USA as a partner, and only 2.6% saw EU as a partner. Vietnam elite was an exception with only 16% seeing China as a partner, and instead 52% seeing US as a key partner. https://www.iseas.edu.sg/wp-content/uploads/2021/01/The-State-of-SEA-2021-v2.pdf
51 . "The State of Southeast Asia 2022," 52.
52 . The trade ratio of 84% was computed by the author based on data available at ASEAN website . https://data.aseanstats.org/trade-annually
53 . "What is RCEP: ASEAN plus 15 countries" accessed on July 17, 2022 at https://www.business-standard.com/about/what-is-rcep

and accusations of influencing operations inside Australia.[54] This was an awkward situation, and a test for RCEP. RCEP was followed by an ASEAN-China Comprehensive Strategic Partnership (CSP) agreement in November 2021,[55] concurrently offset with an ASEAN-U.S. Comprehensive Partnership signed in May 2022.[56] Russia established a trade office to ASEAN in 2021, but also conducted joint military naval drills in December 2021.[57] Amitav Acharya's 'Co-engagement',[58] a better term than hedging, still governs the approach.

But as in any past crisis, state opportunism kicked in. China's assertiveness in the SCS intensified. Grey-zone tactics were fully deployed in Malaysia,[59] the Philippines,[60] Vietnam,[61] and Indonesia[62] (Figure 2). The South China Sea Code of Conduct (CoC) negotiation was once more conveniently put aside, dashing recent hopes. CoC is critical as it drives most of the Southeast Asian's displeasure with China, where 64% see it as a key precondition to improve relations[63]. Even the usefulness of the CoC negotiation is openly questioned, with arguments supporting both sides.[64] To make things worse, China passed a new Coast Guard law in early 2021,[65] authorizing

---

54 . "Timeline: The Downward Spiral of China-Australia Relations," Geopolitical Monitor, January 23, 2022,
https://www.geopoliticalmonitor.com/timeline-the-downward-spiral-of-china-australia-relations/

55 . "Joint Statement of the ASEAN-China Special Summit to Commemorate the 30th Anniversary of ASEAN-China Dialogue Relations," Association of Southeast Asian Nations, November 22, 2021,
https://asean.org/wp-content/uploads/2021/11/Joint-Statement-30th-Anniversary-of-ASEAN-China-Dialogue-Relations-Final.pdf

56 . "ASEAN-U.S Special Summit, 2022 Joint Vision Statement," Association of Southeast Asian Nations, May 14, 2022, https://asean.org/wp-content/uploads/2022/05/Final-ASEAN-US-Special-Summit-2022-Joint-Vision-Statement.pdf

57 . Andrey Gubin, "Russia's blossoming ties with ASEAN," East Asia Forum, February 5, 2022, https://www.eastasiaforum.org/2022/02/05/russias-blossoming-ties-with-asean/

58 . Acharya, ASEAN and the Regional Order, 127.

59 . Joseph Sipalan,. "Malaysia to summon Chinese envoy over 'suspicious' air force activity," Reuters, June 2, 2021, https://www.reuters.com/world/asia-pacific/malaysia-says-chinese-military-planes-came-close-violating-airspace-2021-06-01/

60 . Scott Neuman, "Philippines Calls On China To Remove Massive Fishing Fleet At Disputed Reef", NPR, March 22, 2021, https://www.npr.org/2021/03/22/979923065/philippines-calls-on-china-to-remove-massive-fishing-fleet-at-disputed-reef

61 . Helen Clark, "Oil and Gas Fuelling South China Sea Tensions,", Asia Times, July 22, 2020, https://asiatimes.com/2020/07/oil-and-gas-fueling-south-china-sea-tensions/

62 . Sebastian Strangio, "China Demanded Halt to Indonesian Drilling Near Natuna Islands: Report," The Diplomat, December 2, 2021, https://thediplomat.com/2021/12/china-demanded-halt-to-indonesian-drilling-near-natuna-islands-report/

63 . "The State of Southeast Asia 2022" 37.

64 . "Should ASEAN walk away from the South China Sea Code of Conduct process?," Lee Kuan Yew School of Public Policy, June 7, 2022, Video Recording, https://www.youtube.com/watch?v=tPaTLk6n0Mo

65 . Ministry of Defense of Japan, The Coast Guard Law of the People's Republic of China, https://www.mod.go.jp/en/d_act/sec_env/ch_ocn/index.html

law enforcement operation within SCS's nine-dash line, to suspend what it deems illegal activities, such as constructing installations, and carrying out naval defense operations. This was in direct violation of UNCLOS.[66]

Furthermore, in 2019, China hoarded Mekong's downstream water to Vietnam,[67] which could feel first-hand the potential threat. ASEAN, in a similar fashion as in the case of the South China Sea, advocated mostly dialogue, in line with its long-held tradition, but without much effect.

Figure 2: Main Chinese incursions into South East Asian countries over the Covid period 2019-2021
Source : by author from public reporting
South East Asia Map Copyright: <a href='https://www.123rf.com/profile_pytyczech'>pytyczech</a>

By pushing its pawns on the Southeast Asian chessboard during the pandemic, China provided the Quad with a second life, under the instigation of Japan and Australia. It even expanded its scope to vaccines and other issues, trying to show a good face not solely focused on security.[68] But in September 2021, a diplomatic bomb was dropped. The AUKUS alliance,

---

66 . UNCLOS: United Nations Convention on the Law of the Sea.
67 . Bryan Eyler, "How China Turned Off the Tap on the Mekong River,", STIMSON, April 13, 2020, https://www.stimson.org/2020/new-evidence-how-china-turned-off-the-mekong-tap/
68 . "Covid: US and allies promise one billion jabs for Southeast Asia," BBC, March 12, 2021, https://www.bbc.com/news/world-56381104

a trilateral security partnership between the U.S., the UK, and Australia was announced.[69] It highlighted once more U.S. unilateral decisions in a region of the world without prior consultation with its allies,[70] and reflected Australia obsessive fear of abandonment.[71] AUKUS is largely perceived as an escalation in Southeast Asia, carrying nuclear proliferation risk, triggering an arms race,[72] and opening up an avenue for power projections in the region's security affairs.[73]

Support for these security arrangements is ambivalent. About 60% of Southeast Asians support the Quad, especially true in Singapore and the Philippines.[74] On the other hand, AUKUS is seen in a much more ambiguous light, especially by Indonesia, the largest power in ASEAN.[75] But Malaysia too,[76] a member of the five powers defense arrangement that has joined together Australia, New Zealand, Britain, Malaysia, and Singapore since 1971, has its own misgivings. Opinions are mixed on security benefits in deterring China, and the cost incurred, such as a loss of ASEAN centrality or the risk of escalation, *"potentially adding fuel to the SCS dispute"*.[77] AUKUS is also seen as the outcome of ASEAN's own limitations and security blind spots. Nevertheless, at ease with the contradictions required by hedging, Indonesia conducted the 'Garuda Shield' military exercise in 2022, which included AUKUS nations[78] (limited military exercises were conducted with

---

69 . The White House. Joint leaders statement on AUKUS (September 2021). https://www.whitehouse.gov/briefing-room/statements-releases/2021/09/15/joint-leaders-statement-on-aukus/

70 . Evan Laksamana, "AUKUS mixed reception a symptom of strategic fault-lines in Southeast Asia." East Asia Forum, October 17, 2021, https://www.eastasiaforum.org/2021/10/17/aukus-mixed-reception-a-symptom-of-strategic-fault-lines-in-southeast-asia/

71 . Allan Gyngell, & Sam Roggeveen. "Fear of abandonment: A Dialogue on Australian Foreign Policy, Past and Future". The Interpreter, May 31, 2017, https://www.lowyinstitute.org/the-interpreter/fear-abandonment-dialogue-australian-foreign-policy-past-and-future

72 . William Choong, & Ian Story. "Southeast Asian Responses to AUKUS: Arms Racing, Non-Proliferation and Regional Stability," Yusof Ishak Institute , no. 134, October 14, 2021, 2, https://www.iseas.edu.sg/wp-content/uploads/2021/09/ISEAS_Perspective_2021_134.pdf

73 . Dino Patti Djalal, "ASEAN Responses to AUKUS Security Dynamic". East Asia Forum, November 28, 2021, https://www.eastasiaforum.org/2021/11/28/asean-responses-to-aukus-security-dynamic/

74 . "The State of Southeast Asia 2022," 28.

75 . Benjamin Herscovitch, & Gata Priyandita, "Indonesia-Australia: Deeper Divide Lies Beneath AUKUS Submarine Rift," The Interpreter, November 8, 2021, https://www.lowyinstitute.org/the-interpreter/indonesia-australia-deeper-divide-lies-beneath-aukus-submarine-rift

76 . Sebastian Strangio, . "Indonesia and Malaysia Reiterate Concerns About AUKUS Pact," The Diplomat, October 19, 2021, https://thediplomat.com/2021/10/indonesia-and-malaysia-reiterate-concerns-about-aukus-pact/

77 . Aristyo Rizka Darmawan. "AUKUS Adds Fuel to the South China Sea Dispute," East Asia Forum, November 1, 2021, https://www.eastasiaforum.org/2021/11/01/aukus-adds-fuel-to-the-south-china-sea-dispute/

78 . Aristyo Rizka Darmawan, "Indonesia - US Garuda Shield Exercises: Strategic but not Without Risks," Fletcher Forum, http://www.fletcherforum.org/home/2022/10/24/

China in May 2021).[79]

The COVID-19 crisis years were a mixed record for Southeast Asia. It put in the spotlight the interdependence of the region and the rest of the world. Southeast Asians always depend on someone for something. Therefore, one would expect resilience to be the region's priority in a post-COVID-19 world. On the other hand, Southeast Asian countries have joined the largest trading blocs but had to cope with bickering great powers and ever-rising mistrust.[80] Mao's years of interference in Southeast Asia are as fresh as the U.S.'s subversion years, and still incite a general defiance toward great powers.

In many ways the COVID-19 crisis actually did not affect the state's legitimacy across ASEAN, and possibly reinforced it (with the exception of Myanmar for different reasons).[81] This was in stark contrast to the U.S. and UK, that suffered setbacks in their legitimacy, along with some European countries,[82] which further fed the perception of a declining West.

3. Russia–Ukraine war: 'Rowing Between Reefs'[83] in Southeast Asia... Again

On February 21, 2022, Russia recognized the two breakaway Ukrainian regions of Donetsk and Luhansk. This was the first shot fired in the February 24 invasion of Ukraine. In Southeast Asia, reactions were mixed, if not uninterested. Singapore was an exception. Taking a more global view of the conflict's impact and its own interests, it aligned quickly with Western positions.[84] Myanmar's Junta, unsurprisingly considering its reliance on

---

indonesia-us-garuda-shield-exercises-strategic-but-not-without-risks
79 . Laura Zhou, "China, Indonesia Hold Joint Naval Exercises Near Jakarta," South China Morning Post, May 9, 2021, https://www.scmp.com/news/china/diplomacy/article/3132821/china-indonesia-hold-joint-naval-exercises-near-jakarta
80 . "The State of South East Asia 2022.", 52.
81 . Maritime ASEAN states improved their fragility index from 67 to 58, while Continental ASEAN went from 85 to 76- https://fragilestatesindex.org/country-data/
82 . Ibid.
83 . In 1948, Prime Minister Mohammad Hatta posited: "Do we, Indonesians, in the struggle for the freedom of our people and our country, only have to choose between Russia and America?" No, he answered: "We must remain the subject who reserves the right to decide our own destiny and fight for our own goal, which is independence for the whole of Indonesia' The policy born that day, known here as mendayung antara dua karang - translates to "rowing between two reefs" , https://www.newmandala.org/indonesias-jalan-tengah-in-the-new-age-of-great-power-rivalries/
84 . Ministry of Foreign Affairs Singapore. Minister for Foreign Affairs Dr Vivian Balakrishnan's Ministerial Statement on the Situation in Ukraine and its Implications. February 28, 2022, https://www.mfa.gov.sg/Newsroom/

Russia in the aftermath of its February 2021 coup, aligned with the Russian position (but the National Unity Government represented at the UN General Assembly, instead of the Junta, voted in favor of the ES 11/1 resolution[85]). Southeast Asians did not identify clearly who the aggressor was, and who the victim was. This was not new. After all, there had been little reaction to the invasion of Crimea, Russia's Donbas conflict, or even the shooting down of the Malaysian MH17 flight.

Within days, sanctioning Russia was on the UN agenda. Several resolutions were proposed to the General Assembly. The ES 11/1 resolution (March 2) on '*Aggression against Ukraine*', and ES 11/2 resolution (March 24), '*Humanitarian consequences of the aggression against Ukraine*', were approved by 141 and 140 countries respectively.[86] Most Southeast Asian countries approved these, except Vietnam and Laos, who opposed. Cambodia was the surprising vote, conceivably hedging.[87] India and China abstained, along with 35 other countries.

The ES 11/3 resolution (April 7), intended to suspend Russia from the Human Rights Council[88] following allegations of war crimes in the Ukrainian town of Bucha. Support was much weaker, with only 93 votes in favor. 'Abstentions' climbed to 58, and 'against' to 24. Southeast Asians remained neutral or opposed to the proposal, a sharp shift from earlier resolutions. Philippines voted in favor, however. It is certain that Russia's shadow might have facilitated the shift,[89] but overall, the sense was that a Global South, if coerced, preferred to side with Russia, as an expression of independence rather than as support for Russian's act of war. The resolution was perceived as being too rushed and so triggered a prudent abstention from many countries.

Lately, the November 14th resolution A/ES-11/L.6 that request Russia to be made responsible for making reparations to Ukraine, was only approved by 94 out of the 193 members.[90] Abstention was record high with

---

85. . The vote was supported by the National Unity Government. See UN vote result.
86. . General Assembly of the UN, "Eleventh Emergency Special session 2022," at https://www.un.org/en/ga/sessions/emergency11th.shtml
87. . Vannarith Chheeang, "Cambodia hedges," East Asia Forum, September 13, 2022.
88. . UN Regional Information Center for Western Europe, "UN General Assembly votes to suspend Russia from the Human Rights Council," April 8, 2022. https://unric.org/en/un-general-assembly-votes-to-suspend-russia-from-the-human-rights-council/
89. . Shannon Tiezzi, "Which Asian Countries Voted to Suspend Russia's UNHRC Membership?," The Diplomat, April 8, 2022. https://thediplomat.com/2022/04/which-asian-countries-voted-to-suspend-russias-unhrc-membership/
90. . Daphane Psaledakis,"U.N. General Assembly calls for Russia to make reparations in Ukraine", Reuters, 14 November 2022. https://www.reuters.com/world/europe/un-general-assembly-calls-russia-make-reparations-ukraine-2022-11-14/

73 countries. In Southeast Asia, only Myanmar, Singapore and Philippines voted in favor of the resolution, while China opposed it on legal ground.[91]

Through its mutinous vote, Southeast Asia has reiterated its opposition to any diplomatic isolation of Russia, any breakdown of dialogue, in line with a long-held ASEAN tradition of keeping communication lines open, no matter what. After all, there is a strong belief that isolating countries only pushes them toward worse behavior, closing off incentives for improvement and dialogue in total opposition to the prevailing Anglo-Saxon approaches. As an example, the suspension of Russia from the G8 in 2014 was seen as a mistake,[92] and was rather considered as an alienation policy, rightly or wrongly, leading to the current situation.

In March 2022, the Western alliance decided to expand UN resolutions to economic sanctions, and to implement a whole set of decisions aimed at crippling Russia under the banner of the international community. Economic sanctions against Russia were certainly not new. Piles of sanctions have already been imposed on Russia since 2013.[93] This is to say that Russia already had ample time to prepare for a new round of bans, hence its pivot to Asia following its annexation of Crimea.

However, these new sanctions were unprecedently broad.[94] The pressure on the Global South to endorse the West's economic sanctions was enormous. Most of the countries did not follow, and focused on their immediate national interests, mostly defined by domestic matters and pandemic recovery plans. A mapping among the G20 revealed that less than half of its members actually subscribe to the sanctions led by the G7

---

91 . "China opposes UN General Assembly draft," Global Times, November 11, 2022, http://www.ecns.cn/news/politics/2022-11-16/detail-ihcfwzyq0204253.shtml
92 . Kishore Mahbubani, "Has China Won or Lost from the Ukraine War?," The Edge, Video Recording, July 9, 2022, https://www.youtube.com/watch?v=z5wcPONET7s
93 . "A timeline of EU and US sanctions and Russia countersanctions", Cambridge, https://static.cambridge.org/content/id/urn:cambridge.org:id:article:S1049096519001781/resource/name/S1049096519001781sup001.pdf
94 . Chad Bown, "Russia's war on Ukraine: A sanctions timeline," PIIE, October 7, 2022, https://www.piie.com/blogs/realtime-economics/russias-war-ukraine-sanctions-timeline

and EU[95] (Figure 3). In Asia, Singapore[96], South Korea[97], and Taiwan[98] only followed in a very limited way.

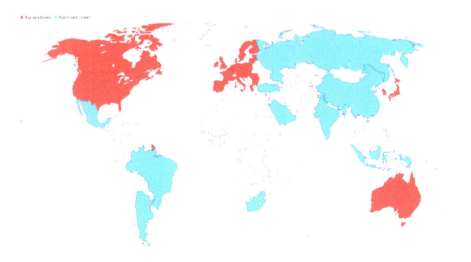

Figure 3: A G20 divided
source: Bloomberg at https://www.bloomberg.com/toaster/v2/charts/20dc2c78c1c64a468dfb85f64c22a2ff.html?brand=politics&webTheme=politics&web=true&hideTitles=true

Some countries, notably China, India, and Indonesia, ignored selectively the sanction regime[99] and have kept procuring discounted energy from Russia.[100] Facing an inflationary environment, domestic stability is paramount. Japan, South Korea, and even Taiwan decided to continue

---

95 . Alan Crawford, Jenni Marsh, Antony Sguazzin, "The US-Led Drive to isolate Russia and China Is falling Short," Bloomberg, August 5, 2022, https://www.bloomberg.com/news/articles/2022-08-05/the-us-led-drive-to-isolate-russia-and-china-is-falling-short?leadSource=uverify%20wall

96 . Singapore placed export controls on software, equipment and technology. It froze the assets of and bans transactions with VTB Bank, VEB.RF, Promsvyazbank and Bank Rossiya, and barred transactions with the Central Bank of Russia, Ministry of Foreign Affairs, Singapore, March 05, 20022, https://www.mfa.gov.sg/Newsroom/Press-Statements-Transcripts-and-Photos/2022/03/20220305-sanctions

97 . South Korea placed export controls on software, equipment and technology and sanctioned seven Russian banks and their subsidiaries. It banned trade in new Russian government bonds., Reuters, https://www.reuters.com/graphics/UKRAINE-CRISIS/SANCTIONS/byvrjenzmve/

98 . Taiwan placed export controls on software, equipment and technology, Reuters, https://www.reuters.com/graphics/UKRAINE-CRISIS/SANCTIONS/byvrjenzmve/

99 . Richard Heydarian, "Southeast Asia will not be Russia's lifeline, " Nikkei Asia, September 23, 2022, https://asia.nikkei.com/Opinion/Southeast-Asia-will-not-be-Russia-s-lifeline

100 . Yukong Huang, "The US and EU are better off without Asia's support for Russia energy sanctions," Carnegie Endowment for International Peace, July 7, 2022, https://carnegieendowment.org/2022/07/07/u.s.-and-eu-are-better-off-without-asia-s-support-for-russia-energy-sanctions-pub-87447

purchasing gas from Russia,[101] while China offered some gas tankers to Europe![102] The U.S. kept silent when Japan steadfastly maintained its interest in the Russian 'Sakhalin 2' gas pipeline,[103] while the U.S. was vocal about the European Nord Stream 2. As much as the UN sanctions were endorsed by the international community, the economic sanctions were Western. The rest of the world offered little support, even among U.S. allies in Asia Pacific.

As far as Southeast Asia is concerned, rather than values, the "*ledger of interests leads the policy-making*".[104] Actually, Russia weighs very lightly in this balance of interests despite its efforts to engage Southeast Asia in the last decade. Russia is hardly on the mind, as reflected by its absence from the '*State of Southeast Asia 2022*' survey. Its trading, including energy and agricultural products, represented no more than 1% of the top five ASEAN countries' trading flows in 2019.[105] Ties back to the Soviet era could indeed be invoked, but this too was limited to a few countries. Potential Russian retaliation was not even a remote threat. Reasons for ASEAN relative neutrality must be found elsewhere.

In 2021, well before the Russia–Ukraine war, commodity prices had already increased. But food security is a core national interest for most countries who are still net staple importers.[106] Their reliance on Ukraine, Russia, and a few others meant that they saw no need to add hurdles to the post-COVID-19 recovery phase that would feed undesirable inflation and politically-costly social unrest.

---

101 . Rurika Imahashi, "Japan, South Korea, Taiwan buy 5.5 b USD of Russian fuel: Think tank," Nikkei Asia, August 23, 2022, https://asia.nikkei.com/Politics/Ukraine-war/Japan-South-Korea-Taiwan-buy-5.5bn-of-Russian-fuel-think-tank2
102 . Misa Hama, "China throws Europe an energy lifeline with LNG resales," Nikkei Asia, August 24, 2022,https://asia.nikkei.com/Politics/International-relations/Indo-Pacific/China-throws-Europe-an-energy-lifeline-with-LNG-resales
103 . "Japan to keep interest in Sakhalin 2 gas project", The Mainichi, August 20, 2022, https://english.kyodonews.net/news/2022/08/3028766a788a-japanese-utilities-consider-renewing-deal-with-new-sakhalin-operator.html
104 . Mc Donald Laurier Institute webinar, Why Russia war in Ukraine matters to Canada and the IndoPacific, August 5, 2022 Gorona Grgic at https://www.youtube.com/watch?v=OE7OXB0iY2Y
105 . ASEAN trade stands at 2.5 Trillions USD, https://research.hktdc.com/en/article/Mzk5MzcxNjEz. Russia trade with ASEAN stands at 18-20b USD, ASEAN Russia Economic relations, at https://www.aseanbriefing.com/news/aseans-trade-relations-with-russia/ and ASEAN – Russia trade statistics, https://asean.org/our-communities/economic-community/asean-russia-economic-relations/
106 . Paul Teng, "Global Food Insecurity – Food Import: Reducing ASEAN's Dependency," RSIS, July 5, 2022, https://www.rsis.edu.sg/rsis-publication/nts/global-food-insecurity-food-import-reducing-aseans-dependency/#.Y4dm63bP3IU https://www.rsis.edu.sg/rsis-publication/nts/global-food-insecurity-food-import-reducing-aseans-dependency/#.Y0kJsy8RpsF

It has been suggested that supplies of arms and weapons were the reason why Russia was not sanctioned by Southeast Asians. This is largely overstated, even if taking into account the legacy of military assets. Granted, Russia has been a large supplier to regional weaponry, but this role dwindled after 2014 and the U.S.'s imposition of CAATSA[107], which inflicted sanctions on Iran, Russia, and North Korea. Myanmar and Vietnam accounted for more than 75% of these weapons deals, while the Vietnam procurement pipeline was waning already.[108] Therefore, putting aside Myanmar and Vietnam, Southeast Asian countries did not really risk the ire of Moscow by toeing the line with the West.

But there is sanction fatigue in Southeast Asia, a victim of past U.S. unilateral bans and even extraterritorial U.S. laws (Myanmar, Thailand, Cambodia; U.S. military cooperation over the East Timor crisis with Indonesia). At present, there are still lingering concerns about the future of U.S. trade sanctions against the region.[109] Furthermore, the bombing of Serbia, operations in Libya, and the Iraq war were all started without backing from the UN Security Council. These did not trigger any sanctions against instigator states. This prompted the Kenyan foreign minister to remind Western countries in February 2022, that *"powerful states, including members of this Security Council, breach international law with little regard"*.[110] Dr Evan Ellis from the U.S. Army War college highlighted that *"to a certain degree, Latin Americans genuinely feel that the U.S. is a bully too, so there is a shade of grey in terms of that moral ambiguity"*.[111] These statements would reverberate equally in Southeast Asia. Indeed, sanctions are perceived as an expression of the West's hegemony rather than an instrument of the international community. They have not convinced the Global South of their utility.[112] The Indonesian foreign ministry spokesman drove this point

---

107 . Countering America's Adversaries Through Sanctions Act (CAATSA).
108 . Ian Storey, "The Russia-Ukraine War and its Potential Impact on Russia's Arms sales to South East Asia.", table 1, Yusof Ishak Institute, no. 47, 5 May 2022, 3, https://www.iseas.edu.sg/articles-commentaries/iseas-perspective/2022-47-the-russia-ukraine-war-and-its-potential-impact-on-russias-arms-sales-to-southeast-asia-by-ian-storey/
109 . Hiroshi Kotani, "Southeast Asia feared next on list for US trade sanctions.", Nikkei Asia, April 9, 2018, https://asia.nikkei.com/Economy/Trade-war/Southeast-Asia-feared-next-on-list-for-US-trade-sanctions
110 . Bill Chappell, "Kenyan UN ambassador compares Ukraine's plight to colonial legacy in Africa," NPR, February 22, 2022, https://www.npr.org/2022/02/22/1082334172/kenya-security-council-russia?t=1660318083915
111 . Jallen Small, "Mexico, Brazil leaders Ignore Their UN delegates, Refuse to Sanction Russia," Newsweek, April 3, 2022, https://www.newsweek.com/mexico-brazil-leaders-ignore-their-un-delegates-refuse-sanction-russia-1685001
112 . Farwa Sial, "Sanctions and the changing world Order: Some Views from the Global South," Developing Economics, September 1, 2022, https://developingeconomics.org/2022/09/01/sanctions-and-the-changing-world-order-some-views-from-the-global-south/

home when stating "*We see time and time again that sanctions do not mean the resolution of a particular issue*".[113] This is largely echoed in other parts of the world. Defiance has been the payback for 'double standards', as Southeast Asians were not in the mood of contributing to 'lawfare' toward a non-Western country.

Additionally, Southeast Asians largely see this crisis as yet another European war in which they are reluctant to meddle.[114] Rightly or wrongly, it is not perceived as directly concerning Southeast Asia's security, again with the notable exception of Singapore, which took a more holistic view. In addition, commentary about the Russia–Ukraine conflict and whose side is right is seen as very confusing for outsiders. Southeast Asians cannot sort out clearly who is to blame for the deep origin of the conflict, and are therefore reluctant to take a position.[115] Russia is not seen as an adversary, even less as an enemy, in what is perceived to be a European problem, and possibly a proxy war between NATO and Russia.[116] In short, Russia is still a dialogue partner despite the crisis and is openly supported in Indonesia[117], and Malaysia[118], for example. After all, strongman leadership, such as demonstrated by Putin, remains lauded by some ASEAN leaders.

So, Southeast Asia's non-alignment with Western sanctions comes as much from a different 'interest ledger', threat perception, as it is a determination to affirm independence. Southeast Asia has repositioned itself in the international system as it has contemplated the West's waning influence. It focuses on its own regional and domestic interests, all bolstered by a renewed self-confidence. The Indonesian foreign ministry spokesman

---

113 . Nivell Rayda, Picharyada Promchertchoo, Tan Vincent, "Indonesia calls for negotiation and diplomacy after Russia attacks Ukraine, will not impose sanctions," Channel News Asia, February 24, 2022, https://www.channelnewsasia.com/world/putin-russia-ukraine-invasion-indonesia-thailand-philippines-malaysia-response-2517031

114 . "David Hutt, "Ukraine conflict: What's behind Southeast Asia's muted response?," DW News, July 3, 2022, https://www.dw.com/en/ukraine-conflict-whats-behind-southeast-asias-muted-response/a-61039013

115 . Muhammad Kharisma, "A View from Southeast Asia: ASEAN, Indonesia, and the Ukraine war, Italian Institute for International Political studies, May 26, 2022, https://www.ispionline.it/en/pubblicazione/view-southeast-asia-asean-indonesia-and-ukraine-war-35058

116 . Mc Donald Laurier Institute webinar, Why Russia war in Ukraine matters to Canada and the IndoPacific, August 5, 2022 Frederick Kliem https://www.youtube.com/watch?v=OE7OXB0iY2Y

117 . Erwida Maulia, "Indomie diplomacy: How inflation drove Jokowi to Kyiv and Moscow," Nikkei Asia, July 5, 2022, https://asia.nikkei.com/Politics/Ukraine-war/Indomie-diplomacy-How-inflation-drove-Jokowi-to-Kyiv-and-Moscow

118 . "Unpacking pro Russian narrative in Southeast Asia," ISEAS webinar, Yusof Ishak Institute, April 22, 2022, https://www.iseas.edu.sg/media/event-highlights/webinar-on-unpacking-pro-russian-narratives-in-southeast-asia/

epitomized this position by stating that *"we will not blindly follow the steps taken by another country. We will make a decision based on our domestic interests"*.[119] This crisis is an opportunity to state this clearly to the Western bloc.

However, all Southeast Asian countries rely heavily on international law and the post-Second World War order, benefiting from it even if it is dominated by the West. Globalization rests on a multilateral regime supported by a rule-based order. Singapore's Prime Minister Lee Hsien Loong reminded his citizens of this point a few times when stating *"that is a big worry for us in Singapore because we depend on globalization to make a living"*.[120] On one hand, Russia sets a precedent that is an issue for Southeast Asia, for Singapore and small countries, in relation to their larger neighbor and China; on the other hand, nobody wants to be labelled as Western lackeys by participating in the economic sanctions. As such, ASEAN's compromise response is perceived by its critics as weak at best.

Very quickly, Russia's participation in the G20 hit the world news. Indonesia, the chair in 2022, was under immense pressure to comply with the G7's bidding.[121] The G7 opposed Russia's presence, while China and most other countries supported Russian involvement. In April 2022, invitations were sent to all anyway; Ukraine was invited too as a balancing act. During preparatory meeting, several walkouts were staged by both G7 members[122] and Russia,[123] while full participation was still in the balance until the last minute.

In the run up to the Bali Summit, Indonesian President Joko Widodo attended the G7 as spokesman for the G20 membership.[124] He pushed

---

119 . Rayda, Promchertchoo, Vincent, "Indonesia calls for negotiation and diplomacy after Russia attacks Ukraine, will not impose sanctions."
120 . "In full: PM Lee's dialogue with the Council on Foreign Relations," Channel News Asia, March 31, 2022, https://www.channelnewsasia.com/singapore/pm-lee-hsien-loong-dialogue-council-foreign-relations-2597991
121 . Sydney Allen, "Indonesia is caught between Russia and the West ahead of the November G20 conference," Global Voices, April 15, 2022, https://globalvoices.org/2022/04/15/indonesia-is-caught-between-russia-and-the-west-ahead-of-the-november-g20-conference/
122 . Richard Partington, "US, UK and Canada walk out of G20 meeting over war in Ukraine," The Guardian, April 20, 2022, https://www.theguardian.com/world/2022/apr/20/us-uk-and-canada-walk-out-g20-meeting-war-in-ukraine-russia
123 . G20 meeting over condemnation of Ukraine war", Benar News, July 8, 2022, https://www.benarnews.org/english/news/indonesian/russian-fm-walks-out-of-g20-meeting-over-condemnation-of-ukraine-war-07082022150549.html
124 . "Presiden Jokowi: G7 dan G20 Harus Segera Atasi Krisis Pangan", June 29, 2022, https://www.menpan.go.id/site/berita-terkini/dari-istana/presiden-jokowi-g7-dan-g20-harus-segera-atasi-krisis-pangan

the global food crisis onto the agenda,[125] possibly motivated by domestic concerns too.[126] In the following days, he visited Ukraine, emphasizing how *"it is important for all parties to provide security guarantees for the smooth export of Ukrainian food, including through seaports"*.[127] Very little has filtered out regarding his June 29 Kremlin visit, but Joko Widodo appeared to have secured a vague promise of fertilizer supply and grain from Russia.[128] The UN–Russia grain deal was settled on July 22, 2022,[129] while fertilizers were still being discussed in September.[130] But, in a twist, Russia pulled out of the agreement on October 29 after Ukrainian's attacks on Sebastopol.[131] However, at the G20, the Turkish President Erdogan announced that the grain deal would most likely be renewed,[132] while U.N. Secretary-General Antonio Guterres is said to have provided assurances to Russia on payment *modus operandi* for its own grain exports.[133]

Nevertheless, despite all these adversities, the G20 has succeeded to cover food security and allocated $81 billion to vulnerable countries.[134] The G20 has further gained prominence as the only global inclusive forum. The Xi-Biden conclave provided a cautious sense of optimism on the trajectory of US-China relationship in an attempt to compartmentalize bilateral issues from global public goods. Vladimir Putin's last minute no-show, and its foreign minister Sergey Lavrov's early departure, all contributed to Xi Jinping's stardom at the G20, unhindered by the Russia controversies. The G20

---

125 . "A global food crisis," World Food Program, https://www.wfp.org/global-hunger-crisis
126 . Radityo Dharmaputra, "Jokowi's visits to Russia and Ukraine are more about domestic gains than the global interest," The Conversation, July 6, 2022, https://theconversation.com/jokowis-visits-to-russia-and-ukraine-are-more-about-domestic-gains-than-the-global-interest-186217
127 . Ministry of Foreign Affairs Republic of Indonesia. President Jokowi: The Visit to Ukraine Shows Indonesia's Concern for Ukraine. June 30, 2022, https://kemlu.go.id/portal/en/read/3752/berita/president-jokowi-the-visit-to-ukraine-shows-indonesias-concern-for-ukraine
128 . Ibid.
129 . Tuvan Gumrukcu, "U.N. expects Ukraine-Russia grain deal to be implemented in a few weeks –officials,". Reuters, July 23, 2022, https://www.reuters.com/world/un-expects-ukraine-russia-grain-deal-be-implemented-few-weeks-officials-2022-07-22/
130 . "Explainer: How UN plan for Russian ammonia export could help global fertiliser market," September 15, 2022, Reuters, https://www.reuters.com/markets/commodities/how-un-plan-russian-ammonia-export-could-help-global-fertiliser-market-2022-09-14/
131 . Pavel Polityuk, & Michelle Nichols, "UN Chief delays travel to try to bring Russia back into Black Sea grain deal," Reuters, 30 October, 2002, https://www.reuters.com/world/europe/russia-suspends-participation-deal-ukraine-grain-exports-tass-2022-10-29/
132 . Patrick Wintour, "Erdogan confident the grain deal will continue," The Guardian, November 16, 2022, https://www.theguardian.com/world/2022/nov/16/erdogan-russia-ukraine-grain-deal-black-sea
133 . Ibid.
134 . Ministry of Foreign Affairs of the Republic of Indonesia "G20 Bali Leader's Declaration Bali, Indonesia 15-16 November." 16 November 2022, https://kemlu.go.id/portal/en/read/4171/siaran_pers/g20-bali-leaders-declaration-bali-indonesia-15-16-november-2022

communique was issued timely, influenced by Indian diplomats, repeating Modi's famous quote that *"today's era must not be of war"*.[135] China pushed back on some wording in the communique, but nevertheless released veiled critics toward Russia prior to the G20.[136] It appears increasingly as a reluctant party in the Russia-Ukraine war. In a very volatile environment, Indonesia proved itself able to navigate between great powers, before handing over the G20 presidency to India.

More importantly, no matter how narrow Russia is in its relations with ASEAN, it is seen as part of some strategic hedging for Vietnam, Myanmar, Thailand, Malaysia, and even Indonesia. As such, Russia potentially still has a role to play in the uncertain future and conceivable hedging triangles. For ASEAN, facing a shrinking diplomatic space and hedging alternatives, sanctioning Russia at this point was, and is, a non-starter. But be that as it may, Russia's pivot to Southeast Asia has in fact been jeopardized significantly by its invasion of Ukraine, *"notwithstanding the Russian leader's popular appeal as well as widespread scepticism toward the West in parts of the region"*,[137] writes Heydarian, a Filipino political scientist.

Whatever the diplomatic theater, for most of the Global South, the critical agenda is domestic, namely securing food and economic recovery, rather than engaging in grand strategies and holistic values. The vision of Southeast Asians is best encapsulated by Indian External Affairs Minister S. Jaishankar's punchline that *"Europe has to grow out of the mindset that Europe's problems are the world's problems, but that the world's problems are not Europe's problems"*,[138] and again from Jaishankar: *"the common man should not be burdened by the fallout"* from the conflict.[139] These sentiments have become the policy guidelines for the whole region.

---

135 . Ibid.
136 . Arpan Rai, "Chinese officials speak out in unprecedented criticism of Russia on eve of G20 ," The Independent, November 15, 2022, https://www.independent.co.uk/independentpremium/world/putin-ukraine-g20-russia-xi-jinping-biden-b2225694.html
137 . Richard Heydarian, "Southeast Asia will not be Russia's lifeline," Nikkei Asia, September 23, 2022,https://asia.nikkei.com/Opinion/Southeast-Asia-will-not-be-Russia-s-lifeline
138 . External Affairs Minister S Jaishankar, "Russia-Ukraine War I Jaishankar Calls Out West Again", GLOBSEC 2022 Bratislava Forum, Video Recoding, at 00':22" https://www.youtube.com/watch?v=j2FdQD_EagO
139 . "India against Ukraine conflict, but can't burden common man with fallout, says Jaishankar," The Print, April 6, 2022,https://theprint.in/india/india-against-ukraine-conflict-but-cant-burden-common-man-with-fallout-says-jaishankar/904665/

4. Impact on Southeast Asia: 'ASEAN centrality' in Rapidly Shifting Structures

The impact of COVID-19, followed by the Russian invasion, are a wake-up call for Southeast Asia, and lessons have been learned. As in Ukraine, flashpoints could quickly turn into a hot war as vulnerabilities and dependencies are uncovered.

Evidently, all eyes are on Taiwan and the South China Sea. In March 2022, Lee Hsien Loong, articulated the general opinion, *"we should also think in Asia Pacific about the path into conflict and how it can be avoided. What structures can you build; what processes; what engagements; what strategic accommodations can be made, in order to head off such a failure of deterrence"*.[140] The concern is that several competing views exist among Great and Middle Powers on these alternative structures.

While trade ties did not prevent this conflict from erupting, this crisis is a stark reminder that trade is power.[141] Currency and energy networks are potential weapons,[142] all underwriting strategic autonomy. Also, visible to all is that the U.S. behaves as a *"dysfunctional great power"*,[143] with its unresolved domestic issues hampering its capacity, and legitimacy, to address world problems.[144] At last, it is seen that China may not remain the growth engine it once was,[145] with an ageing population and its focus on its domestic market. Both countries are retreating from international trade, and are digging into their positions entrenched during the COVID-19 pandemic and the on-going Russia-Ukraine war, with after-effects for ASEAN.

On the other hand, Southeast Asians have become more self-confident about their 'Asian Governing Model',[146] despite the headwinds faced by most

---

140 . In full: PM Lee's dialogue with the Council on Foreign Relations.
141 . Stephen D. Krasner, "State Power and the Structure of International Trade," World Politics 28, no. 3 (1976), 320 https://doi.org/10.2307/2009974.
142 . Margarita Balmaceda, "Europe's Gas Crisis and Russian Energy Politics: Experts Respond", Ukranian Research Institute Harvard University, https://huri.harvard.edu/tcup-commentary/europes-gas-crisis-russian-energy-politics
143 . Tom McTague, "The Decline of the American World," The Atlantic, June 24, 2022, https://www.theatlantic.com/international/archive/2020/06/america-image-power-trump/613228/
144 . Francis Fukuyama,"Francis Fukuyama on the end of American hegemony," The Economist, November 8, 2021,https://www.economist.com/the-world-ahead/2021/11/08/francis-fukuyama-on-the-end-of-american-hegemony
145 . Roland Rajah, Roland & Alyssa Leng, "Revising down the rise of China," Lowy Institute, March 14, 2022, https://www.lowyinstitute.org/publications/revising-down-rise-china
146 . Bruce Gilley, The Nature of Asian Politics (New York: Cambridge University Press, 2014). 16.

states. Remarkably, the ASEAN states' fragility is improving,[147] reinforcing for most their legitimacy premium. A proxy for the risk to peace and security, the Normandy index scores 6.24 for ASEAN.[148] That is better than the world average for half of the ASEAN countries. Firms and societies are hopeful about their future,[149] and their economic performance has surpassed China's in 2022.[150] As a result, ASEAN states will no longer accept lecturing from the West, proudly asserting their political and cultural identity as aspiring middle powers. Whilst the pushback against the West is real and deep,[151] it demands to be converted into a constructive force.

The compounded effect of COVID-19, the Russia–Ukraine conflict, the intensifying of mistrust, and the erosion of multilateralism, has an impact on structure, agency, and interactions. However, interactions and relationships depend on trust.

Mistrust among great powers was magnified by the finger pointing, the vaccines saga, and the collective failure to collaborate during the COVID-19 crisis (unlike the U.S.-Soviet collaboration to eradicate small pox and polio via the World Health Organization[152]). Now the Russia–Ukraine war is driving another wedge. In such a situation, common interests are insufficient to trigger meaningful collaboration.

On the West's side, the Atlantic alliance has become much stronger than it had been in decades. NATO appears to have been reinforced from this event, even declaring global intentions in the Indo Pacific.[153] One can only hope that there is not another overreach.

---

147. To learn more about state fragility in the world, refer to https://fragilestatesindex.org/
148. The Normandy Index at https://www.europarl.europa.eu/thinktank/infographics/peaceandsecurity/index.html#/map
149. "SEA change: The new wave of optimism in Southeast Asia", HSBC, December 7, 2021. https://www.business.hsbc.com/en-gb/insights/growing-my-business/sea-change-the-new-wave-of-optimism-in-southeast-asia
150. Cliff Venzon, "Emerging Asia growing faster than China for 1st time in 30 years," Nikkei Asia, September 21, 2022, https://asia.nikkei.com/Economy/Emerging-Asia-growing-faster-than-China-for-1st-time-in-30-years
151. Tanguy Struye de Swielande, "Nous ne nous rendons pas compte de l'étendue du front occidental," La Libre, August 10, 2022, https://www.lalibre.be/debats/opinions/2022/08/10/nous-ne-nous-rendons-pas-compte-de-letendue-du-front-antioccidental-WD4FPYY3KBBMLBN5P7N4ZWW354/
152. Bruce Bones, "Major Power Rivalry and the Management of Global Threats," Discussion Paper no. 7, Council on Foreign Affairs, November 2021, https://cdn.cfr.org/sites/default/files/report_pdf/Jones_MajorPowerRivalry.pdf
153. "Relations with Asia-Pacific partners" NATO, July 12, 2022, https://www.nato.int/cps/en/natohq/topics_183254.htm

China's assertiveness during the COVID-19 crisis only drove the Quad closer, even prompting some tacit endorsement from Southeast Asians.[154] As for AUKUS, its announcement has undermined regional powers' trust in Australia's rash decisions and lack of transparency.[155] Nevertheless, the balance of threats in the region substantiates the resilience of the Quad,[156] making its integration into ASEAN's security arrangement a core issue.

On the Asian side, the Russia–Ukraine war might also reinforce East Asian geoeconomic power, putting China at its center of gravity. Some have argued that this would be a return to the hierarchical ancient East Asian world order,[157] absorbing Russia geoeconomically,[158] and extending its influence in Central and Southeast Asia, with *Eastphalia* displacing *Westphalia*.[159] We are nowhere near this, but reiterating past proposals, in May 2022, China offered itself as an Asian security provider via its global security initiative, promoting its proposal across ASEAN.[160] This was restated at the latest Shanghai Cooperation Organization (SCO) meeting.[161] Furthermore, it has not escaped China, and the BRICS, that the West quickly cut off Russia from the SWIFT bank network.[162] In 2022, the BRICS restated its aim to de-dollarize their economies,[163] followed by the SCO,[164] and possibly BRI too.[165]

154 . Sarah Teo, "The Quad and ASEAN – where to next?," East Asia Forum, June 25, 2022, https://www.eastasiaforum.org/2022/06/25/the-quad-and-asean-where-to-next/
155 . Grant Wyeth, "A Year after AUKUS, What challenges Loom Largest?,". The Diplomat, September 15, 2022, https://thediplomat.com/2022/09/a-year-after-aukus-what-challenges-loom-largest/
156 . Frederick Kliem, "Why Quasi-Alliances Will Persist in the Indo-Pacific? The Fall and Rise of the Quad," Journal of Asian Security and International Affairs 7, no. 3, (2020), 295.
157 . Kang, "International Order in Historical East Asia", 86.
158 . Mohammadbagher. Forough, "What will Russia's Invasion of Ukraine Mean for China's Belt and Road?," The Diplomat, March 18, 2022, https://thediplomat.com/2022/03/what-will-russias-invasion-of-ukraine-mean-for-chinas-belt-and-road/
159 . Kim Sun Wong, "Eastphalia Revisited: The Potential Contribution of Eastphalia to Post Westphalian Possibilities," Pacific Focus 33, no. 3 (2018):452 ,https://doi.org/10.1111/pafo.12127
160 . Parameswaran, "Managing the Rise of China's Security Partnership in Southeast Asia", Wilson Center – Asia program, July 2019, https://www.wilsoncenter.org/sites/default/files/media/documents/publication/2018-07_managing_the_rise_of_chinas_security_partnerships_in_southeast_asia_-_parameswaran.pdf
161 . Ovigwe Eguegu, "Will China's Global Security Initiative catch on?", The Diplomat, June 8, 2022 at https://thediplomat.com/2022/06/will-chinas-global-security-initiative-catch-on/
162 . Philip Blenkinsop, "EU bars 7 Russian banks from SWIFT, but spares those in energy," Reuters, March 2, 2022, https://www.reuters.com/business/finance
163 . "BRICS urged to boost national currency settlements to counter US' abuse of dollar hegemony," Global Times, May 19, 2022,https://www.globaltimes.cn/page/202205/1266097.shtml
164 . "China-led SCO bloc agrees to expand trade in national currencies," Reuters, September 16, 2022,
https://www.reuters.com/markets/commodities/china-led-sco-bloc-agrees-expand-trade-national-currencies-2022-09-16/
165 . Diana Choyleva, & Dinny McMahon, "Belt and Road's next chapter will be all about the

In the middle of the 2022 crisis, Russia successfully issued more than $2.5 billion of bonds in renminbi.[166] A few Southeast Asia nations are now also joining the dollar decoupling bandwagon,[167] while Indonesia is thinking of joining the BRICS.[168] How far all this can go is unclear at this point, but the strategic intent is increasingly shared, and, unlike in the past, the financial infrastructures are in place.[169] Furthermore, the revitalized SCO controls 52% of the world's gas reserves, while China's expanding energy networks in Central Asia will alleviate the Malacca Straits dilemma and its choke points.[170] All combined, it provides deadly leverage, even blackmail, against anticipated sanctions if conflicts erupt. Energy, microchips, and currencies emerge as international political choke points.

The Russia–Ukraine conflict is threatening the foundation of Southeast Asia's prosperity as ASEAN's *raison d'être* is trade.[171] The West, especially the U.S., wants to bring the world back to the more exclusive free-trade agreement principles of the past that excluded non-allies. A decade ago, the D-10,[172] a loose coalition of democracies launched by then Assistant Secretary of State Kurt Campbell was supposed to consolidate trade, technology,

yuan." Asia Nikkei. October 25th, 2022. https://asia.nikkei.com/Opinion/Belt-and-Road-s-next-chapter-will-be-all-about-the-yuan

166 . Brian Evans, "Russia's largest oil producer completes its very first yuan-denominated bond sale as Moscow leans further toward China's currency". Market Business Insider, September 16, 2022, https://markets.businessinsider.com/news/bonds/russia-rosneft-completes-a-bond-sale-in-yuan-ruble-currencies-2022-9

167 . Tom Hancock, "China's Trade Dominance Is Boosting Renminbi's Reserve Status," Bloomberg, July 25, 2022, https://www.bloomberg.com/news/articles/2022-07-25/china-s-trade-dominance-is-boosting-renminbi-s-reserve-status?leadSource=uverify%20wall

168 . Nian Peng, "Great Power Conflict Fuels BRICS Expansion Push," The Diplomat, 13 July 2022,https://thediplomat.com/2022/07/great-power-conflict-fuels-brics-expansion-push/

169 . Zongyuan Zoe Liu & Mihaela Papa, . Can BRICS De-Dollarize the Global Financial System? (Cambridge: Cambridge University Press, 2022), 63, DOI:10.1017/9781009029544

170 . "Malacca Dilemma is a word coined in 2003, by the then Chinese President Hu Jintao. It is a term that represents the potential factors that could hinder China's economic development through choking oil imports. The strategic location strait of Malacca Falls between Sumatra Islands and Malay Peninsula and has Singapore to its east. This narrow stretch of water could be easily blocked by the rival nations of China." - "The Malacca Dilemma and Chinese Ambitions: Two Sides of a Coin," The Diplomat, July 7, 2010, https://diplomatist.com/2020/07/07/the-malacca-dilemma-and-chinese-ambitions-two-sides-of-a-coin/

171 . Anthony Reid, Southeast Asia in the Age of Commerce 1450-1680: the Lands below the Winds (Yale University Press, 1993).

172 . U.S State of Department. The Summit for Democracy. https://www.state.gov/summit-for-democracy/

supply chain among its members.[173] The recent '*friend-shoring*' concept,[174] and closer to home, the Indo-Pacific Economic Framework for Prosperity (IPEF)[175] proposed by the U.S operate along the same line of thought. As a result, the golden age of inclusive globalization involving adversaries is potentially over, as globalization might take on a new architecture.[176]

This is a direct challenge to Southeast Asia's multilateral engagement and its omni-enmeshment policy, embodied by 'ASEAN centrality', and best defined by former Indonesian foreign minister Natalegawa as "*the setting of norms and principles in the nature of great powers engagement in the region*", while having ASEAN in the "*driving seat in shaping the region political, diplomatic and economic architecture*".[177] This centrality was effective as long as no counter-center was present, China was 'biding its time', and the U.S. was accommodating.[178] These provided some diplomatic space to ASEAN, which is now being challenged both externally and internally.

The region is witnessing the rise of illiberal democracies, with an accelerating democratic regression during the COVID-19 crisis,[179] which could potentially weaken 'ASEAN centrality'. In Indonesia, new nationalism directed toward its neighbors, such as Malaysia, is becoming more evident.[180] The region's fragile economic security is also a potential pitfall. As a result, observers have highlighted that the risks to 'ASEAN centrality' might even be greater from internal factors than from external factors and great power competition.[181]

---

173 . Robert Manning, & Mathew Burrows, "The Problem with Biden's democracy Agenda," War on the Rocks, July 27, 2021, https://warontherocks.com/2021/07/the-problem-with-bidens-democracy-agenda/

174 . Su-Lin Tan, "Yellen says the U.S. and its allies should use 'friend-shoring' to give supply chain a boost," CNBC, 19 July 2022,https://www.cnbc.com/2022/07/19/us-treasury-secretary-on-supply-chain-resilience-use-friend-shoring.html

175 . The IPEF framework includes four so-called 'pillars': supply chain resiliency, digital economy rules, clean energy and infrastructure and taxation and anti-corruption. IISD, 25 September 2022, https://www.iisd.org/articles/policy-analysis/indo-pacific-economic-framework

176 . "Hostile influence ops targetting Singapore "a clear and current danger": Vivian Balakrishnan," The Strait Times, August 21, 2022, https://www.youtube.com/watch?v=Mp2ZXHRGYqw

177 . Natalegawa, Does ASEAN matter, 71.

178 . Emmerson, The Deer and the Dragon 19.

179 . James Gomez, "Covid-19 accelerates democratic regression in Southeast Asia," Australian Institute of International Affairs, December 9, 2020, https://www.internationalaffairs.org.au/australianoutlook/covid-19-accelerates-democratic-regression-in-southeast-asia/

180 . Edward Aspinall, "The New Nationalism in Indonesia," Asia and the Pacific Policy Studies 3, no. 1, (2016), 3: 72 DOI: 10.1002/app5.111.

181 . Acharya, ASEAN and the Regional Order, 132.

The deepening of economic regionalization is therefore seen as having the potential for diversification and acting as a bulwark against the rise of protectionism,[182] with RCEP at its center. To be clear, ASEAN will not drop Western-led institutions for the Chinese-led BRI and its development bank, AIIB.[183] Sticking to its trade-mark balanced approach, it will keep both and extract benefits from all, while not taking sides.

But is the diplomatic space really shrinking? Below the great powers, an unprecedented horde of emerging middle powers are making their aspirations known. The GDP of Asian middle powers is about $15 trillion,[184] nearing that of China, while the G18 (G20 minus the U.S. and China), is about $38 trillion,[185] or 50% of the G20's GDP. Middle powers collectively do have agency under certain conditions,[186] while *"ASEAN centrality is not ASEAN only,"* as sensitively put by Australia's Foreign Minister Wong.[187] New triangularities are surfacing, such as Japan–Indonesia–Australia[188], Korea–Indonesia–Australia[189], and India–Japan–ASEAN[190], which are potentially capable of shaping the region's environment. As former Indonesian Ambassador to the U.S. Dino Patti Djalal aptly nailed it, *"there is an important role for middle powers, such as Australia, and groupings, such as ASEAN, to push for a strategic entente between the two major powers, who, trying to resolve things alone, are likely to make less progress"* .[191] However, all of

---

182 . See Seng Tan, "Can east Asia regionalism be a bulwark against a 'post liberal' West?", East Asia Forum, November 18, 2017, https://www.eastasiaforum.org/2017/11/18/can-east-asian-regionalism-be-a-bulwark-against-a-post-liberal-west/.
183 . Acharya, .ASEAN and the Regional Order, 130.
184 . World Population Review, https://worldpopulationreview.com/countries/by-gdp
185 . Ibid.
186 . Arta Moeini, et al. "Middle Powers in the Multipolar World," The Institute for Peace & Diplomacy,, March 2022,https://peacediplomacy.org/wp-content/uploads/2022/03/Middle-Powers-in-the-Multipolar-World-2.pdf
187 . Senator the Hon Penny Wong, Special lecture to the IISS – A shared Future : Australia, ASEAN and Southeast Asia, July 6, 2022 https://www.foreignminister.gov.au/minister/penny-wong/speech/special-lecture-international-institute-strategic-studies-shared-future-australia-asean-and-southeast-asia
188 . Philip Green OAM, Department of Foreign Affairs and Trade- Australian Government, "Australia-Japan-ASEAN: Strengthening the Core of the Indo-Pacific," https://www.dfat.gov.au/news/speeches/Pages/australia-japan-asean-strengthening-the-core-of-the-indo-pacific
189 . "Krisis Indo-Pasifik, Korsel dan Indonesia Bisa Pelopori Kerja Sama Negara Menengah," Tempo, https://dunia.tempo.co/read/1635452/krisis-indo-pasifik-korsel-dan-indonesia-bisa-pelopori-kerja-sama-negara-menengah
190 . Jagannath P Panda, "India Japan ASEAN triangularity: Emergence of a Possible Indo-Pacific Axis? (London: Routledge, 2022).
191 . Djalal, "ASEAN responses to AUKUS security dynamic."East Asia Forum, November 28, 2021 https://www.eastasiaforum.org/2021/11/28/asean-responses-to-aukus-security-dynamic/

these mini-laterals must overcome the mistrust that has built up over the years.[192]

ASEAN might have to contend with a centrality limited to topics where it has a recognized capacity, as *"middle powers can aspire to wield a significant amount of influence in a multipolar world...they cannot hope to shape superpowers' grand strategies by themselves"*.[193] But even such a limited objective must be crafted energetically, and the diplomatic megaphone must be grasped.

5. Conclusion

Ultimately, despite the great powers' competition, there is no substitute for ASEAN, which does not mean that it should be complacent. Even Japan, the most trusted regional power, or India, cannot be substitutes for ASEAN because of the overall lack of legitimacy.[194] ASEAN's direction will hinge on Indonesia, Singapore, and the few most powerful states[195] in their attempt to create a third pole for ASEAN's strategic autonomy.[196]

ASEAN centrality requires solving a collective-action problem, despite ASEAN not being a supranational structure. As the region's institutional assets, the 'ASEAN way',[197] based on group's consensus and non-interference,[198] establishes a slow-brewing consensus-building process. The resultant community acts as a substitute for the lack of supra-nationality. But these communities are fragile and are challenged externally and internally, because the 'ASEAN way' has a lot of drawbacks in dealing effectively with an increasingly competitive environment. The sovereignty dear to Southeast

---

192 . "More than half Indonesians (56%) say they trust the United States, a 16-point fall since ten years ago. The shift is even starker when it comes to Australia: 55% express trust in Australia, a 20-point drop from 2011 levels.... falling levels of trust for regional countries are also evident. While 65% of Indonesians say they trust Japan, this figure has dropped 15 points since 2011. Four in ten Indonesians (42%) trust China to act responsibly in the world, a decline of 18 points over the past decade. Trust in India has also fallen ten points, with only 41% saying they trust the country." - Lowy Institute, "Australia," https://interactives.lowyinstitute.org/features/indonesia-poll-2021/topic/australia/
193 . Gabriele Abbondanza, "Whither the Indo-Pacific? Middle power strategies from Australia, South Korea and Indonesia," International Affairs 98, no. 2, (2022): 421, https://doi.org/10.1093/ia/iiab231
194 . Acharya, ASEAN and the Regional Order, 132.
195 . Ibid.
196 . Abbondanza, "Whither the Indo-Pacific?", 421.
197 . Emmerson, The Deer and the Dragon, 2.
198 . Rizal G. Buendia, "Is the 'ASEAN Way' the Way to ASEAN Security?," Political Reflection Magazine 4, no. 4 (2018), 36-39, https://cesran.org/is-the-asean-way-the-way-to-asean-security.html

Asian nations obstructs the delegating of some powers to ASEAN for a common good. Yet, in a world where bipolarity/unipolarity is no longer prominent, the 'ASEAN way' might prove to be a better fit for the reality of the emerging world order. Inclusiveness, pluralistic leadership, open regionalism, and cooperative security might provide a better diplomatic value proposition.[199]

Pandemic and war have accelerated prior trends, and the inevitable transformation of ASEAN. It finds itself at a crossroad again as it was in 1967, or in 1994, when it incorporated the ASEAN Regional Forum, or in 2007 with the ASEAN charter. ASEAN must have the self-confidence to pursue its course, to lead the change,[200] and to articulate more forcefully its positions,[201] while addressing its structural weaknesses, both urgently and assertively. Or it will face the risk of irrelevance among the fast-changing international structures.[202]

---

199 . Acharya, ASEAN and the Regional Order, 130.
200 . Natalegawa, "Does ASEAN matter"; Acharya, ASEAN and the Regional Order, 233.
201 . Djalal, "ASEAN responses to AUKUS security dynamic".
202 . Ja Ian Chong, "Is ASEAN still 'in the 'driver's seat or asleep at the wheel?,", East Asia Forum, March 11, 2018, https://www.eastasiaforum.org/2018/03/11/is-asean-still-in-the-drivers-seat-or-asleep-at-the-wheel/

CHAPTER III

China and a New World Order After Ukraine

Marcus Vinicius De Freitas

China's rise has been impressive. Though facing enormous challenges as its global relevance has grown, the Chinese have taken measures to alter the poverty legacy from the past and create a new future of prosperity. The period of *Reform and Opening up* profoundly changed the face of China. Of course, many criticisms are still levied against China: human rights, lack of democracy, authoritarianism, and increased assertiveness in the international arena. Despite these, the Chinese social-inclusion and development record, based on an economic model that has effectively developed significant positive welfare results, is admirable. Such results have increased Chinese ambitions, particularly in terms of reshaping global governance and the liberal world order, which, established after the Second World War, has grown old and less effective. China has pursued new multilateral arrangements for building a new world order. Still, the COVID-19 pandemic and the war in Ukraine have slowed down the process and increased tensions with the West. How China responds to such challenges affects the Global South, particularly in the transition period.

Introduction

China has spent five decades under reconstruction. Through policies started under the Reform and Opening-up program[1] in 1978, the face of China has changed substantially. From a backwards agricultural country, humiliated by Western powers and Japan in the nineteenth and early twentieth centuries, it has become the largest economy in the world in purchasing power parity (PPP) terms. This is no miracle. Hard work, visionary leadership, and the wise use of its most widely available commodity—its hard-working people—changed the nation's course.

Additionally, the Chinese social-inclusion and development record has delivered compelling results. The Chinese have navigated several periods of turbulence, domestically and internationally. As a result, China became the second-largest economy in the world in 2010.[2] In 1978, when Reform and Opening Up started, its nominal gross domestic product (GDP) was US$214 billion. Currently, it is estimated at US$19.9 trillion. China has become a global factory. Its services sector is growing steadily and has become more comprehensive.

China has also faced global economic crises. By seeking to learn from previous experiences and learning lessons, the country has emerged from challenges in good shape and has reinvented itself as a nation that can reverse any possible negative trends. China went from an impoverished nation in 1949, with significant concerns around food security and living standards, when compared to Hong Kong and Taiwan, to a prosperous country, facing economic challenges, but with a much better outlook for the future. The Communist Party of China (CPC) has made practical changes to preserve its legitimacy and power, achieving growth, development, and global stature. China has reinvented itself and its population to meet the challenges imposed by globalisation and the twenty-first century, embracing modernity with a positive perspective on the future.

The rise of China to become the second-largest economy in the world and a familiar player in the global economy and politics has not been without criticism. Its economic performance and impending risks have generated

---

1 . The Chinese Reform and Opening Up (改革开放; Gaigé kaifang) was the program implemented by Deng Xiaoping that introduced significant economic reforms in the country, termed Socialism with Chinese Characteristics, which led to the accelerated economic growth of China after 1978. This program also led to a profound change in Chinese Communism, abandoning the Soviet model.

2 . BBC News, "China's economy is now the world's second largest," https://www.bbc.com/news/av/business-12445925 (accessed October 31, 2022).

increasing domestic inequalities and environmental degradation, and have even created concerns about the sustainability of China's economic growth and its readiness as a rising power. Additionally, the rise in unfavourable views of China has grown because of China's initial handling of the coronavirus pandemic. This disapproval has undermined confidence in Chinese President Xi Jinping. Though given a third term during the 20th CPC Congress, the COVID-19 pandemic has negatively impacted Xi´s leadership.

China has sought to address such complaints through an active vaccine diplomacy effort to supply the Global South with millions of doses of Chinese-made vaccines.[3]

The issue of the debt trap of African nations has also been an argument used by the West in relation to Chinese financing of infrastructure projects. The U.S. State Department issued a report in 2020, *The Elements of the China Challenge*,[4] in which they affirmed that the Communist Party of China has undertaken debt-trap diplomacy to compel nation states to aid China in reshaping the world order. Reactions among African countries, in particular, have been mixed, since China is the only country willing to make significant investments in the continent. Additionally, some have debunked the debt-trap idea, particularly considering that China has not been involved in any asset seizures or sought to exercise control over governments.[5]

Finally, the human rights issue has been used to shame China´s record on Xinjiang and the Uyghur situation.[6] According to the U.S. government, more than a million Muslims have been arbitrarily detained in China's Xinjiang region, with the Chinese government building re-education camps to crack down on Uyghurs. China has responded to this accusation by saying it needs to control terrorism on its territory, and that the re-education process is needed to avoid religious fundamentalism.

---

3 . China was the first country to pledge to make COVID-19 vaccines a global public good. At the early stage of the pandemic outbreak, President Xi Jinping proposed that COVID-19 vaccines should be made a global public good, targeting developing countries. China provided billions of vaccines to more than 120 countries and international organizations, covering almost all African countries.

4 . Office of the Secretary of State, The Policy Planning Staff, The Elements of the China Challenge, November 2020, https://www.state.gov/wp-content/uploads/2020/11/20-02832-Elements-of-China-Challenge-508.pdf

5 . Deborah Brautigam and Meg Rithmire, The Chinese 'Debt Trap' is a Myth, The Atlantic, February 6, 2021, https://www.theatlantic.com/international/archive/2021/02/china-debt-trap-diplomacy/617953/ (accessed October 28, 2022).

6 . Lindsay Maizland, China´s Repression of Uyghurs in Xinjiang, Council on Foreign Relations, September 22, 2022, https://www.cfr.org/backgrounder/china-xinjiang-uyghurs-muslims-repression-genocide-human-rights (accessed Ocotber 30, 2022).

This chapter aims to provide an understanding of China's perspective on the new world order it seeks to establish, the war in Ukraine, and the challenges ahead as China and Russia solidify their partnership and influence in the Global South.

1. The Asian Century and Changes to the Liberal World Order

Asia has consolidated its more prominent leadership position on the global stage.[7] Asia has three of the four largest global economies in PPP terms: China, India, and Japan. With approximately 4.8 billion people, equivalent to 59.76% of the total world population, Asia has most of the world's population. In 2000, Asia accounted for 32% of global GDP in terms of PPP; by 2017, its share had risen to 42% in PPP terms (34% in real GDP terms),[8] and it should reach 52% (46% in real GDP terms) in 2040. Between 2000 and 2017, on the other hand, Europe's share of global output declined from 26% to 22% and North America's (US and Canada) from 25% to 18%. By 2040, Asia will rise from 23% of total global consumption to 39%.

Previously based on four pillars—economic weight, military power, technological dominance, and the missionary dissemination of its values—U.S. power has been circumscribing its primary sources of power to military strength and the control of the predominant currency in the global market. With the evolution of cyber warfare and reducing rationale for large-scale military engagements, military power is increasingly relegated to a secondary role. However, there is an increasing desire to ignite a new 'cold war' between the United States and China,[9] mainly influenced by NATO and a hegemonic perspective on the part of the United States. Based on a Thucydides trap concept, such a perspective has led to global political instability and decreasing interest in international cooperation, particularly after President Donald Trump took office.

Confidence in the strength and resilience of the dollar as the global reserve currency has been tested and has declined, particularly since the 2007 economic crisis. A lack of confidence in the dollar has been growing,

---

7 . Praneeth Yendamuri and Zara Ingilizian. In 2020 Asia will have the world's largest GDP. Here's what that means, World Economic Forum, December 20, 2019, https://www.weforum.org/agenda/2019/12/asia-economic-growth/ (accessed October, 28, 2022).
8 . China and the world: Inside the dynamics of a changing relationship, McKinsey Global Institute, July 2019
9 . Michael Hirsh, We are in a Global Cold War, Foreign Policy, June 27, 2022. https://foreignpolicy.com/2022/06/27/new-cold-war-nato-summit-united-states-russia-ukraine-china/ (accessed on October 25, 2022).

mainly since the U.S. economy saw its economic strength deteriorate and reduce its participation in the global market share. For Asia, this lack of confidence comes from how the United States reacted to the Asian financial crisis in the 1990s, when Asian countries did not receive the expected economic support to overcome the problem.

The frequent use of dollar-derived financial controls for political intervention in third countries to address exclusively U.S. interests has undermined trust in the currency. As a result, some countries have sought alternatives for other types of reserve values. The dollar, which still accounts for more than 40% of cross-border payments and almost 90% of international trade settlements,[10] has been able to maintain its relevance based on a historical tripod: strong institutions (including an independent central bank), efficient courts, and a record of relatively low inflation. Circumstances may change, however. As the economic situation of the US deteriorates, for instance, with a higher level of inflation (currently at a historic 40-year high), countries are affected by importing such inflationary trends into their economies.

Instead of adapting and changing course, the West has resisted changes to the post-Second World War institutions in order to perpetuate a global political and financial order that no longer corresponds to reality, given the significant emergence of new global players. The absence of reforms in the World Bank, International Monetary Fund, and the United Nations Security Council shows an effort to keep things as they are. The request for a more inclusive global order comes from Brazil, Turkey, Indonesia, Russia, Iran, and China. The central challenge is that the current institutional framework for dealing with global challenges does not match the scope, scale, and nature of the challenges of the twenty-first century, which require a much more comprehensive grasp than the current framework.

Transitions are always complicated. They may lead to wars. Criticisms of Asia, particularly China, will continue to grow, and the scenario of constant conflict will become the new normal. However, the shift of power from the Atlantic to the Pacific constitutes a new reality. The COVID-19 pandemic and the war in Ukraine have given rise to a more confrontational approach to China and Russia, with countries considering options for near-shoring and friend-shoring. Though a possible strategy the amount of time required

---

10 . Serkan Arslanalp, Barry J. Eichengreen, and Chima Simpson-Bell. (2022), "The stealth erosion of dollar dominance: active diversifiers and the rise of non-traditional reserve currencies" (2022), Working Paper, No 2022/058, International Monetary Fund, Washington, March 24.

to build the same level of competitiveness in infrastructure as China has done over the last forty years will require decades to secure the same level of delivery and just-in-time supply.

Atlantic-based developing countries should strategize on transforming the Asian century into an opportunity for greater global integration, either through cross-investment and trade or by substantially deepening commercial, political, and strategic relationships. On the economic side, companies from such countries should be encouraged to increase their presence in Asia if they want to remain relevant players in the global context and boost their competitiveness and productivity. China, where growth has slowed over the last five years, still has a large domestic market to tap into. If the Chinese goal is to reach GDP per capita of $20,000 to $25,000 by 2049, as planned by the Xi administration, the trickle-down impact of such growth will impact the world positively.

The western led liberal order, as currently constituted, must change to accommodate the rise of Asia, or, should the current level of inflexibility and the lack of compelling interest to change remain, accept the fate of irrelevance as new frameworks are created to meet the global challenges.

2. China and the Twenty-First Century

As the People's Republic of China (PRC) approaches its centenary in 2049, the country has engaged in a significant transition: from the global factory to the world's largest consumers market, with an unprecedented and considerable growing purchasing power in the history of humankind, a disruptive factor that the world will need to learn to deal with in seeking greater prosperity and welfare.

Economic globalisation has brought China from the periphery to the core of the international system. Since 1978, China has become the world's largest economy (on a PPP basis), manufacturer, trader, and holder of foreign exchange reserves. However, China has recently seen its real GDP growth slow, mainly due to the COVID-19 pandemic. The success of the Chinese economy is essential for its current political ruling party system to remain in power. President Xi Jinping understands this challenge and has addressed this concern by referring to the country's rejuvenation to increase faith in the Communist Party of China (CPC), preserve the so-called mandate of heaven,[11] and deliver effective welfare improvement. China faces

---

11 . During the Zhou Dynasty in China (1050–221 BCE), the concept of the Mandate of Heaven

the middle-income trap[12] and has sought to secure survival for the current political establishment—responsible for China's most prosperous period in history—and to step in as the U.S. slowly moves down the ladder as the world superpower.

The return of China to the international system became a reality on October 25, 1971, on the approval of the United Nations General Assembly Resolution 2758, where the One China Principle was recognized. Through centralized planning, with five-year growth plans, high levels of savings, and massive investment in education, China has slowly opened its economy to the world and positioned itself as the largest trading partner of more than 120 countries.[13]

The world is navigating through the most turbulent waters, witnessing one of the most significant historical transitions. The relationship between China and the U.S. has become tenser, with no mitigating factors altering this path. As China ascends, an intertwined but increasingly conflictual relationship has become the new normal between the world's foremost powers. The differences between the two countries could not be starker: (i) different economic and political models, (ii) different social fabrics, and (iii) different perspectives on global governance.

The current global governance framework will likely change as China attains greater prominence and relevance. Deciphering what this new world order with Chinese characteristics is likely to be, is essential for understanding what lies ahead. As China devises this new world order, some leading factors play a critical role:

- **Economic power prevails over military might**. China has made clear that it does not intend to become the world's leading military power or its policeman. The country faces constraints resulting from a complicated

---

was created, in which it was understood that China could only have one legitimate ruler at a time, who would rule with the approval of the gods and to deliver welfare to the people. Though the ruler had great power, he had a moral obligation to use such force for the people's good. If the rule was unfair, this mandate of heaven could be lost, leading to the ruler's downfall.

12 . An economic situation where the middle-income country (usually a gross national product per capita around $10,000) is not capable of competing internationally in labor-intensive goods, since wages are relatively high, and cannot compete in higher value-added activities because productivity is still relatively low, leading to slow growth and falling wages.

13 . China has become a top trading partner of over 120 countries and regions including the United States, the European Union, as well as Japan. China's booming foreign trade brings benefits to the world, China International Import Expo (2021). https://www.ciie.org/zbh/en/news/exhibition/news/20210321/27370.html (accessed October 24, 2022).

neighbourhood, in which any significant movement could spark an arms race. With four nuclear-armed neighbours—India, North Korea, Pakistan, and Russia—in addition to South Korea and Japan, which mirror the presence of the United States in Asia, geography forces China to be cautious about the perception of its use of military force.

- **Technology will be the leading force of growth, development, and alliances.** Chairman Xi Jinping has stressed the importance of technology as a driving force for the rejuvenation of China and for reaching a higher level of development. In line with that, China has declared its goal of enhancing its global technological presence, reaping the benefits of a first-mover advantage in the Fourth Industrial Revolution.

- **A new world order based on less preaching and more pragmatism.** The fact that the United States, led by its professed moral compass, contributed to much of the existing global pollution and military confrontations over the past 70 years, has been criticized as hypocritical. Though still recognizing the vital role of the United States, many countries in the Global South point to examples of situations in which the preaching did not truly match the actions, leading to grievance and extreme discomfort.

  The same can be said about the record of the European Union, or at least its core member states, who are the former colonial powers. As domestic challenges arise, the EU will likely remain a relevant yet secondary player in the new world order. Though the war in Ukraine may have increased the bullishness of the transatlantic alliance between the United States and Europe, in relation to China and Russia, the asymmetries of the sanctions imposed may affect the alliance's unity.

- **Which political system is the best fit to deliver results and lead to prosperity for citizens?** Liberal democracy is in a crisis, and the ascent of populism in some countries is clear evidence of failings more profound than ever thought. In many liberal democracies, voters have become used to the perspective of electing and immediately regretting their choices, a real sense of buyer's remorse whenever an electoral cycle comes to an end. For instance, the elections held in 2021 in Peru, with the election of Pedro Castillo, and Chile in 2022 with Gabriel Boric, reflect this sense of buyer´s remorse on the part of the electorate, and the immediate incapacity of the newly-elected governments to deliver effectively the promised results. This feeling of discontent with how Western democracies—and their corresponding establishment elites—have operated shows the divorce in practice from the definition of democracy: the government of the people, for the people, and by the people. The concept of democracy, which in the West is more related to freedoms of opinion, press, and religion, in the Chinese context, is more about government delivery of social welfare and guarantee of basic needs.

Based on the principles listed before, China has introduced to the world some strategies that reflect its view of the world order and how it would like to work on the governance side. For instance, the Belt and Road Initiative (BRI), launched and promoted by the Chinese government, provides some hints of how China envisages the world's future functioning by deepening and enhancing the Chinese presence globally within a new framework of political and economic cooperation.

3. The Russia-Ukraine War and its effects on the World Order

Though Mikhail Gorbachev tried to prevent the collapse of the Soviet empire through the economic and political changes he introduced—*perestroika* and *glasnost*, respectively—this proved ineffective and extemporaneous. The result was the official dissolution of the Soviet Union on December 26, 1991. The post-mortem pointed to the Soviet behemoth's incapacity to renew and innovate to meet domestic and international challenges. Additionally, the support expected from the West, particularly the United States, did not come as expected.

The end of the Soviet empire consolidated the primacy of the United States in the international system. President George H. Bush oversaw the beginning of a new world order with the U.S. at the top. However, the U.S. global hegemony was undermined by Bush's successor, Bill Clinton, who turned his attention primarily to domestic issues. Basing his campaign and focus on the economy, Bill Clinton was not an internationalist like his predecessor, nor did he feel it was in the interest of U.S. public opinion to focus on international issues.

As Russia faced a challenging transition period, it slowly became a less relevant player in the global arena. Many Soviet states also became independent; some moved into the Western orbit. The capitalist promise of the Western lifestyle and bad memories from the Soviet period stimulated former Soviet states to move away from Russian influence. This impacted Russia profoundly as it saw its relevance diminish abruptly and intensively.

President Barack Obama even classified the country as a regional power.[14] For Russian president Vladimir Putin, the whole process of the collapse of the Soviet Union and its descent into a less relevant position became the greatest geopolitical tragedy of the twentieth century,[15] especially given the role of the Soviet Union in the Second World War and the respect Putin felt Russia still deserved.

The Russian invasion of Ukraine—an attempt by Putin to keep Russia relevant as a global player—has become the greatest threat to European peace since the end of the Second World War. The war derives from Putin's grievances about the geopolitical collapse of the Soviet Union and the expansion of the North Atlantic Treaty Organization (NATO) into areas previously under Russian influence. Additionally, Putin's actions have sought to reestablish identity based on historical ties and origins, disregarding the possibility of sovereign, independent political destinies in Ukraine and Belarus. For Putin, the current national identities are artificial and fragile, fostered by the U.S., with the aim of weakening Russia and its role in global affairs.

In this attempt, Putin implemented a so-called Special Military Operation to invade Ukraine, and has broken the most important tenets of international law since 1945: annexations should not happen, and wars should only take place in case of legitimate self-defense or when authorized by the United Nations Security Council. The ousting of Muammar Ghaddafi in Libya and Saddam Hussein in Iraq, which were not sanctioned by the United Nations General Assembly nor supported by the United Nations Security Council, had undermined these fundamental principles of state interaction.

After the military operations of February 24, 2022, marking the commencement of the war in Ukraine, the global order will never be the same. Regardless of the strategies adopted and the eventual results—whether Russia wins or loses—the redesign of the worldwide chessboard has become irreversible. The West had applied an ever-growing number of sanctions to Russia to protect the existing international order. Initially, such sanctions received support from most countries. Still, as Ukraine has become more of a proxy war for the U.S. to retain its global hegemony, the

---

14 . Scott Wilson, "Obama dismisses Russia as 'regional power' acting out of weakness", Washington Post, March 25, 2014, National Security. https://www.washingtonpost.com/world/national-security/obama-dismisses-russia-as-regional-power-acting-out-of-weakness/2014/03/25/1e5a678e-b439-11e3-b899-20667de76985_story.html (accessed October 5, 2022).

15 . Associated Press, "Putin: Soviet collapse a 'genuine tragedy'", NBC News, April 25, 2005, https://www.nbcnews.com/id/wbna7632057. (accessed October 5, 2022).

Global South became less supportive of the actions against Russia.

Joe Biden has affirmed the goal of inflicting pain on Russia through sanctions.[16] To this end, despite the asymmetry of the impact of sanctions on their territories, he managed to convince EU countries to go along. Russia, which has coexisted with sanctions since 1917 and more recently since 2014, has resisted longer than expected. Despite the Western effort to convert Russia into a pariah state, Putin has achieved some substantial territorial gains, which remain contested as the war in Ukraine continues.

History has shown that hegemonic powers rise and decline. Hegemony has proven to be cyclical. In the current scenario, the U.S. dominance in the global order has been declining for quite some time. During the post-Cold War period, the U.S. became more inward-looking, with more significant concern for the domestic rather than the global agenda. For a short period, the world became unipolar, with the U.S. remaining the most powerful country in the global system. Although Washington still is militarily superior, its interventions in the Balkans and Iraq, and, with NATO support, in Afghanistan, have diluted much of its moral capital and the perception of invincibility. Also, though Europe has preserved relative unanimity in its actions in response to the war in Ukraine, its long-term goals remain fragmented because of the asymmetric impact of the war and related sanctions on its member states.

Countries with significant economic ties to Russia are more affected by the adverse effects of such sanctions, particularly in relation to oil and gas supplies. Increasing energy costs, economic deacceleration, and growing political instability have become a reality in many countries still facing the dire consequences of the COVID-19 pandemic and its harmful impacts on supply chains and rising inflation worldwide.

The Global South has also suffered the consequences of the war in Ukraine. It has in fact been most adversely impacted, and the rest of the world is bearing the costs of this war.

From reduced supplies of fertilizers to increased energy prices, the Global South—like its European counterparts but with fewer means to respond—still faces the challenges imposed by COVID-19 and an ever more distant economic recovery. Famine and agricultural scarcity have returned

---

16 . White House, State of the Union Address, 2022. https://www.whitehouse.gov/state-of-the-union-2022/, (accessed October 29, 2022).

to the global agenda.[17] Food insecurity has become a global concern. An estimated 29.3% of the global population—2.3 billion people—were moderately or severely food insecure in 2021, with no access to adequate food. With the war in Ukraine, these numbers will likely grow.

4. China and the War in Ukraine

The Chinese perspective on the war in Ukraine is very different from that of Europeans and Americans. The latter understand the Russian invasion as a turning point in global affairs. For China, however, this is just another war of intervention, like those in Korea, Vietnam, Iraq, Libya, and Afghanistan. The difference, however, is that since it is Russia this time, the West seems more worried about losing global dominance.

In 1954, the leadership of the People's Republic of China enumerated the principles that would guide its foreign policy—the 'Five Principles of Peaceful Coexistence'.[18] These were mutual respect for sovereignty and territorial integrity; mutual non-aggression; non-interference in each other's internal affairs; equality and mutual benefit; and peaceful coexistence.

Through these principles, China made explicit the assumptions of its foreign policy that are often not understood in the West. In the West, the focus of *realpolitik* prevails—diplomacy's relentless pursuit of national interest from a pragmatic and objective viewpoint, whereby the sovereignty of a country can often be disrespected if it opposes the interests of the other state, particularly when a country has greater power to sustain the action.

In the name of realpolitik, the United States has often limited the rights of sovereign states, sanctioning and imposing the idea of state-building according to a preconceived formula of democracy. We have often seen regime change—the replacement of a country's constituted leadership—to be the main objective of Western foreign policy, leading to situations of institutional chaos that can never be recovered. This was the case in Libya, Iraq, and Afghanistan, among others, in recent history. A repetitive issue has occurred whenever this policy has been applied: who will take over power and what guarantees are there of a significant improvement in the situation?

---

17 . FAO, IFAD, UNICEF, WFP and WHO. The State of Food Security and Nutrition in the World 2022. Repurposing food and agricultural policies to make healthy diets more affordable (2022). Rome, FAO.
18 . Wen Jiabao. Carrying Forward the Five Principles of Peaceful Coexistence in the Promotion of Peace and Development, Chinese Journal of International Law (2004), Volume 3, Issue 2, 363–368, https://doi.org/10.1093/oxfordjournals.cjilaw.a000522 (accessed October 15, 2022)

China has developed an alternative concept reaffirming that sovereignty is an equal and inviolable right of states, regardless of the geographic extent, political regime, or economic situation. By applying the Five Principles, China has avoided interfering in other states' foreign affairs.

Since the beginning of tensions between Russia and Ukraine, China's position has remained consistent: i) maintain the solidity of the relationship with Russia—not the same concept of ally understood by the NATO Charter; ii) uphold the sanctity of the principle of non-interference in the affairs of other states; and iii) promote global economic growth. Thus, China has abstained from issues related to the tension between Russia and Ukraine, aiming to maintain equidistance in the situation—and possibly to act as a mediator if needed—and to reiterate its commitment to multilateralism since the United Nations is the ideal forum for the discussion of conflict situations such as that in Ukraine.

Though China and Russia have announced a no-limits strategic partnership[19] to counter the influence of the United States, with no forbidden areas of cooperation, the war in Ukraine has not shifted the terms of the association, which covers the following areas:

- Continued Russian support for China regarding Taiwan's status as an inalienable part of China;

- Opposition to NATO enlargement, particularly on the borders of Russia and its area of influence;

- Opposition to Australia, the United Kingdom, and United States (AUKUS) alliance, and the threat of an arms race in the Pacific;

- Cooperation in technological areas, particularly artificial intelligence and information security;

- Action against developing missile defense systems and global hegemony claims by countries that impose their democracy standards.

The Chinese understand this as a partnership, not as an alliance that would force them to support Russia in its military actions. The Chinese non-alignment position is strange to Western countries. The Chinese believe an automatic alignment obscures the understanding of the fundamental factors

---

19 . "Moscow, Beijing declare Russian-Chinese friendship has no limits, no 'forbidden areas'", Tass Russian Agency, February 4, 2022, https://tass.com/politics/1398071 (accessed 25 November, 2022)

that guide a dispute and forces countries to make decisions that will harm them and, possibly, will need to be reversed. This is indeed the case for several European countries that, initially under pressure from Washington, decided to implement sanctions on Russia that will be economically harmful to them and that, eventually, may have to be abandoned because of the impossibility of implementation or the costs thereof.

In the Chinese concept of a community with a shared future, countries' sovereignties must always be respected with the impossibility of intervening in domestic affairs. Multilateral organizations must therefore reassume a more relevant and primal role to ensure win-win cooperation—one favorite Chinese expression—to obtain better results in improving the global order.

Therefore, the current Chinese position in Ukraine has been consistent with its history and precedents. The policy of the Five Principles of Peaceful Coexistence remains valid. As Confucius taught, *"the man without constancy cannot be a comforter or a doctor"*. In line with Confucian thought, China has kept a strategic silence to act effectively in the resolution of any conflict. A conflict resolution—or even a cease-fire—will be necessary as soon as the global costs of the war pile up and the world is forced into a worldwide recession.

To summarize, the Chinese perspective on the war in Ukraine has been the following:

- Russia, the West, and the United States are responsible for the war in Ukraine, mainly because the West has ignored Russia's regional security concerns;

- The involvement of the U.S. in the conflict only prolongs the war. The U.S. seeks to recreate a Cold War narrative that is not positive for the world, with NATO aiding U.S. geopolitical goals of continued hegemony and expansionism;

- Sanctions are ineffective instruments to dissuade Russia, and only reflect the U.S. effort to enhance its geoeconomic reach.

The Chinese are aware of the toxic impact of the war in Ukraine and how Western countries have used the conflict and the Chinese position to threaten China's global reputation and image, because of its close ties to Russia.

Finally, China has little interest in a long-term, high-intensity conflict. This would affect its path to economic growth and income-level goals for 2049, when the People's Republic of China will celebrate its centenary. Beijing does not want to see Russia's defeat, which could lead to the installation of a pro-Western regime in Moscow, or even the country's disintegration. This would add one more hostile state to its neighborhood and affect regional stability. Thus, a cease-fire would be the best solution for Beijing, which does not accept submission to the U.S. hegemonic will.

China has adopted a pragmatic approach when dealing with such types of conflicts and has tried, whenever possible, to extend its interests and consolidate its presence. For instance, the negotiations carried out by the Chinese with the Taliban in Afghanistan demonstrate this pragmatic approach when dealing with conflict.

5. Chinese Pragmatism in Afghanistan

After the rapid rise of the Taliban to take over the government of Afghanistan after twenty years of U.S. presence, China adopted a cautious approach. China has a 76 kilometer border with Afghanistan. In China's Silk Road Strategy, Afghanistan is considered an essential gateway to European markets.[20] Additionally, the China-Pakistan Economic Corridor (CPEC) is a crucial economic agreement within the Chinese strategic framework for Central Asia, particularly in energy and infrastructure. The Chinese have built rail and road connections and sought to deconstruct any existing rifts in the relationship between Pakistan and Afghanistan, so that the projects move forward without turmoil.

China has been the largest foreign investor in Afghanistan, particularly in natural resources and infrastructure. However, the investment numbers from China have not been as high as expected, since the Taliban have not shown enough capacity or effort to crack down on ties to separatists in the Xinjiang region.[21]

China has invested in oil extraction in the northern region of Afghanistan, telecommunications, and the construction of fiber-optic

---

20 . Belt and Road Initiative is a Chinese-developed model for international economic, political, and development cooperation under the Five Principles of Peaceful Coexistence, aiming to increment connectivity with heavy Chinese financing to build a community of shared future.

21 . Bloomberg, "China's failure to invest in Afghanistan is frustrating the Taliban," The Times of India, October 1, 2022, World section, http://timesofindia.indiatimes.com/articleshow/94468965.cms?utm_source=contentofinterest&utm_medium=text&utm_campaign=cppst (accessed 17 October, 2022).

connections.[22] However, such investments could not expand because of the political situation and unstable security. The stability promised—and never achieved—by the United States and NATO countries, did not provide Afghanistan with substantial economic development, with the country still facing reduced export capacity.

The Chinese understand that regional stability will positively affect the continuity of their initiatives and investments related to the New Silk Road. With this, it intends to contain terrorist organizations, such as the Islamic Movement of East Turkestan, a radical Uighur group active in the Xinjiang region, which seeks, through terrorism, the independence of this Chinese region.[23]

With economic development, many elements that foster political instability in Afghanistan will likely disappear. What matters to China is a stable Afghanistan so that it can reach European consumer markets more quickly and without turmoil related to anti-government, terrorism, or anti-Chinese actions.

Chinese pragmatism in the Afghan situation is an example of China's commitment to non-interventionism as a long-term foreign-relations principle, despite its growing economic interests in Afghanistan. This should provide a greater understanding of how the Chinese envisage a new world order.

6. China and Taiwan after the War in Ukraine

Though the issue of Taiwan has been raised many times during the war in Ukraine, the Chinese have emphasized the relevance of the Shanghai Communiqué of 27 February 1972, issued jointly by the United States and the People's Republic of China, regarding Taiwan's status as a Chinese domestic affair. No foreign country would have the right to interfere.

In the communiqué, the United States acknowledged that *"all Chinese*

---

22 . A $3 billion investment deal with state-owned Metallurgical Corporation of China, awarded a 30-year contract to explore the Mes Aynak region, still needs to become a reality.

23 . The West has accused China of creating reeducation camps in Xinjiang with the purpose to seek secession from China, with the Uyghurs wanting to establish their own state. The West accuses China of building a network of surveillance and human rights violation against the Uyghur population, which is approximately of 12 million people, mostly Muslim, living in the Xinjiang Uyghur Autonomous Region (XUAR). BBC News, "Who are the Uyghurs and why is China being accused of genocide?" , BBC News, May 24, 2022, China section, https://www.bbc.com/news/world-asia-china-22278037 (accessed October, 30, 2022).

on both sides of the Taiwan Strait claim that there is only one China and that Taiwan is part of China". Hence comparing Taiwan to Ukraine has no basis since Taiwan is a domestic affair for China.

The Russian invasion of Ukraine has shed light on a hypothetical conflict with Taiwan. Several publications have tried to compare Ukraine with Taiwan, but have yet to understand the profound differences between the two situations. Though China may have increased the number of air surveillance operations in Taiwan's Air Defense Zone, China has taken a discernible long-term perspective on unifying Taiwan with mainland China without a major war.

Though the United States has tried to change direction in its recognition of the One China Principle, particularly after U.S. House Speaker Nancy Pelosi visited Taiwan in early August 2022, China has only launched military activities to build a potential blockade around Taiwan's main island and to remind the Taiwanese not to flirt with possible independence efforts, which would only generate more regional instability. The Chinese understood the Pelosi visit as an attempt by the Biden Administration to renege on the U.S. understanding of the One China Principle, and to destabilize China, particularly with the re-election of Xi Jinping as Chairman of the Communist Party of China and President of the People's Republic of China.

7. China-Russia Relations

China will gain geopolitically either from a Russian victory or defeat in Ukraine. That is why Beijing has avoided violating sanctions. With a clear commitment to rebuilding the international system of global governance, Beijing has avoided taking actions that may damage its economic path to prosperity. Any missteps could disrupt China's goals and create significant challenges in a world that desperately needs to recover from the COVID-19 pandemic.

China has taken measures to support Russia against the sanctions the West has imposed.[24] However, the Chinese have been cautious not to accelerate any attempt by the West to cut off the country from technology, trade, or global influence. As a result, China has supported Russia's acquisition of goods but provides no explicit military support, which could subject China

---

24 . U.S.-China Economic and Security Review Commission. Timeline of key events leading up to the invasion, including points of Russia-China communication and engagement, https://www.uscc.gov/research/china-russia-interactions-leading-invasion-ukraine (accessed October 20, 2022).

or Chinese entities to sanctions. There is no evidence that China is willing to change this path, which has proven profitable for the country, particularly in terms of acquiring oil and natural gas at differentiated prices.

As part of the BRICS, China has strengthened its relationship with Russia over the years. Since 2013, Xi Jinping and Vladimir Putin have met 39 times. Russia is part of the Chinese revisionist global power strategy and an essential partner in global defense. A victory by Russia would consolidate this strategy quicker, while a defeat would lead China to postpone its grand plan for a few years or decades. It is clear, however, that despite both countries' engagement and mutual interests, China is not likely to divert from its current strategy of meeting Xi's development targets.

8. China at 73

From the days of 1949 up to its 73rd anniversary, the People's Republic of China has faced countless challenges and accomplished an economic miracle. China is moving fast towards its former position as the world's most significant economic power. The Chinese rise has caused discomfort, particularly in some Western countries, which are losing global primacy and hegemony. The rise of China will transform the world in two fundamental ways. First, it is a country of more than 1.3 billion people, which has grown substantially in the last thirty years, with increasing consumption power. Second, for the first time in modern history, the core country of the global system will be a developing country from the East with civilizational roots different from those we know. And, differently than expected, China will not become westernized. China is a civilization-state, which is reflected in its worship of traditional values, social relationships, and the merits of Confucianism.

The function of the Chinese government and the Communist Party of China (CPC) is to preserve this civilization and to be the cement that holds the country together. Unity for the maintenance of Chinese culture is the most critical value. This unity has allowed the country to become a global power and to benefit from the globalization process that came to it, despite its enormous cost to both the environment and the sweat equity of the Chinese people. The results are that more than 700 million people have been lifted out of poverty. In this process, China has become the most prominent global consumer market.

9. China and the Global South After the War in Ukraine

As a country of the Global South, China remains committed to expanding its ties, enhancing its reach, and deepening its economic relations. China understands the Global South as a priority for it to consolidate its role as the largest economy in the world and as a global influencer.

The goal is to reach a per-capita income of between $20,000 and $25,000 by 2049, when the People's Republic of China reaches its centenary, which would affect the Global South in a very particular and profound way. If this objective is achieved, the disruptive effect on global production will be immense, and the increase in Chinese consumption will impact every corner of the globe. As China includes more of its population in the consumer market, food consumption and natural resources will be more widely sought. Though there is a movement for nearshoring[25] and friend-shoring,[26] it will take the world many decades to build the same just-in-time infrastructure China has developed over the last 40 years. Additionally, the Chinese educational system has an added element of intense competition, which could encourage the best brains to remain in Chinese universities.

The Chinese economic model is not exportable. China has emphasized this aspect. It has also reaffirmed that it does not seek hegemony. Deng Xiaoping insisted that China should not seek hegemony or impose its values or ways on other countries. He said: *"China is not a superpower, nor will she ever seek to be one. If one day China should change her color and turn into a superpower, if she too should play the tyrant in the world and everywhere subject others to her bullying, aggression, and exploitation, the people of the world should identify her as social-imperialist, expose it, oppose it, and work together with the Chinese people to overthrow it".*[27]

During President Xi´s time in power, however, China has become more assertive on the world stage, particularly regarding significant reform of global governance and the international order.[28] This is particularly important

---

[25] . Nearshoring is a policy in which business processes are transferred to companies in a nearby country to benefit from geographic and cultural proximity.
[26] . Friend-shoring or ally-shoring has become a strategy pursued by the U.S. government to influence companies to move their sourcing and manufacturing to countries with which the U.S. has a friendlier relationship, and to insulate supply chains from China and Russia.
[27] . Marcus Vinicius De Freitas. 2019. Reform and Opening-up: Chinese Lessons to the World. Policy Paper, May 2019, PP 19/05, Policy Center for the New South, 2019.
[28] . This assertiveness by Chinese diplomacy has been derogatorily referred to as "Wolf Warrior Diplomacy", a shorthand expression to denote a new, assertive brand of Chinese diplomacy, differently from past behavior of keeping a lower profile, and cautious and moderate interaction with other countries. Chinese diplomats felt under attack but also

to address since the world of the 2020s is very different from the end of the Second World War, when the current global order was built. As a result of this new active role, China's status as a rising power is consolidating with great strength.

Xi´s thoughts on diplomacy reflect China's new global role, relevance, and essentiality. China has become an indispensable partner for many countries worldwide, and its influence is expanding ever more. It should not be a surprise that China would seek a more assertive position, which is not only a natural result of the new role it plays in the global order, but also a demand by the countries that have felt left out of the current world order and see in China's rise a new possibility to share a more significant stake and be able to contribute to the improvement of a new global order. China has played a dual role: strengthening the current institutions where possible and creating new alternatives for global governance. As to hegemony, the position of the current administration—as well as that of the Communist Party of China—is that the country shall not seek to become a hegemon. The Chinese word for hegemony (霸权 – pinyin *Bàquán*) denotes a sense of tyranny, which would oppose the historical Chinese perspective of peace and harmony in international relations.

Therein lies an enormous opportunity for the Global South in a new world order, where China believes trade and cooperation to be the fundamental instruments for global interaction, and not the predominance of one country over the others. This approach to global power would be different from any experience the West has led over the last five centuries.

The Chinese engagement and presence in the Global South has been hugely significant. For the last three decades, China has become a significant financier of infrastructure projects in Latin America, Africa, and Asia, to support countries in their most relevant needs and with a long-term perspective for economic growth. The Chinese appetite for infrastructure projects, in particular, is related to a Chinese proverb "If you want to get rich, build a road first" (要想富先修路 – pinyin Yào xiang fù xian xiu lù). Infrastructure is essential for any economic development. China has also forgiven billions of dollars in debt to developing countries that have not been able to meet their financial commitments.

Additionally, China has become the first or second trading partner for most countries in the Global South, allowing them to export ever-

proud of the way China has handled the pandemic crisis.

growing numbers of products, commodities and goods in general. Though a large economy in the region, India has been more moderate in promoting international investments in Asia and other parts of the world, mainly because of its domestic conditions.

Finally, the Asian century will not have—and should not repeat—the same features of the current Western-centered global system, particularly considering that China will be at the helm. China does not view itself as a missionary country, does not wish to spread its political system to other countries, and does not perceive itself as the last bastion of democracy in the world.

10. Conclusion

The world is in transition. The 2020s will be considered the beginning of the Asian Century because of the disruptions resulting from COVID-19 and the war in Ukraine. China will certainly be of utmost importance in this new period of world history.

Profound transformation and adjustments will occur, and globalization still offers even more benefits that can raise the level of global prosperity. Though there are discussions and strategies about diverting production from Asia to different parts of the world, particularly after COVID-19 and the war in Ukraine, the reality is that in the short and medium terms, countries will have a difficult time displacing China as the leading supplier, mainly because China has taken all the necessary steps to guarantee its logistical advantages.

As perceived by China, a new world order should be more open to the worldwide community. The Chinese affirm: "*The greatness of the sea results from its ability to absorb water from all sources*". Building a more inclusive world order will bring about an improved global reality. By absorbing contributions from all sources, the net result will be a global power structure that is more equal, particularly for the developing world. Napoleon Bonaparte is credited with the phrase: "*Let China sleep. Because when she wakes up, the world will shake*". Napoleon was correct. China has woken up. The world will never be the same again.

CHAPTER IV

Turkey's Policy Response to War-Induced Economic Downturn and Geopolitical Shifts

Serhat S. Çubukçuoğlu

Turkey is an emerging country in the G20, with a young population and growing economy. It is located at the crossroads of trade routes between Europe, Asia, and Africa, with a lucrative local market. The Turkish economic trajectory has been through ups and downs over the past thirty years, after opening to free-market liberalism. Despite initial successes with reforms, deregulation, and democratization, the Justice and Development Party's (AKP) policies since 2002 have rested on unsustainable levels of consumption, trade deficits, and foreign debt. The war in Ukraine has presented an opportunity to return to economic orthodoxy, but the government has rather adopted a nationalist discourse to distance itself further from international financial norms. There is a tendency for localization and self-sufficiency, coupled with social-welfare policies reminiscent of embedded liberalism, which is a middle ground policy between liberal orthodoxy and economic nationalism. The system of executive presidency grants overwhelming powers to the government, which has taken radical measures to achieve export-driven high growth in the lead up to elections in 2023. Even before the war, Turkey leveraged its geopolitical significance and positioned itself as a regional balancer between the U.S./NATO and Eurasia, but this has put the country in a precarious position where it must manage complex, transactional relations with shrinking margins for political maneuverability. Because of its economic fragility, Turkey may have to choose a side in the war if a possible recession bites deeper into the country's economic backbone.

1. Introduction

Turkey is a developing country in the G20 group of nations, situated at the crossroads of Europe, Asia, and the Middle East. Historically, it is the heir to the Ottoman Empire that controlled a thriving overland trade route for nearly six centuries. It opened itself as a free market economy in the 1980s and adapted to the fast pace of neoliberal globalization from the early 2000s. From an insider's point of view, interlinkages between its history, geography, and foreign policy are conspicuous. Central to Turkey's strategic culture is survivability in a chaotic region marked by social cleavages, civil strife, and proxy wars. It walks a fine line between the NATO alliance, as a frontier country, and Eurasia's emergent powers of Russia, China, and Central Asia. Since the start of the Ukraine crisis, Turkey has leveraged its geopolitical clout to exert an assertive posture in its sphere of influence, which now stretches from the deserts of the Sahel to the Caucasus, and Eastern Ukraine to the Persian Gulf. As a pivotal country between competing poles of power, it exacts a comparative advantage from its geography, and a competitive advantage with its highly successful, battle-proven defense industry.

Throughout the twentieth century, Turkey had a bumpy relationship with the West. The much-hyped accession process for European Union (EU) membership, which continued on-and-off since the 1960s, ground to a halt in the mid-2000s and has not restarted. During the Cold War, the U.S. supplied weapons to Turkey only as part of its wider agenda to encircle the then-Soviet Union. It stationed nuclear warheads on Turkish air bases, prompting the USSR to attempt the same in Cuba in 1962. Similarly, from Moscow's point of view, NATO's plans at present to expand eastward toward Ukraine and Georgia are its Cuba Moment. On one hand, Turkey is home to NATO's land command and several strategic assets such as the X-band radar in Malatya-Kürecik and Patriot missiles for early-warning and missile defense; on the other, it controversially purchased Russian S-400 surface-to-air missiles to defend its airspace for the next few years until its indigenous defense systems are robustly in place. That resulted in its expulsion from the US-led F-35 Joint Strike Fighter program, and imposition of measures under the Countering America's Adversaries Through Sanctions Act (CAATSA) that are normally reserved for rogue states such as Iran and North Korea. These complex relations are reflected in the multi-layered conflicts in Ukraine, Syria, Libya, and the Caucasus. With Russia's invasion of Ukraine, Turkey assumed heightened importance as a bulwark on NATO's south-eastern flank for its control over the only maritime access route to the

Black Sea and as a gateway for air passage rights from Russia to the Western world. It also regained some of the attention lost after the end of the Cold War, as demonstrated at the crucial NATO Summit in Madrid in June 2022. Since Finland's and Sweden's applications to join NATO require unanimous approval, Turkey's precarious stance towards the alliance's enlargement led western policymakers to pay more attention to Ankara's legitimate concerns on regional security.

The reality of a multipolar world today presents more options for a medium-size power like Turkey to act assertively to defend its interests. Despite U.S. President Joe Biden's efforts to re-unite the world under an American-led, rules-based neoliberal world order, the fragmented international system favors more transactional, business-like deals on sidelines, rather than a steadfast approach to diplomacy through multilateral institutions. It also paves the way for emergence of new alliances, especially among the regional powers of the Global South, including Turkey, Azerbaijan, and Qatar. In this context, the activism in Turkish foreign policy also extends to North Africa, the Indian Ocean, and the Persian Gulf. The country's strengthening economic and diplomatic ties with the islands of the Indian Ocean, Mauritius for instance,[1] also lead to new circumstances of power dynamics in the Indo-Africa sphere,[2] an unthinkable event in the early 2000s. In the war-induced global turmoil, these dynamics raise questions about political economy and macroeconomic drivers of Turkey's pre-war and post-war foreign policy, its role as a power balancer, and how they relate to geopolitical shifts in the region. This chapter aims to fill this gap and present Turkey's politico-economic trajectory before and during this tumultuous period.

2. Pre-War Macroeconomic and Political Situation

Since Turkey opened itself as a free market economy in the 1980s, the pace of neoliberal globalization has created opportunities for business growth, capital accumulation, and foreign direct investment (FDI) in key sectors including banking, construction, textiles, and tourism. However, imbalances of liberalization, consumption-led economic growth, and large

---

[1] . "Republic of Mauritius- Mauritius-Turkey: First Meeting of the Joint Committee under the Free Trade Agreement," November 18, 2016, http://www.govmu.org/English/News/Pages/Mauritius-Turkey-First-meeting-of-the-Joint-Committee-under-the-Free-Trade-Agreement.aspx.

[2] . Darshana M. Baruah, "What Is Happening in the Indian Ocean?," Carnegie Endowment for International Peace, March 3, 2021, https://carnegieendowment.org/2021/03/03/what-is-happening-in-indian-ocean-pub-83948.

budget deficits common to most poorer countries of the Global South since the 1990s, led to sovereign debt and foreign exchange rate crises in the early 2000s. General elections in 2002 brought the conservative Justice and Development Party (AKP) to government in Ankara, led by Recep Tayyip Erdogan, who has held power and guided the economy in a self-styled way since then. In its early years, the AKP government accomplished key reforms, regulatory changes, and democratic progress towards a healthier economic order, especially with the "*impetus provided by the EU membership process*".[3] During this early era, or the golden age of the AKP, the Turkish economy grew on average by 6% annually. This trend continued until 2011, when the country's role-model status as a secular-democratic, Muslim-majority, developing country began to deteriorate in the wake of the Arab Spring uprisings.

By 2022, Turkey's productive capacity was already under stress because of lack of domestic savings, high foreign debt, and double-digit inflation. The COVID-19 pandemic in 2020 transformed the global geopolitical landscape within a matter of weeks and laid bare the unsustainability of the consumerist, debt-laden, growth-driven economic model in Turkey. Whereas the early 2000s were characterized by the rise of neoliberal policies, economic integration, and civil society freedoms, the new era between 2016 and 2022 ushered in economic nationalism, localization, and protectionism because of centralization of authority under the executive president's self-styled leadership. Turkey's main challenges in this period were lack of transparency, loss of market confidence to attract FDI, and inadequacy of foreign exchange reserves. Although the COVID-19 pandemic precipitated an economic downturn in 2020-21, it is the AKP government's political considerations and international relations that have determined Turkey's macroeconomic policy response to the war-induced economic crisis in 2022.

There are important political drivers behind the government's policy prescriptions and main priorities, which have led Turkey to select certain policies over others. The AKP's decision-making model in the early period of 2002-2016 fits within neoliberal globalization, whereas the six years since the failed coup attempt in 2016, including the pandemic era and the Ukraine crisis, conform to embedded liberalism. In the face of rising property, food, and fuel prices since February 2022, and having to choose between populist growth and high inflation versus unpopular low inflation

---

3 . Ziya Öniş, "Sharing Power: Turkey's Democratization Challenge in the Age of the AKP Hegemony," Insight Turkey, April 1, 2013, https://www.insightturkey.com/articles/sharing-power-turkeys-democratization-challenge-in-the-age-of-the-akp-hegemony.

and unemployment trade-off, the government has succumbed to the former.

a. Economic Stability, Financial Markets, and Investment Climate

Overall, Turkey was in a weak state to weather an economic crisis prior to the onset of the war in Ukraine. Since the 1980s, free-market oriented reforms, privatization, and deregulation opened the Turkish economy to international trade and investment. Convertibility of the Turkish Lira (TL), institution of the floating exchange-rate regime, and liberalization of the financial system enabled small and medium size enterprises (SMEs) to tap into credit markets, increase exports, and create wealth for a greater share of the population. After 2002, the first decade of AKP rule saw significant economic growth and the rise of a strong middle class in the rural heartland of Anatolia. Nonetheless, despite regulatory reforms, redistribution of wealth, and the rise of new business elites to challenge the dominance of established big businesses, Turkey's growth depended on unsustainable levels of domestic consumption and trade deficits, arising from the high proportion of imports to value-added exports.[4] The government considered usury as the source of all economic evils in Islamic terms and intervened in the central bank's management to impose loose monetary policy. President Erdogan argued against economic orthodoxy that high interest rates cause inflation; he believed that a low interest-rate policy is the cure to the disease.

Owing to global capital liquidity in the 2000s, as cheap credit inflow buoyed Turkish capital markets, private sector businesses borrowed heavily in foreign currency-denominated instruments and invested in unproductive assets, icluding housing, shopping malls, and hotels, rather than technology-intensive capital. Cronies in the non-foreign-exchange-earning construction sector and real estate invested huge sums of credit-funded capital into mega projects, such as high-rise office towers in Istanbul's financial center. Although real estate counts for 57% of FDI inflows to Turkey, thanks to the granting of citizenship to holiday home buyers, it hovers on average at $4.5 billion per year,[5] which is only a fraction of the country's current account deficit.[6] Furthermore, emergence of an affluent middle-class and internal migration has accelerated urbanization and over-population in

---

4 . "Turkey Current Account Balance: % of GDP, 1998 – Sep 2022 | CEIC Data," CEIC Quarterly Country Data, 2022, https://www.ceicdata.com/en/indicator/turkey/current-account-balance--of-nominal-gdp.
5 . "Turkey (FDI) Foreign Direct Investment: Real Estate: Net | Economic Indicators | CEIC," CEIC Turkey FDI: Real Estate, 2018, https://www.ceicdata.com/en/turkey/foreign-direct-investment-flow-by-industry-annual/fdi-real-estate-net.
6 . "Real Estate - Invest in Türkiye," Presidency of the Republic of Türkiye, 2022, https://www.invest.gov.tr/en/sectors/pages/real-estate.aspx.

Istanbul, a city that pulses to the beat of globalization. Erdogan pioneered building of modern infrastructure across the country, especially in city centers, based on his earlier experience as mayor of Istanbul between 1994-1998. To complement extensive highway networks, the automotive industry achieved remarkable output and productivity growth rates, earning the title of Turkey's flagship export industry, and enabling backward linkages and positive spillover effects to SMEs.[7]

Whereas the sovereign debt and financial crises characterized the 1990s and early 2000s, banking reforms including the Basel III capital adequacy ratio from 2002 onwards, put Turkish banks on a solid path to recovery and resilience. Turkey followed a prudent fiscal policy and paid its debt to the International Monetary Fund (IMF), terminated stand-by agreements in 2008, and even donated money to the IMF to assist underdeveloped countries of the Global South, such as Somalia.[8] Nonetheless, government policy to encourage construction, tourism, and textiles, to reduce high levels of unemployment, rather than high-technology sectors, industrial development, and differentiated services, forced businesses to fit into the straitjacket of easy credit, quick-turnaround-type non-productive investments. In accordance with policy choices, asset specificity increased in rent-seeking activities. Because of vested political interests, capital-intensive factors of production began to concentrate in a few lucrative sectors including energy, defense, and transport. After 2012, as foreign capital inflows began to dry up, inadequate savings accumulation crippled credit markets and the credit crunch put extraneous strain of interest burden on the SMEs, which had borrowed in foreign-currency denominated assets. The informal economy grew while inefficient taxation in the form of high indirect taxes on the poor, and low direct taxes on high-income individuals, caused severe economic dislocations. Rent-seeking, corruption, and cronyism diffused across the country.

Still, Turkey has a relatively diversified urban-industrial economy without dependence on a single export commodity like oil. Until 2022, the country's main economic concern was the current account deficit. The impact of import dependency in energy was severe, making the sector the single largest contributor to the current-account shortfall. Turkey ran large

---

[7] . Erol Taymaz and Kamil Yılmaz, "Political Economy of Industrial Policy in Turkey: The Case of Automotive Industry," TÜSİAD – Sabancı Üniversitesi Rekabet Forumu, no. 2016–1 (n.d.): 53.

[8] . "Turkey Pays Part of Somalia's IMF Debt for Relief Initiative - Türkiye News," Hürriyet Daily News, November 6, 2020, https://www.hurriyetdailynews.com/turkey-pays-part-of-somalias-imf-debt-for-relief-initiative-159791.

trade deficits with developed countries of the West, as well as emerging markets of the Global South. Importing 75% of its total energy demand, it depended on foreign natural gas and oil resources to meet most of its domestic consumption. By the end of 2021, out of $50 billion paid for energy imports, about $20 billion went towards imported gas, which is sourced from a variety of countries including the U.S., Russia, Azerbaijan, and Iran. Despite the high energy bill, the trade deficit gradually dropped over the past decade from 5.7% to 2.6% of gross domestic product (GDP), and for the first time, Turkey posted a current account surplus of 1.2% of GDP in 2019.[9] The main reasons for the upturn in the current account were the TL's depreciation against the U.S. dollar, reduced luxury goods trade, and a slow-down in intermediate input imports for industrial production, rather than an increase in productivity.

Notably, Turkey has arable land for development and a relatively cheap labor force in comparison even to labor-abundant China. But Turkey also has weaknesses in its economic structures and democratic institutions, which are major bottlenecks that hinder the investment climate, and therefore job creation. From 2016 to 2020, the FDI stock declined from $19 billion to $8.6 billion and briefly rose to $14.2 billion in 2021, but only temporarily. In contrast with economic overheating in 2010, marked by a record 8.4% growth rate and per-capita income in 2015 at $11,085, the Turkish economy grew only 0.9% in 2019 and per-capita income dropped to $9,213.[10] During this turbulence, the financial sector, which is 70% owned by firms in Europe and the Gulf monarchies, maintained its role as the backbone of the economy to channel savings to investments. The sector showed mixed performance but weathered a severe speculative foreign-exchange attack on the TL in 2018, maintained its liquidity, and prevented a bank run. Amid regulatory pressures, lower profitability, and worsening macroeconomic environment, the return on equity in the banking sector dropped from 14.8% in 2018 to 11.4% in 2019, but the sector entered the COVID-19 pandemic in 2020 with $8.4 billion annual net profit.[11]

Perhaps the most remarkable achievement of the AKP government in macro-policy terms was to keep the budget deficit at 2.9%, below the

---

[9] . "Economic Outlook: Republic of Turkey - Ministry of Trade," September 2021, https://www.trade.gov.tr/data/5b9229ab13b876136466584b/Economic%20Outlook%20September_2021.pdf.

[10] . "GDP Growth (Annual %) - Turkiye | Data," The World Bank Group, 2021, https://data.worldbank.org/indicator/NY.GDP.MKTP.KD.ZG?locations=TR.

[11] . "Turkey's Banking Sector Posts $8.4B Net Profit in 2019," AA (blog), January 30, 2020, https://www.aa.com.tr/en/economy/turkeys-banking-sector-posts-84b-net-profit-in-2019/1719225.

EU's Maastricht Criteria of 3% of GDP,[12] an important accomplishment in the context of the EU's economic policy as a benchmark for the Turkish economy since 2004. Moreover, Turkey's debt-to-GDP ratio in 2013 was 32%, among the lowest in Europe and less than half of the euro area's overall debt ratio.[13] To maintain public debt at a manageable level, attract FDI, and diversify financial instruments in the Turkish market, the government established a sovereign wealth fund in 2016 and transferred assets of large state-owned firms to the fund, which had assets of $245 billion by the end of 2020.[14] Among the fund's goals are to become a regular issuer of debt in international markets, to rely on dividends from the companies it owns, and to re-cycle proceeds from asset sales to fund its operations. The fund has become the prime vehicle to facilitate initial public offerings for mining, oil, and gas companies in Turkey, and to attract financial resources for critical projects in the defense industry without straining the central budget. Nonetheless, Turkey's trade deficits, high consumption, and shortage of productive investments have hampered sustainable growth.

b. Political-Economy Drivers of the Pre-War Macroeconomic Situation

The AKP government has leveraged Islamism as identity politics and has strived to create a strong, pious middle-class in the country's Anatolian heartland since 2002. This became the support network for the AKP, but it also enabled formation of partisan identities and nationalist-populist policies. There were high stakes involved in the distribution of benefits and costs, and the AKP's voter base did not want to relinquish their new-found privileged status once in power. Notably, Erdogan issued a statement comparing the country's government in principle to "*corporate management*" and likened himself to a chief executive officer.[15] He suppressed traditional corporatist interests of the city elites and nurtured "*Anatolian Tigers*" as the new class of conservative entrepreneurs for his voter base.

---

12 . "Economic Outlook: Republic of Turkey - Ministry of Trade."
13 . "Central Government Debt, Total (% of GDP) - Turkiye | Data," The World Bank Group, 2021, https://data.worldbank.org/indicator/GC.DOD.TOTL.GD.ZS?end=2020&locations=TR&start=2002.
14 . "Turkey Wealth Fund to Retry Bond Sale as It Plans IPO of Assets - Bloomberg," December 1, 2020, https://www.bloomberg.com/news/articles/2020-12-01/turkey-wealth-fund-to-retry-bond-sale-as-it-plans-ipo-of-assets.
15 . Recep Tayyip Erdogan, "'Ülkeyi anonim sirket gibi yönetmek çok önemli,'" Ahaber, May 24, 2018, https://www.ahaber.com.tr/video/gundem-videolari/ulkeyi-anonim-sirket-gibi-yonetmek-cok-onemli.

It is important to highlight that the open-economy politics approach that the AKP has adopted emphasizes the relative political leverage of constituents and their organizational influence on decision-making. In a strongman regime like Turkey, firms with long-term, diversified interests engage in political activity to protect their assets, such that *"the politician relies on the group's support whereas the group relies on the politician's delivery of benefits"*.[16] The AKP has eleven million active party members in Turkey, as opposed to only two million members in its nearest contender, the Republican People's Party (CHP). Plus, labor unions in Turkey are weak and social welfare is secondary to profitability. During the AKP's first decade up until 2012, the government firmly committed itself to the neoliberal globalization model. Economic management was based on *"twin external anchors"*,[17] the IMF and the EU, to restore credibility after the 2001 sovereign debt crisis. Under the IMF's fiscal discipline, credit-rating agencies upgraded Turkey and reinforced the upswing sentiment by establishing *"the conventional judgment regarding Turkey's creditworthiness"*.[18] From the 1990s onwards, IMF's neoliberal policies under the Washington Consensus opened Turkey to intensive cross-border movement of goods, services, and capital, supported by the cornerstone Customs Union agreement in 1995 with the EU. The AKP continued economic reforms through deregulation, liberalization, and privatization policies between 2002 and 2008.

The government divested underperforming state-owned assets and enacted reforms in education, healthcare, and research and development, to increase productivity and competitiveness. In 2004, Turkey started accession negotiations with the EU, providing an impetus to undertake further economic, legal, and political reforms. The bilateral trade volume reached €167 billion in 2021 and the EU remained Turkey's largest export market.[19] However, Turkey's absence from the EU's decision-making bodies left it in a relatively disadvantaged position against worsening terms of trade. Turkey lost an estimated €300 billion since 1995 due to non-tariff barriers, exclusion of the services and agriculture sectors from the Customs Union, and the EU's comparative advantage in manufactured goods.[20]

---

16. James E. Alt et al., "The Political Economy of International Trade: Enduring Puzzles and an Agenda for Inquiry," Comparative Political Studies 29, no. 6 (1996): 703.
17. Andrew Finkel, Turkey: What Everyone Needs to Know (Oxford: Oxford University Press, 2012), 53.
18. Ernesto Vivares, The Routledge Handbook to Global Political Economy: Conversations and Inquiries, 1st ed. (New York: Routledge, 2020), 225.
19. Eurostat, "Turkey-EU - International Trade in Goods Statistics," Statistics (Brussels, Belgium, February 2022), https://ec.europa.eu/eurostat/statistics-explained/index.php?title=Turkey-EU_-_international_trade_in_goods_statistics.
20. Yavuz Özdemir and Güner Koç Aytekin, "Avrupa Birliği (AB) Gümrük Birliği'nin Türkiye

The main positive aspect of this period was that Turkey further opened its market to free trade and began to specialize in production of certain manufactured goods including household appliances, construction materials, and textile fabrics, as well as agricultural products including fruits, vegetables, and olive oil. With the rise of an entrepreneurial middle class, Turkey diversified its partnerships and widened its export markets in the Global South, namely the Middle East, Africa, and Central Asia. The Ministry of Foreign Affairs opened embassies in even the farthest corners of Africa that acted practically as trade representative offices. In just fifteen years, Turkey increased its number of African embassies from twelve to forty-two.[21] Nonetheless, this opening up to emerging markets of the East coincided with worsening relations with the West. Turkey has traditionally been a capital-scarce, labor-intensive country that has faced declining terms of trade for agricultural products. Like many developing countries of the Global South, its infant industries could not compete on manufactured goods within the European Customs Union. Turkey has occupied a "*subservient place on the periphery of a capitalist world system*" since the late Ottoman era,[22] and it has tried to break free of this uneven exchange between the industrial core in Europe and the agrarian periphery in Asia-Africa. Gradually, it reorganized itself as an alternative industrial base and established trade partnerships with labor-intensive markets of the Global South to improve its terms of trade.

The key guiding principle for foreign policy during the AKP's first decade was the "*zero-problems with neighbors*" approach to consolidate the "community of Muslim believers, or the Ummah" around a vibrant regional economic union with its center in Turkey.[23] Erdogan and his close aide at the AKP, Ahmet Davutoglu, embraced the transformation of Islamism within a neoliberal globalist vision based on the primacy of conservative democracy and free market capitalism. Countries including Jordan, Qatar, Tunisia, and Syria looked at Turkey as a role model of a secular-democratic, Muslim-majority country. The model of export-led economic growth via expanding trade partnerships in the near neighborhood suited Turkey's vision of becoming a new regional economic hub. The AKP enjoyed unprecedented

---

Ekonomisine Etkileri," Ufuk Üniversitesi Sosyal Bilimler Enstitüsü Dergisi, no. 9 (2016): 15, https://dergipark.org.tr/en/download/article-file/1359119.

21 . Anatolia News Agency, "'Number of Turkish embassies in Africa rises from 12 to 42' | Anatolia News Agency," October 19, 2019, https://www.aa.com.tr/en/africa/-number-of-turkish-embassies-in-africa-rises-from-12-to-42/1619429.

22 . Erik Jan Zürcher, Turkey: A Modern History, 3rd ed. (London: I.B. Tauris, 2004), 6.

23 . K.E. Calder, Super Continent: The Logic of Eurasian Integration (California: Stanford University Press, 2019), 41.

"prosperity and influence, thanks to Turkey's slow but growing integration into global markets".[24]

The model worked until the Arab Spring uprisings in 2011. Up to that point, the government had been wildly over-optimistic about the economy's prospects. However, with the drop in confidence because of regional political instability, Turkey's access to credit inflows and export markets began to lessen. As the government intensified its pursuit of a leadership role in regional politics, alongside an Islamist ideology, it intervened in a diverse set of intractable conflicts from Syria and Tunisia to Egypt and Libya. The earlier *"zero problems with neighbors"* policy collapsed and the AKP government began to the put blame on the United Nation's failure to adapt to changing global circumstances and the need to make its peace-making mission more effective.[25] In a motto, the "world is bigger than five",[26] Erdogan expressed his self-styled skepticism about the Western order and his objections to the current structure of the UN Security Council (UNSC), because of its shortcomings to maintain peace and security.

Challenged by violent popular protests, corruptions scandals, and economic downturn after 2013, Erdogan drew a link between alleged international plots such as the 'interest lobby' and the rapid depreciation of the TL. The nadir in Turkish politics was the 2016 failed coup attempt, orchestrated by a Gülenist terrorist cult (FETÖ),[27] the leader of which resides in Pennsylvania. After the failed coup, Erdogan found a *"golden opportunity"* to re-define himself in the domestic arena as the champion of a neo-nationalist economic agenda.[28] This is evident in his scorn for the West's *"imperialist forces"*, such as the IMF, a phenomenon that he refers to as the curse from higher levels of the global neoliberal class structure, superimposed on the national order.[29] As the national economic champion,

---

24 . Halil Karaveli, "Erdogan's Journey: Conservatism and Authoritarianism in Turkey," Foreign Affairs 95, no. 6 (2016): 121–30, https://www.jstor.org/stable/43948388.
25 . Berdal Aral, "'The World Is Bigger than Five': A Salutary Manifesto of Turkey's New International Outlook," Insight Turkey, December 13, 2019, https://www.insightturkey.com/articles/the-world-is-bigger-than-five-a-salutary-manifesto-of-turkeys-new-international-outlook.
26 . "Presidency Of The Republic Of Turkey: 'Our Motto "the World Is Bigger than Five" Is the Biggest-Ever Rise against Global Injustice,'" January 10, 2018, https://www.tccb.gov.tr/en/news/542/89052/our-motto-the-world-is-bigger-than-five-is-the-biggest-ever-rise-against-global-injustice.
27 . "Turkey Failed Coup: Who Are the Gulenists?," BBC News, July 28, 2016, sec. Europe, https://www.bbc.com/news/world-europe-36920535.t
28 . "Where Turkey Goes Next," The Economist, July 16, 2016, https://www.economist.com/europe/2016/07/16/turkeys-failed-coup-gives-its-president-a-chance-to-seize-more-power.
29 . Selçuk Tepeli, "Habertürk: Cumhurbaşkanı Erdoğan: Üst akıl Türkiye üzerinde oyun oynuyor | Gündem Haberleri," April 3, 2016, https://www.haberturk.com/gundem/

Erdogan played a *"two-level game"*[30] to manage the balancing act between pressing domestic factors and powerful international influences. He harnessed power through interest group coalitions to squeeze his opponents in domestic politics, and strengthened his negotiation position against foreign actors, effectively reaching an equilibrium between his domestic constituents and international interlocutors. Economic policies from 2016 to 2020 empowered the central authority and gave a free hand to Erdogan to manage shared beliefs about what constitutes appropriate or acceptable deviations from disciplined monetary or fiscal policy.[31] From the start of his executive presidency and strong-man rule in 2018, the government remained insulated from feedback about how its policies are affecting the economy and focused instead on building scarcely used roads, bridges, and lofty office buildings. Despite the initial success, as the pandemic-induced economic crisis and rising inequality exacerbated political instability across Turkey, as in the rest of the Global South, the country entered 2022 with pre-existing economic vulnerabilities.

3. Macroeconomic and Political Response to the War in Europe

The war in Ukraine induced an exogenous economic shock in 2022 that transformed the global geopolitical landscape within a matter of weeks. Global economic crises can undermine government control over macroeconomic policy and create new policy coalitions.[32] Indeed, the resultant mounting economic pressure from supply-side, demand-side, and asset-side triple shocks left central bankers and governors around the world scrambling to reinstate public confidence and bail out state-owned enterprises by raising interest rates, while rolling back stimulus packages to tame inflation. In Turkey, the construction, logistics, energy, and tourism-catering sectors were hit hardest. In contrast to the rest of the world, the AKP government resorted to aggressive monetary loosening. Interest rates, falling since mid-2019, turned negative in real terms. This has had a detrimental effect on households. As commercial banks kept credit interest high despite an opening wedge between the central bank's policy rate and the inflation-

---

haber/1219150-cumhurbaskani-erdogan-ust-akil-turkiye-uzerinde-oyun-oynuyor.

30 . Robert D. Putnam, "Diplomacy and Domestic Politics: The Logic of Two-Level Games," International Organization 42, no. 3 (1988): 427.

31 . Vivares, The Routledge Handbook to Global Political Economy: Conversations and Inquiries, 223.

32 . Benjamin J. Cohen, International Political Economy: An Intellectual History (Princeton: Princeton University Press, 2008), 128.

adjusted rate, the rich got richer, and the poor got poorer.

With the rise of the U.S. dollar against other currencies, low-income countries in the Global South like Turkey must pay more for imports of essential goods such as food and fuel. Although Turkey has plenty of robust energy supply contracts with Russia, Iran, and Azerbaijan, supply-chain disruptions, high unemployment, and exorbitant fuel prices in the winter of 2022-2023 are bound to engulf the country and undermine the AKP's plan to quickly resuscitate the economy. This makes it harder for Turkey to play the regional balancer role and brings into question the central dilemma of having to sustain a partnership of convenience with Russia while still being a key member of the NATO alliance. As the war drags on and economic recession sets in, Turkey may have to make hard choices about its economic ties and diversification of partnerships.

An example of this is Turkey's decision, under threat from U.S. sanctions, to leave the Russian payment clearance system (MIR), an alternative to the SWIFT system for financial transactions worldwide. Turkey's tourism industry, which is a major destination for Russians, struggles because of economic sanctions including the ban on usage of MIR-authorized credit cards.[33] In parallel, 60% of Turkey's foreign trade is with the EU and it must maintain this delicate relationship to sustain foreign-currency inflows. Despite this, President Erdogan reiterated Turkey's intention to join the Shanghai Cooperation Organization (SCO),[34] a Eurasian economic integration bloc led by China and Russia,[35] at the latest summit in September 2022 in Samarkand, Uzbekistan where Erdogan pacificated the summit as a dialogue partner upon Russian President Vladimir Putin's invitation. Many observers thought of this as a bargaining ploy against the U.S./NATO to strengthen Turkey's hand. Turkey is not alone in diversification of regional partnerships, however. Conspicuously, long-time U.S. allies Saudi Arabia, Egypt, and Qatar are already SCO dialogue partners,[36] while the UAE, Bahrain, and Kuwait are also on the path to do the same.[37]

---

33 . "Turkey's Tourism Industry Struggles as Russian Visitors Face Sanctions," Euronews (blog), September 16, 2022, https://www.euronews.com/2022/09/16/turkeys-tourism-industry-struggles-as-russian-visitors-face-sanctions.

34 . "Turkey's Erdogan Targets Joining Shanghai Cooperation Organisation -Media," Euronews (blog), September 18, 2022, https://www.euronews.com/2022/09/18/uzbekistan-sco-turkey.

35 . "Shanghai Cooperation Organisation | SCO," 2022, http://eng.sectsco.org/docs/about/faq.html.

36 . "Saudi Arabia, Egypt, Qatar to Become SCO Dialogue Partners," Asharq Al-awsat, September 18, 2021, https://english.aawsat.com/home/article/3195761/saudi-arabia-egypt-qatar-become-sco-dialogue-partners.

37 . "Bahrain, Kuwait, Maldives, Myanmar, UAE May Become SCO Dialogue Partners —

a. Economic Stability, Foreign Relations, and Turkey's Precarious Position

As the effects of the war started to be felt, the non-oil states of the Global South faced massive import costs because of higher oil and gas prices. In Turkey, capital outflows and foreign debt stock caused the TL to depreciate by over 90% against the U.S. dollar and the TL/$ exchange rate hit 18.6 TL/$1 as of November 2022[38]. As unemployment soared, surging energy and food prices and supply-chain disruptions increased the combined foreign-currency debts of Turkey's government, banks, and companies to over 65% of GDP by July 2022.[39] Following an unorthodox monetary policy under Erdogan's influence, the central bank lowered the nominal interest rate to 12% in the hope of taming inflation, but the effect was the opposite with annual inflation reaching 80% officially and 180% on an unofficial basis.[40] Another important factor in high inflation is the food basket price. Grain is still a key ingredient in Turkish homes as in much of the developing world, and the country is a net importer of food. Despite media hype, the grain deal that Turkey helped to negotiate between the UN, Russia, and Ukraine, does not alleviate food shortages. Most of the shipments are in small amounts and go to the not-so-underdeveloped world.[41] Ukraine complains that Russia exports stolen grain while Russia claims that the grain deal benefits European countries rather than the Global South.

Since household consumption accounts for most of GDP growth in Turkey, the war-induced economic downturn has impacted SMEs severely. Before the war, drastic measures such as tax deferral, social security assistance, debt restructuring, and repayment holidays increased the ratio of fiscal stimulus to the GDP. But in 2022, Erdogan's economic program has prioritized exports and growth instead of fighting inflation and indebtedness. The government supports monetary stimulus policies to achieve high economic growth (5%+) in preparation for presidential elections in 2023. Turkey outperformed most G20 nations with 2.1% quarterly GDP growth in Q2-2022 thanks to a combination of earlier interest-rate cuts, fiscal spending,

---

Kremlin," TASS (blog), September 13, 2022, https://tass.com/politics/1506931.

38 . Ezgi Erkoyun and Nevzat Devranoglu, "Turkish Lira Slips toward Record Low in Post-Rate-Cut Selloff," Reuters, August 19, 2022, sec. Middle East, https://www.reuters.com/world/middle-east/turkish-lira-flat-after-shock-rate-cut-weakening-2022-08-19/.

39 . "The World Bank: Türkiye," Text/HTML, World Bank, 2022, https://www.worldbank.org/en/country/turkey/overview.

40 . "Turkey's Inflation Hits New 24-Year High beyond 80% | Reuters," Reuters (blog), September 5, 2022, https://www.reuters.com/world/middle-east/turkeys-inflation-touches-new-24-year-high-802-2022-09-05/.

41 . "Ukraine Grain Deal: Where Are the Ships Going?," BBC News, August 30, 2022, sec. Europe, https://www.bbc.com/news/world-europe-62717010.

and a government-led consumption drive. For 2022, the OECD revised its growth rate expectation upward for Turkey to 5.4%.[42]

By contrast, despite economic growth, the overall state of the economy has worsened, especially with the inflow of 7 million migrants from various countries, most notably from Syria. Turkey still hosts the largest number of displaced people under temporary protection in the world. This is a sensitive political issue in the run-up to the elections, and has led the government to consider mending ties with the Assad regime in Damascus to facilitate the return of at least one million refugees. In parallel, the AKP's mid-term economic plan is to achieve a 5% growth rate, 65% inflation, and $47 billion current account deficit by the end of 2022. This is a very ambitious target. End-of-year annual growth returned positive to an all-time high of 11% in 2021, but GDP per capita decreased in U.S. dollar terms, which is regarded as a pyrrhic victory because of inflation and the TL's depreciation. The current account deficit widened to 4.5% of the GDP largely because of high energy prices.[43] The gaping current-account deficit is something that often worries those who invest in developing economies of the Global South and Turkey is no exception.[44] The AKP hoped that a devalued TL would increase exports, boost employment, and reduce the current account deficit, but the net effect was a transfer of wealth from the wage-earning population to big capital owners. The central bank's net reserves stand at negative $50 billion as of October 2022, because it has depleted the country's precious foreign currency to maintain a competitive exchange rate. The short-term external debt stock-stood at $135 billion as of July 2022.[45] Common problems in the Global South, including the foreign currency crunch, debt distress[46], and a high ratio of imports to exports, persist.

---

42. "OECD, Türkiye'nin 2022 büyüme tahminini yükseltti," NTV, September 29, 2022, https://www.ntv.com.tr/ntvpara/oecd-turkiyenin-2022-buyume-tahminini-yukseltti,qbELasYQmFShvdt0sOZglw.
43. "The Central Bank of the Republic of Türkiye - Balance of Payments Statistics," The Central Bank, July 2022, https://www.tcmb.gov.tr/wps/wcm/connect/en/tcmb+en/main+menu/statistics/balance+of+payments+and+related+statistics/balance+of+payments+statisticss.
44. "The Pound Is Plumbing Near-Historical Depths. Why?," The Economist, September 26, 2022, http://www.economist.com/britain/2022/09/26/the-pound-is-plumbing-near-historical-depths-why.
45. "The Central Bank of the Republic of Türkiye - Short Term External Debt Statistics," August 19, 2022, https://www.tcmb.gov.tr/wps/wcm/connect/EN/TCMB+EN/Main+Menu/Statistics/Balance+of+Payments+and+Related+Statistics/Short+Term+External+Debt+Statisticss/.
46. Mark Malloch-Brown, "The Global South's Looming Debt Crisis—and How to Stop It," Foreign Policy (blog), March 16, 2022, https://foreignpolicy.com/2022/03/16/global-south-sovereign-debt-crisis-covid-economy-imf-reform/.

b. Political-Economy Drivers of the Post-War Macroeconomic Situation

Between 2016 and 2022, Turkey was characterized by weak institutions and checks and balances, with societal preferences debated only nominally. There was a close circle of inmates, family members, and crony capitalists involved in discussions over decision-making, and conflicting interests were arbitrated behind closed doors. This era followed the dictum, *"for my enemies, the law; for my friends, everything"*.[47] Separation of powers, an independent judiciary, and the rule-of-law eroded over time, leading to the empowerment of rent-seeking groups. Competition for political power in Turkish society was conducted via financial contributions and patrimonial rentier networks. Nepotism, erosion of liberal values, and arbitrariness weakened bureaucratic institutions and turned the legislative body into a rubber-stamp parliament. The realist President Erdogan believes that institutions do not have an independent standing, much less a life of their own, and his balancer role between Russia and NATO/West should be understood from this angle. Unlike President Biden who firmly believes in U.S.-led neoliberal institutionalism, Erdoggan prefers side deals in a personal fashion, and positions himself as an indispensable strongman figure to mediate between Russia and the U.S.

Starting in 2022, Turkey has increasingly leaned towards the consensus of embedded liberalism, which *"encouraged trade and growth while insulating domestic population from the most severe consequences of globalization"*.[48] Embedded liberalism, according to John Gerard Ruggie, is a compromise between liberal orthodoxy and economic nationalism. It is predicated on domestic interventionism to soften the effects of unimpeded multilateralism, such as government subsidies for developing industries.[49] The overall perception in the AKP government is that globalization has delivered but not without costs; there is a widening 'control gap', meaning that the government is struggling to sustain its authority against rival transnational

---

47 . Fernando Henrique Cardoso, "New Paths: Globalization in Historical Perspective," Studies in Comparative International Development 44, no. 4 (2009): 304, http://dx.doi.org/10.1007/s12116-009-9050-3.

48 . Stephen M. Walt, "Russia's Defeat in Ukraine Would Be America's Problem," Foreign Policy (blog), September 27, 2022, https://foreignpolicy.com/2022/09/27/russia-defeat-ukraine-america-problem-hubris/?utm_source=PostUp&utm_medium=email&utm_campaign=Editors%20Picks%20OC&utm_term=50668&tpcc=Editors%20Picks%20OC.

49 . John Gerard Ruggie, "International Regimes, Transactions, and Change: Embedded Liberalism in the Postwar Economic Order," International Organization 36, no. 2 (1982): 393.and Change: Embedded Liberalism in the Postwar Economic Order,\\uc0\\u8221{} {\\i{}International Organization} 36, no. 2 (1982

forces.⁵⁰ The focus has therefore shifted to improvements in efficiency, and state capacity to act in national interests and effectively address challenges of neoliberal globalization. On the path to *"globalized social democracy"*,⁵¹ the accepted policy program in Turkey stipulates that the new era of economic modernization should go hand-in-hand with government social welfare programs and an active civil society. There is *"mistrust of markets and the return of statism"*,⁵² and Turkey relies on Erdogan's charisma as a leader to warm up ties with populist countries like Russia and Central Asian Turkic states. The new era offers rather more economic unorthodoxy and adventurous schemes than rationality, and Erdogan insists on keeping his personal control over the economy.

On the decision-making mechanism, fewer veto points within a majoritarian political system like Turkey's increases policy flexibility and the ability of the government to respond effectively to external shocks. A strong presidency and the winner-takes-all nature of the Turkish system grants unprecedented executive powers to the governing party. If the main concern in the pre-war era was the need to reduce uncertainty, the overwhelming impetus for the ruling polity in the new era is to take risks and lessen the impact of the economic downturn. Under the government's neo-nationalist economic model since the war, it has become more attractive for Turkey to produce goods locally, closer to demand centers, and to serve as a logistics hub by capitalizing on its geopolitical significance. In the new era of the war, it has expedited development of a military-industry-media complex, a world-class healthcare system, airline connections with many parts of the world, and digitalization of the education system, to take advantage of knowledge economies as regionalization gains pace, and the wedge between Eurasia and the Euro-Atlantic space widens. High-value exports require low fixed-costs, marketing connections, and differentiation advantage to compete in global markets, which only the large industries with economies of scale can afford. Turkey aims to increase its leverage, know-how, and brand equity to gain competitive advantage in the post-war era by moving up the value chain.

In contrast to rapid liberalization during the Middle East-centric era of the previous decade, the AKP's authoritarian foreign policy elite and its nationalist coalition partner, the MHP, prioritize closer ties with Turkic Eurasia, Russia, Pakistan, and China. Africa is still an important partner

---

50 . Cohen, International Political Economy: An Intellectual History, 139.
51 . Cardoso, "New Paths," 310.
52 . Cardoso, 307.

for investment opportunities, defense cooperation, and natural resources. The government's vision promotes solidarity among Eurasian and African states to help resist Western neoliberal globalism and replace it with a more equitable distributive globalism, which adds more layers of multipolarity. As Turkey's political prospects in the EU and with the U.S. become dimmer, so that Turkey is no longer an irreplaceable strategic partner for Washington, or anything other than a bulwark against migration towards Europe, Erdogan believes that the rise of new partners in Asia and Africa could offer geopolitical and economic benefits. Using platforms such as the recently expanded Turkic Council of states with common cultural heritage in Central Asia, Caucasus, and Europe, this policy shift towards fair trade with closer partners is not specific to Turkey. In a multipolar world, mid-size, regional powers of the Global South are increasingly more confident to negotiate and defend their interests on the global stage. As such, economic restructuring and regionalism sit side by side to render more explanatory power to Turkey's more independent, activist foreign policy. In essence, Turkey is looking, in this new period, to shift towards greater alliances within its wider region.

4. Conclusion

Turkey emerged as an open market economy in 1980s and quickly adopted the neoliberal model. The economic trajectory of the country's last thirty years has been marked by booms and busts, partly because of populist policies and partly because of structural constraints and external factors. The Turkish government's impressive reform agenda until 2008 reflected a genuine desire to integrate with the EU and become a member of the developed world, while maintaining its Muslim heritage. However, over time, the fatigue of waiting on the EU's doorstep and migration inflows have undermined the AKP's initial enthusiasm for liberal reforms and democratization. The resultant cronyism, lack of transparency, and inflationary pressures have reduced capital inflows and caused economic unpredictability. As Turkey entered 2022 with pre-existing vulnerabilities, its policy shifted to localization, self-sufficiency, and export-led growth, subordinating international norms to national economic goals. This has not shielded the country from rising inflation because of increasing food and energy prices but has enabled a shift in its foreign policy posture to a more independent, activist stance, while the war has amplified its geopolitical significance.

Turkey tries to keep a balance between the U.S./NATO and Eurasia amid a growing set of problems including migrant flows and civil wars. It builds relationships with the wider region to increase multipolarity with Russia, China, Central Asia, and the Indo-Pacific, expecting an upward shift in their influence on the global stage after the war. There will certainly be more cooperation in future between growing regional actors as it serves their interests better. Nonetheless, faced with managing these complex interests, Turkey is in a precarious position, with the risk of needing to navigate between opposing alliances if the war in Europe is prolonged.

CHAPTER V

India's Rise to Global Stature: The Challenges of Strategic Autonomy

Rahul Sharma

India followed the principles of non-alignment for a greater part of its post-independence history but was seen by the West to be more pro-Soviet Union during the Cold War. The collapse of the Soviet Union and the emergence of a unipolar world has seen India's relationship with United States evolve in the past two decades to new strategic levels. However, India's traditional reliance on Russia for military supplies has seen its ties with Moscow endure the changing times. The war in Ukraine has tested that relationship, as India becomes a bigger and more important player in geopolitics, and the world demands that it takes sides. Given its growing economic heft, and its tense relationship with China because of long-standing border issues, the United States is keen for India to become more involved in coalitions against both Russia and China. This would be a difficult choice for New Delhi, which believes it should be allowed to make its own choices in its national interests. So, for sourcing cheap oil and defense products from Russia, while continuing to define its neighborhood policies, India is increasingly talking about strategic autonomy like many other developing nations, indicating a growing divide between the Global South and the North. While the developing world sees India as an example to follow, the West will push New Delhi to redefine its foreign policy stance. Can India, it its own journey to become a developed country, continue to remain relevant in a polarized world as it becomes the world's most-populated nation and a bigger economy? It can, provided it plays the balancing game well, and is seen to be a bridge between the Global South and North.

"India must reach out in as many directions as possible and maximise its gains. This is not just about greater ambition; it is also about not living in yesterday. In this world of all against all, India's goal should be to move closer to the strategic sweet spot". – S. Jaishankar, India's External Affairs Minister[1]

1. Following History

In September 2022, just after India marked its seventy-fifth anniversary of independence from British colonial rule, a conversation between Russian President Vladimir Putin and Indian Prime Minister Narendra Modi in the Uzbek city of Samarkand, about Russia's invasion of Ukraine, indicated not much had changed since 1949.

"Today's era is not of war," Modi told Putin, urging him to *"move onto a path of peace"*.[2] Soon after Russia invaded, India was being berated by the West for not criticizing Moscow for the invasion, which has created new challenges for the world – from a nuclear threat to food insecurity and rising energy prices.

When Russia invaded Ukraine, India—which was trying hard to evacuate more than 20,000 of its students from the war zones—was accused by world leaders, diplomats, historians, and other experts, of siding with Russia, and was asked to reflect on where it would stand if history books were written about that moment in time. Looking back, however, India was not doing anything different from what it has long done.

The forces driving parties to war can be checked only by the most persistent and patient effort to bring and hold all sides together, an anonymous Indian official wrote in a 1949 essay in *Foreign Affairs*, not by helping to build up the strength of one side, which in itself, and through its example to others, can have no other result than that of widening the cleavage, pulling down the bridges, and pushing the world a little nearer to the brink.[3]

---

[1] . Subrahmanyam Jaishankar, The India Way: Strategies for an Uncertain World (New Delhi: HarperCollins Press, 2020), 42.
[2] . Rishabh Pretap, Larry Register, Heather Chen "Indian leader Narendra Modi tells Putin: Now is not the time for war," CNN, September 17, 2022, https://edition.cnn.com/2022/09/17/world/modi-putin-russia-ukraine-war-rebuke-intl-hnk/index.html.
[3] . Indian Official, "India as a World Power," Foreign Affairs, July 1949. https://www.foreignaffairs.com/articles/india/1949-07-01/india-world-power

This conviction, the unidentified official said, was the mainspring of India's foreign policy. *"It impels her—not toward isolationism or any fictitious neutrality—but to extend the hand of friendship to all, provided only that the price of friendship is not conformity or subservience; to retain and develop all existing friendly contacts as well as to establish new ones,"* the official wrote.[4]

That conviction still holds, as India continues to fast shed its colonial past and cements its place in the world community as a strong and proud nation, a large, fast-growing economy that can feed its population—likely to be the world's largest very soon—and ensure that the aspirations of its 1.4 billion people are met at a time when the world is battling triple challenges of food security, energy security, and climate change.

The 'New India' that is beginning to assert itself vigorously in a multipolar world wants to confidently portray its civilizational advantages, from the time when it was the world's second-biggest economy and when, along with its ancient neighbor and now adversary China, it controlled trade and commerce across the land and seas.

India believes that its agenda for its centenary as a nation will be achieved through five pledges. It wants to be a developed country by 2047.[5] Second, it wants to liberate itself from a colonial mindset, which many believe has not allowed the country to grow. Externally, India's External Affairs Minister S. Jaishankar, told the 77th Session of the UN General Assembly in New York in September 2022, it means reformed multilateralism and more contemporary global governance.[6]

Third, India's rich civilizational heritage, which includes care and concern for the environment, will be a source of pride and strength for its people. Four, Jaishankar, said, India will promote greater unity and solidarity, which means coming together on global issues, including terrorism, pandemics, or the environment.

---

4 . Ibid
5 . A developed nation is usually defined as one where people have easy access to quality healthcare and education, advanced technology and infrastructure, diverse economic sectors, and a relatively high per-capita gross domestic product (GDP)
6 . Ministry of External Affairs- Government of India, "Shri G. Balasubramanian concurrently accredited as the next Ambassador of India to the Republic of Benin", September 25, 2022, https://www.mea.gov.in/Speeches-Statements.htm?dtl

"And five, we will instill consciousness of duties and responsibilities. This applies to nations, as much as it does to citizens. These five pledges affirm our age-old outlook that sees the world as one family. We believe that national good and global good can be entirely in harmony," Jaishankar added.[7]

India's future trajectory is thus mostly defined and the destination clear as the nation begins to use some of its advantages—a large population and a growing economy—to race past several other countries, even as it continues to increase its defense, social, and educational weight to position itself well to keep its pledges ahead of the centenary of its independence from British colonialists.

However, to rise, India will also have to prepare to battle the new challenges facing the contemporary world, some of which will define the remaining part of this century, of which the first two decades have been difficult.

The world underwent three massive, unexpected shocks in the past 20 years: the 9/11 terrorist attacks on the United States, which triggered the long, bloody wars in Iraq and Afghanistan; the 2008 financial meltdown that rocked the world's biggest economies and led to a global recession; and the disastrous COVID-19 pandemic that shut the world down for months. Each of these events redefined global relationships.

And just as nations were coming out of COVID-19 lockdowns and preparing to rebuild their devastated economies hit by high energy prices, food shortages, and loss of jobs, the war in Ukraine with a clear and present nuclear threat has increased the uncertainties that have to be faced by all.

Simmering tensions between the United States and China, a looming global recession, the war in Europe which is slowing down global output, uncertainties in the South China Sea, a broken supply chain, massive climate-related challenges, potential new pandemics, trade imbalances, nations beginning to look inward as a safeguard against the ills of the world, put India in a place where it will need to make choices—hard choices—if it is to position itself as a power that matters.

The 'Big Question' that has been around for some time is whether India will rise to the challenges and become the bridge the warring ends of the world might be looking for, and truly become what it believes it has been for the longest time because of its past—the Vishwa Guru (Global Guru)

---

7 . Ibid.

it aspires to be again. Today's India truly believes it can be amongst the world's great powers because it wants to, unlike in previous times when it was more of a reluctant power. There are several potential landmines on the way.

2. The Three Phases

India's foreign policy can be said to have evolved in three phases, though the core focus on its neighbors, especially Pakistan and China, has remained unchanged. That continuity has probably helped India in different ways as the world has evolved since the beginning of this century.

The first phase ran from 1947 when India gained independence to the early 1990s, when suddenly the once-powerful Soviet Union collapsed and broke into different nations, and the world order became unipolar. India, then seen as aligned to Moscow, had to make hard choices. In that period, which coincided with the Cold War, India actively followed the policy of non-alignment, as defined and declared by its first Prime Minister Jawaharlal Nehru. India grew closer to the Soviet Union in the face of an impending war with Pakistan and the American threat in 1971, and fought an ugly border war with China and two with Pakistan, Beijing's all-weather friend. For the West, India, the world's biggest democracy, was the bad guy of geopolitics because, while officially choosing to not take sides, its ties with Moscow were far stronger than those with Washington and its allies.

The fact that the Americans backed Pakistan as its army killed people in its eastern part (now Bangladesh), pushing millions of refugees into India, only made the Indian government, led by then Prime Minister Indira Gandhi, more suspicious of Washington and the Nixon Administration. Richard Nixon and his Secretary of State Henry Kissinger were at that point using Islamabad to open doors to China, as they tried to reach out to Beijing.[8] Some of the past still rankles, even though the ties between the two democracies have prospered immensely in the past 20 years. Building trust is still an incomplete exercise.

---

8 . In its effort to reach out to China and its leaders, the United States received active support from Pakistan. Henry Kissinger made his first secretive visit to Beijing in 1971 to meet Mao Zedong and Chou Enlai, from Islamabad, where he was on a visit but feigned illness to cancel his local appointments and instead fly to Beijing. His visit opened the doors for then U.S. President Richard Nixon make his historic trip to China in 1972.

The second phase began in 1991 when India started opening its economy to the world after a payments crisis and tried to position itself as a rising economic power. *"The government is committed to removing the cobwebs that come in the way of rapid industrialization. We will work towards making India internationally competitive, taking full advantage of modern science and technology and opportunities offered by the evolving global economy,"* Prime Minister P.V. Narasimha Rao said on national television on June 22, 1991, a day after he was sworn in, setting India on a new economic path that was radically different from the inward orientation since 1947.[9]

Rao also took critical steps to shift India's foreign policy by reaching out to the United States and building the first bridges with Washington and other Western nations, as well as Israel—which would become an important friend in the subsequent years.

The first decade of the twenty-first century saw the biggest expansion of the Indian economy, with GDP growth on average in double digits. India's relations with its neighbors—especially China—were also mostly peaceful. China, growing rapidly too, tried to accept New Delhi as at least a regional power. A booming economy made India an important market, not only for the large American and European multinationals, but also for Chinese companies.

The period 1991-2014 saw three prime ministers—Rao, Atal Behari Vajpayee, and Manmohan Singh—shape the country's new foreign policy, despite the fragile foundations of their governments.[10]

While Rao used crisis to reform the economy and consultation to push through the Border Peace and Tranquility Agreement with China, Vajpayee made it acceptable to have the United States as an ally. He also engaged with Pakistan and made India a declared nuclear weapon state. Singh staked the future of his government to push through the civil nuclear initiative with the United States through parliament.

---

9 . Sanjaya Baru, Journey of a Nation: 75 Years of Indian Economy (Rupa Publications India, 2022): 108.
10 . Shivshankar Menon, Choices: Inside the Making of India's Foreign Policy, (Penguin Random House India, 2016): 4.

"There was remarkable continuity in policy among these three prime ministers, with each building on his predecessor's work and all acknowledging each other's contributions," India's former Foreign Secretary Shivshankar Menon wrote.[11]

The third—a more muscular, nationalistic, and sometimes aggressive—phase began with the rise of Narendra Modi and the forceful arrival of his Bharatiya Janata Party (BJP) on the political stage with a strong election win in 2014, followed by a stronger show five years later.

Modi's arrival clearly set expectations of a robust, proactive foreign policy that would leverage India's civilizational strengths, and create equities through the country's network of bilateral and multilateral engagements, as well as its strong, rich, and influential diaspora. The 'New India' today smartly uses a potent cocktail of nationalistic geopolitics and expedient geoeconomics to promote the political, economic, and security interests of the country.

3. A Natural Choice

Non-alignment was a natural choice for India after independence. The once-prosperous landmass lost both its arms once the British decided to carve out West and East Pakistan in a bloody partition, which killed millions of people across the religious divide. Overnight, India lost its historical connection with Central Asia on one side and Southeast Asia on the other. With its global reach constrained, India battled to build a nation out of a treasury left empty by the colonizers. India's trade was devastated, and its population poor and divided when leaders began the process of rebuilding a country emerging from two centuries of occupation.

With the Cold War at its peak, India was expected to take sides. It chose not to, triggering events that eventually severely impeded its chances to become strong and prosperous. However, its decision to follow a policy of neutrality was self-interested as its then leaders—influenced strongly by the results of the Second World War—figured it was best to balance two large powers than align with one.

A year before he died, Nehru, accused of losing a critical border war against China which he had actively courted, wrote that what is called non-alignment had not fared badly. *"This, strictly speaking, represents only one*

---

11 . Ibid., 5.

aspect of our policy; we have other positive aims also, such as the promotion of freedom from colonial rule, racial equality, peace, and international cooperation, but 'non-alignment' has become a summary description of this policy of friendship toward all nations, uncompromised by adherence to any military pacts," he said in an essay.[12]

This implied, basically, a conviction that good and evil are mixed up in this world, that the nations cannot be divided into sheep and goats, to be condemned or approved accordingly, and that if India were to join one military group rather than the other it was liable to increase and not diminish the risk of a major clash between them, Nehru explained.[13]

However, events dictated otherwise, and India became close to the then Soviet Union, which became its biggest defense supplier. The military relationship continued well after the collapse of the Soviet Union and the emergence of Russia. The need for spares from Russia, to fly combat aircraft and sail naval vessels, makes it difficult for India to make a complete break with Moscow quickly. In an event of a war with China or Pakistan, India will have to rely on Russia for critical supplies.

The Non-Aligned Movement (NAM), in which countries including Egypt, Indonesia, Ghana, and Yugoslavia joined India, also allowed New Delhi to carve out a special place in the Global South, which it lost once it began looking West. Many newly independent countries, coming out of centuries of ugly colonial rule between the 1950s and 1970s, looked up to India. Non-alignment ended up becoming a legitimate policy for quite a few of them in Asia and Africa.

However, by the 1990s, most of the original NAM nations, including India, faced crises. Egypt wasn't as strong in the Middle East as before, Indonesia was wracked by the Asian economic crisis which led to the fall of President Suharto, and Yugoslavia broke up in the wake of political changes and strife. In a unipolar world, India had been forced to shift its external policies to ensure its own national interests.

The principles of classical non-alignment have undergone a shift in recent years with the BJP government looking at its purpose and usefulness differently. The government defines it as strategic autonomy that gives India the flexibility to make decisions in the interests of national security. India is

---

[12] . Jawaharlal Nehru, "Changing India," Foreign Affairs, April 1, 1963, https://www.foreignaffairs.com/articles/asia/1963-04-01/changing-india.

[13] . Ibid.

now probably more inward- rather than outward-looking, with a focus on self-reliance to ensure it eventually reaches a point in history when it cannot be forced to take sides.

4. Economic Surge

The years since India's economic opening, after decades of a socialist and regulated economy, saw India's resurgence. Suddenly, India and Indians had the ability to choose. From a time when there was a months-long wait for a telephone connection, Indians could easily get mobile phones. They were spoilt for choice when it came to buying cars and white goods. The economic engine began moving, raising India's confidence to become a worthy member of the global community.

The awkwardness and reluctance in pushing its national interest gradually gave way to a new confidence. Indians could travel across and trade with the world. As new opportunities opened, India began asserting its influence in its neighborhood. From nuclear tests in May 1998, to a confident outreach to larger nations such as the United States and China, all firmly cemented India's belief that it was ready to play a bigger role on the global stage.

To be a great power it is necessary to be a strong economy. Just as the United States flexed its muscles because it was the world's biggest economy and China later followed with years of double-digit growth, India also felt that an economic boom in the first decade of this century positioned it well to become a nation that mattered—a belief that goes back thousands of years.

It was also at this time that the relationship between India and the United States took a more positive turn, thanks to then U.S. President George W. Bush, who pushed for a civil nuclear deal between the two nations in his effort to give New Delhi the legitimacy of a nuclear nation. Shedding decades of mistrust was good news to many in the United States, where Indian-origin people were beginning to lead the technology sector in Silicon Valley. Supported by a diaspora that strongly believed in India's rise, New Delhi used the 1990s and 2000s to position itself for the next big push.

The new understanding and appreciation also saw the United States allowing sales of defense equipment to India, which was beginning to look at alternatives to its stock of Russian arms. The shift was sharp and remarkable. Russia was India's largest supplier of arms in 2000-2010, according to the Stockholm International Peace Research Institute (SIPRI). But from 2012 to 2021, the share of Russian weapons in India's arsenal shrunk by nearly half, as New Delhi actively turned to alternative suppliers including the United States and France.[14]

It wasn't that India didn't want to buy military hardware from the United States before. It did, but it couldn't because of restrictions applied by Washington, where many still saw India through the prism of the past. As political relations improved, so did military ties. In the past decade, the United States has become one the largest arms suppliers to India, selling aircraft, helicopters, and missiles worth $22 billion. Deals worth another $10 billion are in the pipeline.[15]

The war between Russia and Ukraine is only going to hasten the process of India's defense decoupling from Russia. For one, India is worried about the availability of spare parts. Second, India cannot be certain of receiving them in case of a potential border war with China or Pakistan, given Moscow's increasing reliance on Beijing for support and the latter's friendliness towards Russia.

5. Strategic Autonomy

The global power balance is being remodeled in a world that is trying to manage the fallout of the war in Europe while still emerging from the shock of a pandemic, bringing forth long-simmering apprehensions and forcing nations to revisit and recraft their domestic and global priorities. The weakening of multilateral institutions, disillusion with the global economic order, and a desire to fortify against uncertainties and become more self-reliant, mean the status-quo is being challenged like never before.

For India, there are both challenges and opportunities. With the emergence of a new world order in which many see the U.S. and the West weakening, developing nations such as India do not see a need to adhere to the traditional norms of nation blocs. They realize it is probably best to take an issue-based stand when it comes to making a choice between the West and the rest. India, therefore, must pursue its interests by 'leveraging' the

---

14 . Happymon Jacob, "Russia Is Losing India," Foreign Affairs, September 22, 2022, https://www.foreignaffairs.com/india/russia-losing-india
15 . Sandeep Unnithan, "In a graphic: India-US: Brothers in Arms," India Today,September 23, 2021, https://www.indiatoday.in/india-today-insight/story/india-us-brothers-in-arms-1856465-2021-09-23

competition among rival great powers to extract maximum advantage for itself. With the rapidly evolving dynamic underpinned by unpredictability, and by military and economic polarization of positions, India can be expected to follow strategic autonomy. India's non-alignment is not simply a relic of the Cold War; rather, it represents a fundamental and enduring aspect of New Delhi's worldview.

Strategic autonomy brings with it the need to engage with all influencing players on India's own terms. The West needs to engage with India on more realistic terms, while trying to integrate New Delhi as a key player in the Indo-Pacific security arrangements, such as the Quad, which is targeted at China. This begins by helping India wean itself off Russian technology, while recognizing that this will not lead India to abandon its commitment to strategic autonomy.

On the flip side, India can help Western economies diversify their manufacturing and supply chains away from China. The West can still engage with India on a mutually productive footing by taking into consideration India's status as a 'global swing state'—one that will look at its own self-interest and adhere to an issue-based stand. The West can also acknowledge India's security preferences.

New Delhi's deep-rooted commitment to the principle of strategic autonomy is the bedrock of understanding and appreciating India's position as a global swing state. This principle is not specific to the Cold War, or simply a desire for neutrality. Instead, strategic autonomy is fundamental to the way India understands and manages risks in international politics in its journey to assert itself.

As the world re-aligns and India reassesses its global ambitions, China is the big elephant in the room. China's footprints are everywhere, and its financial, trade, and technology prowess gives it that additional heft that it first achieved by integrating deeply with the global economy and becoming the world's factory. The United States played a key role in China's emergence in the hope that Beijing's political system would begin to align itself with the West's. That was never to happen. What happened instead was China's emergence as a real and clear challenger to the supremacy of the United States.

What the United States and successive governments in Washington were unwilling to accept was that communism was the bedrock of the Chinese system, and that was never going to change. Successive Chinese leaders, and more so Xi Jinping, have ensured that the economy has grown stronger within the ambit of the communist ideology, where the party is supreme. In the last decade, Xi has strengthened the party's role, immersing it back into the social, educational, and manufacturing fabric of the country. China's economy might not be expanding at the same frenetic pace of the past two decades, but that doesn't mean it has lost its power to influence and impact the rest of the world.

China has also spent time and money on vastly strengthening its military capability, while building a world-class navy and air force. Beijing has also opened military bases in Africa and Asia to ensure it can manage the sea lanes critical to its energy and trade needs. While the world grapples to contain China and its probable rise as the next superpower, India stands more affected because of its geographical proximity.

6. The Chinese Conundrum

Indians see China looking down at them from across the mighty Himalayas and are constantly reminded of a long border dispute with the neighbor. China's long shadow is a reality India must deal with every day, more so than any other large nation. For decades India has tried to build a mutually respectful and trusting relationship with China, but to no avail.

China has profitably used the uncertainties of the COVID-19 pandemic to expand its geopolitical footprint across the world, from the South China Sea to the Himalayas, raising concerns in the region.

For India, Chinese incursions on its territory are a bigger worry after skirmishes in 2020 between their troops killed soldiers. With Xi's China laying a blueprint for a new world order, countries, especially the United States and the Indian subcontinent, worry over the need for a greater balance in the global matrix.

While many are prone to compare India with China, the reality is that India still has a long journey to make before it can be anywhere near China's economic size. India is expected to grow fastest among all large economies to become the world's third-biggest economy, probably by 2030, according to projections by the International Monetary Fund.[16]

---

16 . "India set to be world's 3rd largest economy by 2030," Report, Fortune India, September 7, 2022, https://www.fortuneindia.com/macro/india-set-to-be-worlds-3rd-largest-economy-by-2030-report/109567

China's historical and all-weather ties with Pakistan create diplomatic and military challenges for India. For one, it raises the possibility of a two-front war for India, and second, it stops India from enhancing its influence in its immediate South Asian neighborhood. No comprehensive agreement has emerged from multiple rounds of border talks with China, and Chinese military incursions into Indian-controlled territory have only increased political and diplomatic tensions between the two capitals.

It is not that Modi did not reach out to Xi and China when he became prime minister. However, he soon realized that close ties with India did not fit in well in the longer-term game plan for China. For China, India might not be an immediate threat, but it is one over the next few decades. And the Chinese tend to take a much longer strategic view of the world than everybody else.

China's national interests clearly clash with those of India's, just as much as they are a hot button for the United States' view of the world. Beijing's rising influence in south Asian counties other than Pakistan also makes India uncomfortable. It doesn't want its backyard to be populated by Chinese troops and interests, as has happened in Sri Lanka, where the government gave China a 99-year lease on a port, allowing Chinese naval ships to dock there.

China's rise creates problems because of the country's unique characteristics, which make it harder for it to become a part of the West-led global order, as has been possible for others such as Japan. The reality now is that the two most powerful nations of our day are at extreme ends of the geopolitical spectrum.[17] India is more acceptable to the West because it is not an isolationist power like China and follows a rules-based political system the West understands and appreciates.

India is transparent; China is not. And, therefore, India can probably be trusted, even though New Delhi will not wholly side with the West. And that is why the United States is willing to give India a longer rope, without pushing it too hard to take a hard stand on critical diplomatic issues facing the world. If India does not want to be an ally, so be it; at least it is a friend. All this has, over the past two decades, allowed India and the United Statea to form a strategic relationship. This had never happened before.

---

17 . S. Jaishankar, The India Way: Strategies for an Uncertain World (New Delhi: HarperCollins Press, 2020), 5-6.

India too has realized that there are more ways to deal with the Chinese threat than merely militarily. The Indian government has, therefore, started putting pressure economically by going after the Chinese companies operating in India, accusing them of financial irregularities and bringing in policies that make it difficult for them to do business in the world's second-most populated country.[18]

Following the border skirmishes in 2020, the Indian government first started by banning several Chinese mobile applications, including TikTok, on grounds they were a threat to national security.[19] Later, security agencies began investigating loan apps and other gaming apps, recommending they be banned too. Chinese mobile phone companies operating in India were also investigated for alleged financial irregularities, prompting China to urge India to "*act in compliance with laws and regulations, and provide a fair, just and non-discriminatory business environment for Chinese companies to invest and operate in India*".[20]

7. A Slower Rise

China's rise, openly supported by American business and successive presidents, came during an era of benign globalization, which has now been consigned to history as nations have turned inward, and are increasingly looking at being self-sufficient after the difficult experiences of lockdowns triggered by the pandemic.

It was also fast. In about two decades China's economy expanded exponentially: "*In 1987, the GDP (nominal) of both countries was almost equal; even in PPP terms, China was slightly ahead of India in 1990. Now in 2021, China's GDP is 5.46 times higher than India. On a PPP basis, the GDP of China is 2.61 times of India. China crossed the $1 trillion mark in 1998, while India crossed nine years later in 2007 on an exchange rate basis*".[21] This gap must be first bridged in a hurry if India wants to race ahead in the game in its quest for power and influence.

---

18. . "More Trouble for Chinese Companies as Indian Tightens Scrutiny," Outlook India, May 31, 2021, https://www.outlookindia.com/business/more-trouble-for-chinese-companies-as-india-tightens-scrutiny-news-199515
19. . Ibid.
20. . Yin Yeping & Chu Daye, "India urged to be fair, reasonable toward Chinese companies investment," Global Times, August 29, 2022, https://www.globaltimes.cn/page/202208/1274154.shtml.
21. . "Comparing China and India by Economy," Statistics Times, May 16, 2021, https://statisticstimes.com/economy/china-vs-india-economy.php

India's rise will also be slower because it is growing at a remarkably uncertain time. The choices India will have to make in the immediate and mid-term future will also be different from the choices China had to make. India's political system too opens up domestic challenges as consensus building can be difficult.

It is obvious that India's rise will be compared to that of China, Jaishankar writes, adding that *"its imprint on global consciousness, its civilizational contribution, geopolitical value and economic performance will all be factors in that exercise"*.[22] However, China and India are two different societies, have two different political systems and have different outlooks. What does that mean? Jaishankar explains[23]:

- To begin with, it would require advancing national interests by identifying and exploiting opportunities created by global contradictions.

- Such an India would pay more attention to national security and national integrity. It would not be hesitant in adjusting its positions where required by its own interests.

- This mindset would also accord primacy to the nurturing of goodwill, beginning with India's immediate neighborhood.

- Making a visible impact on global consciousness would be taking this to the next level. It would encourage a greater contribution to global issues and regional challenges.

India, essentially, will grow with others and not ahead of others, because it can be the bridge that the world might be looking for in times of uncertainty, as it can provide foundational stability in geopolitical relationships and partnerships.

However, as Alyssa Ayres said, it will not always be easy to work with a rising India, which according to her, remains fiercely protective of its policy independence, shuns formal alliances, and remains ever willing to break global consensus, as it has done most famously on trade negotiations. *"It can be a close defense partner, but not in the familiar template of most U.S. alliances. India wants an improved trade and economic relationship, but it will not be easily persuaded by U.S. entreaties for increased market access."*[24]

---

22 . Ibid.
23 . Ibid.
24 . Alyssa Ayres, "Will India Start Acting Like a Global Power?," Foreign Affairs, December 16, 2017, https://www.foreignaffairs.com/articles/india/2017-10-16/will-india-start-acting-global-power

8. The Bridge

This is where India's role as a bridge between the Global South—where it is respected—and the West—which is beginning to respect it—can become critical to resolving contentious issues that impact the world. Whether it is climate change, sustainability, or green energy, digitalization for public good, or even food security, India can take a lead in bringing the world together.

The fact that Modi could publicly tell Putin that it is not the right time for a war, and India's continued imports of cheap Russian oil and abstention from key votes against Russia at the United Nations despite U.S. unhappiness, shows India's current ability to balance relationships. India has also offered Ukraine its support for peace, as it is of a firm view that there can be no military solution to the conflict between Ukraine and Russia.

India's centuries-old ties with Africa and its contribution to the social, educational, institutional, and military development of several African states gives it an opportunity to continue to offer support to them in battling several new challenges in the post-COVID-19 world, as well as during the uncertainties triggered by the war in Europe.

Prime Minister Modi, in a speech in Uganda in 2018, laid down principles that will continue to guide India's engagement with Africa.[25]

He said Africa will top India's priorities, and India will continue to deepen and intensify its engagement with Africa. The development partnership will be guided by Africa's priorities and India will help create *"as much local capacity and create many local opportunities as possible"*.[26]

He further promised to keep the Indian market open and support Africa's development by sharing India's digital experiences to improve delivery of public services, expand financial inclusion, and spread digital literacy. Modi offered help to improve Africa's agriculture and address challenges brought about by climate change.[27]

Importantly, he added that India will strengthen cooperation and mutual capabilities in combating terrorism and extremism, keeping cyberspace safe

---

25 . Ministry of External Affairs- Government of India, "Prime Minister's address at Parliament of Uganda during his State visit to Uganda," July 15, 2018, https://mea.gov.in/Speeches-Statements.htm?dtl/30152/Prime+Ministers+address+at+Parliament+of+Uganda+during+his+State+Visit+to+Ugand.
26 . Ibid
27 . Ibid

and secure, and keeping the oceans open and free for the benefit of all countries.

"The world needs cooperation and not competition in the eastern shores of Africa and the eastern Indian Ocean. That is why India's vision of Indian Ocean Security is cooperative and inclusive, rooted in security and growth for all in the region," Modi said, adding that it was extremely important to ensure that *"Africa does not once again turn into a theatre of rival ambitions, but becomes a nursery for the aspirations of Africa's youth"*. [28]

"Just as India and Africa fought colonial rule together, we will work together for a just, representative and democratic global order that has a voice and a role for one-third of humanity that lives in Africa and India. India's own quest for reforms in the global institutions is incomplete without an equal place for Africa. That will be a key purpose of our foreign policy, he added". [29]

In laying out his vision for bilateral ties with Africa, Modi focused on the needs of the continent and clearly said that India was a good partner to have because it was committed to help improve lives of African people and willing to invest for the long term. So, it isn't so much about India, but more about what Africa needs. No other country, eyeing the continent's vast natural resources, is telling Africa that. *"We understand that Africa wants multiple options to get the best out of the international order and will endeavor to provide that credibly. To that end, we are also open to working with third countries,"* External Affairs Minister Jaishankar pointed out in a speech. [30]

Indeed, India's footprint has slowly but surely expanded in Africa. India is today the fourth-largest trade partner for Africa with bilateral trade hitting $89.5 billion in 2021-22.[31] The Duty-Free Tariff Preference Scheme announced by India, which provides duty free access to 98.2% of India's total tariff lines, has greatly benefited African nations. India is also the fifth-biggest investor in Africa with a total commitment of $70.7 billion.[32] Defense

---

28 . Ibid
29 . Ibid
30 . Ministry of External Affairs- Government of India, "Address by External Affairs Minister, Dr S. Jaishankar at the Launch of Book: India-Africa Relations: Changing Horizons," May 17, 2022, https://mea.gov.in/Speeches-Statements.htm?dtl/35322/.
31 . "India among Africa's top investors, bilateral trade at $ 89.5bn in FY22: EAM," Business Standard, July 20, 2022, https://www.business-standard.com/article/current-affairs/india-among-africa-s-top-investors-bilateral-trade-at-89-5bn-in-fy22-eam-122072000023_1.html.
32 . Ministry of External Affairs- Government of India, "Address by External Affairs Minister, Dr S. Jaishankar at the Launch of Book: India-Africa Relations: changing Horizons."

cooperation has increased too, with India also now focusing on coastal countries, though its maritime security interests are still mostly centered around Mauritius and Seychelles.

As India takes over the presidency of the G20 from Indonesia, it finds itself staring at the huge opportunity to revitalize and redefine the Global South.[33] The year-long presidency that will bring together heads of state and government of the 20 member countries, and another 20-odd invitees, will help showcase India's rise at a time when the world is battling conflicts, trade and political tensions, and major challenges due to climate change.

India is looking to take a leadership role by offering to share its success in digitalization, green energy, and sustainability with the world, to enable learning from ancient and modern practices adopted by India for the betterment of its people. India's ability to weave the right stories and position its narratives underlines its hopes that the Global South will be able to benefit from its learnings.

Therein lie India's advantages. As the world's fifth-largest economy and a country which will very soon have the world's biggest population, India cannot be overlooked. The West wants India to join it against China. Emerging nations see India as a nation to follow. India, therefore, can be a bridge between the two ends of the world, while maintaining its strategic autonomy.

---

33 . The G20 describes itself as a strategic multilateral platform connecting the world's major developed and emerging economies. Together the G20 members represent more than 80% of world GDP, 75% of international trade, and 60% of the world population.

CHAPTER VI

Latin America in the Aftermath of Europe's War

Otaviano Canuto

This chapter examines the impacts and durable consequences of Europe's war (in Ukraine), overlapping with the effects of other components of the 'perfect storm' (pandemic, severe weather phenomenon, hunger, global inflation) for Latin America. First, we deal with the global tectonic shifts that have conditioned the region's economic performance since the 1990s. Second, we outline the range of effects stemming from the 'perfect storm'. The third section discusses how economic relations between China and Latin America have evolved. Finally, we frame the U.S.-China rivalry in a Latin American context.

This chapter examines the impacts and durable consequences of Europe's war (in Ukraine), overlapping with the effects of other components of the 'perfect storm' (pandemic, severe weather phenomenon, hunger, global inflation), for Latin America. Although commodity-dependent countries in Latin America have exhibited some positive surprises in terms of GDP growth, inequality has risen more broadly, and the living conditions of the poor have deteriorated. The mediocre growth performance of the last decade appears to be the underlying trend, in case a reshuffle of the growth pattern is not pursued. First, we deal with the global tectonic shifts that have conditioned the region's economic performance since the 1990s. Second, we outline the range of effects stemming from the 'perfect storm'. The third section discusses how economic relations between China and Latin America have evolved. Finally, we frame the U.S.-China rivalry in a Latin American context.

1. Implications for Latin America of Global Tectonic Shifts

Latin America's economic evolution since the 1990s has been conditioned by three 'tectonic shifts' underlying the global economy. Such tectonic shifts directly impacted three basic prices at the global level, with direct implications for the region's economic trajectory.[1]

First is the shock associated with a decline in labor prices, reflecting the sudden incorporation of workers whose labor services were previously not integrated into the global market economy. That evolved into a supply shock emanating from an increase in the number of manufacturing workers engaged in international trade. We refer to the fall of the Berlin Wall, and the dissolution of the Soviet Union, as well as to China's opening of free trade zones, which happened even before China joined the World Trade Organization in 2001.

Two complementary changes also weighed in favor of this labor-supply movement. Countries implemented reforms toward trade opening, lowering tariff and non-tariff trade barriers. Furthermore, a cluster of technological breakthroughs in information and communications technology (ICT) and transportation (containerization) made possible the geographical fragmentation of manufacturing processes, and the relocation of parts of

---

[1] . Otaviano Canuto, Climbing a High Ladder – Development in the Global Economy (Rabat: Policy Center for the New South, 2021).

value chains according to convenience—including the use of cheaper labor. The phenomenon of integration of Asia into global or regional value chains that was seen in the previous decades was reinforced.

The combination of industrialization being facilitated by those changes and cheap labor in Asia (and Eastern Europe) directly challenged manufacturing in Latin America. The region's previous 'import-substitution industrialization' (ISI) strategy had already initiated a phase of review, as it had clearly started to face limits, even in the cases of relative success, including Brazil, Mexico, and Argentina. To differing degrees, countries in the region partially reversed protectionist trade policies pursued in the previous decades.

However, except for Mexico which opted for integration into North America's value chains through NAFTA, countries in the region were now facing a tougher transition to any 'export-led industrialization' (ELI) strategy. Difficulties in implementing structural reforms that would allow the region to phase out the legacy of ISI policies and compete with low Asian wage-productivity, help to understand the 'precocious deindustrialization' in many countries in the region.

A second tectonic shift corresponded to a change in the financial landscape, arising from declining interest rates in advanced economies and the availability of global finance at lower costs. Even considering risk premiums associated with emerging markets, relative to the sources of finance in advanced economies, capital flows to the former acquired a huge significance, with cycles of boom and bust.

The debt crisis in Latin America and South Korea in the 1980s followed a strong cycle of international bank credit in the previous decade, particularly recycling surpluses of oil producers after the oil price shocks—in what became known as 'petrodollars' through the 'Eurodollar system'. However, the banks' retrenchment after the debt crisis was followed in the 1990s by the arrival of non-banking financial intermediation, fed by declining earnings rates in advanced economies. Subsequent episodes of busts in Asia (1997), Russia (1998), Argentina, and others did not close the financial window of flows to emerging markets.

The third tectonic plate shift and basic price change was more a consequence of the two previous ones. Because of the high growth-cum-industrialization in Asia, with globalization thriving using its cheap labor, prices of natural resources and commodities went through a super-cycle.

A demand shock was associated with an increase in global demand for primary goods, one not matched by a commensurate supply-capacity response. It reflected the relatively high commodity intensity of imports of the larger rising Global South countries, particularly China. The result was a rise in commodity prices—an unusually vigorous upswing phase of a commodity super-cycle. For commodity exporters, including in Latin America, this shock was associated with terms-of-trade gains.

A super-cycle of commodity prices started in the mid-1990s, reaching a peak by the time of the global financial crisis, and hitting the bottom with oil price declines by 2015. In Latin America, except for Mexico and its integration into U.S. value chains, the super-cycle of commodities was gravitationally strong enough to become the basis of economic growth.

One important feature of the upswing phase of the commodity-based economic cycle was that it cascaded down to the bottom of the income pyramid, with poverty reduction and expanding middle classes as outcomes. Several countries in the region created or reinforced social policies that partly conveyed macroeconomic gains to the poor—for example, conditional cash transfers implemented in Mexico, Brazil, and others.

The combination of income gains associated with natural resource-intensive tradable goods and non-tradable services, in addition to capital inflows and exchange-rate appreciation, exercised an additional price and competitiveness pressure on tradable manufacturing production.

As the super-cycle faded out in the 2010s, bringing down GDP growth and affecting fiscal conditions, countries in the region faced higher levels of potential social unrest and political instability. This was the case even in countries, including Chile, Colombia, and Peru, that had adopted fiscal frameworks or policies aiming at mitigating the consequences of cyclical fluctuations of commodity prices. Chile, for instance, established rules under which part of the extraordinary fiscal receipts during copper boom times was set aside as a reserve fund to be used in down times. Brazil attempted to extend the cycle by resorting to public-debt-financed lending by the National Economic and Social Development Bank (BNDES), but that led mainly to a fiscal crisis without commensurate private investment results.[2]

It must be noted that, despite the overall stronger macroeconomic performance in the 1990s and 2000s relative to the 1980s, there was

---

2 . Otaviano Canuto, A Straitjacket to Help Brazil Fight Fiscal Obesity (Rabat: Policy Center for the New South, October 2016).

little convergence of GDP per-capita levels in Latin America with those in the United States. In the meantime, emerging Asia and Eastern Europe underwent rapid convergence.[3]

Political contestation of incumbent governments became a normal feature in the region. With some exceptions—Ecuador—a new 'pink tide' of more left-wing governments has spread in the region, starting with Mexico in 2018 and Argentina in 2019, followed by Bolivia in 2020, along with Peru, Honduras, and Chile in 2021, and Colombia in 2022. In Brazil, the incumbent right-wing government lost the 2022 October election to the center-to-left former President Lula.

In Venezuela, the period of a parallel 'government' led by the opposition, recognized by 54 countries, is coming to an end, and President Maduro's position has strengthened. At the same time, the war in Ukraine has raised the possibility that sanctions will be lifted in exchange for more oil from Venezuela, given Europe's and the U.S.'s need for energy supplies. A major limitation is the lack of investment in the country, which has stopped Venezuela from even using fully its OPEC quota. The change of government in Colombia has also brought a more friendly relationship between the two countries.

One important aspect of Latin America's economic evolution in recent decades has been the continuity of its shallow physical and trade integration. Although slightly superior to sub-Saharan Africa, the degree of physical (infrastructure) and trade integration pales relative to dynamic Asian economies. While the ratio of intraregional exports to total exports in Latin America hovered between 10% and 20% from 1980 to 2010, levels climbed in Asia from 30% to 50% in the same period.[4]

Efforts like the South American Regional Infrastructure Integration (IIRSA), led by the Inter-American Development Bank in the last decade, ended up not receiving appropriate backing by countries in the region. While Peru implemented some IIRSA-related projects, efforts were dispersed after the creation of the Union of South American Nations (UNASUR) in 2008.

---

[3] . Bas B. Bakker et al,"The Lack of Convergence of Latin-America Compared with CESEE: Is Low Investment to Blame?," WP/20/98 , International Monetary Fund, June 2020, https://www.imf.org/en/Publications/WP/Issues/2020/06/19/The-Lack-of-Convergence-of-Latin-America-Compared-with-CESEE-Is-Low-Investment-to-Blame-49519

[4] . Otaviano Canuto and Manu Sharma, M., Asia and South America: A Quasi-Common Economy Approach (Washington, DC: World Bank, Economic Premise No. 65, 2011), http://hdl.handle.net/10986/10076.

Even the Southern Common Market (MERCOSUR)—initially established by Argentina, Brazil, Paraguay, and Uruguay, and subsequently joined by Venezuela and Bolivia—has remained limited as a regional integration process. Despite being signed as a 'common market', still nowadays MERCOSUR resembles more a free-trade zone, full of country exceptions and without a common trade policy. MERCOSUR has signed trade deals with several economies, but significant deals, including with the European Union, remain to be completed and ratified. One may say that the political will to deepen regional integration has not been strong and broad enough to pull the agenda forward.

2. Pandemic, War, Climate Change, and Global Inflation: Multiple Economic Shocks to Latin America

The pandemic hit the region hard, and the economic recovery has been slower than in other regions of the world. As well as a legacy of higher public debt, the pandemic has scarred the labor market and undermined the human capital accumulation of future workers.

The COVID-19 crisis has receded in Latin America but has left a significant toll. Reported deaths related to the pandemic are currently low and have converged to global levels—albeit from much higher levels than previously thought. Average excess mortality during the pandemic was among the highest in the world: 250% in 2020-21, double the global average (120%), and second only to Central Europe and Central Asia.[5] Low vaccination rates in some countries leave them vulnerable to new variants.

In most countries, GDP and employment have moved back to their pre-pandemic 2019 levels. On the other hand, according to the World Bank, expected growth rates may be named as *"resiliently mediocre"*. Banking systems are sound, and debt burdens overall seem not have entered any unsustainable path, differently from many developing countries elsewhere. However, economic growth is not projected to go above the low levels of the 2010s that we discussed in the previous section.

The post-pandemic economic recovery has led to a large unwinding of the rise in income poverty in 2020-21. But the permanent output losses from the pandemic will not be recovered, nor have the longer-term scars of the pandemic in terms of education, health, and future inequality been

---

5 . World Bank, New Approaches to Closing the Fiscal Gap. LAC Semiannual Update. (Washington, DC: World Bank, October 2022), http://hdl.handle.net/10986/38093.

wiped out.[6]

The Russian invasion and the war in Ukraine have further had an economic impact on the region, particularly through the commodity price shock and consequent domestic inflation hikes. While commodity exporters (importers) faced positive (negative) effects on their GDPs, via terms of trade, they all had to face higher levels of inflation, with food and energy prices affecting in particular the lower half of the income pyramid, given the weight of such items in their consumption basket.

Growth rates in the region have been systematically upgraded since January 2022—in contrast to the downgrades of the rest of the world because of the war in Ukraine. GDPs of net importers of food and fuel, including Caribbean and Central American countries, have been negatively affected. Rising prices of these goods have also affected households across the region. On the other hand, the overall rise in commodity prices has been a blessing to regional exporters including Argentina, Brazil, Chile, Colombia, Ecuador, and Peru.

The favorable tailwinds coming from commodity prices are expected to change course.[7] In the case of oil prices, futures markets point to a fall in coming years, after rising by 41% in 2022. Russia's invasion of Ukraine lifted base metal prices, but these are expected to end 2022 5.5% lower on average, and to decrease by a further 12% in 2023. The IMF report forecasts precious metal prices to drop more moderately, by 0.9% in 2022 and an additional 0.6% in 2023.

Food commodity prices, which also climbed after Russia's invasion of Ukraine, had returned to prewar levels by mid-2022, finishing a two-year rally. However, this was not before adding 5 percentage points to food price inflation for the average country in 2021, an estimated 6 percentage points in 2022, and 2 percentage points in 2023.

Higher frequency and greater extent of adverse weather events, probably already reflecting climate change, have also constituted a source of price shocks on food and energy. In the last few years, more frequent floods and droughts have affected the supply of food and energy in China, India,

---

[6] . Otaviano Canuto, "Permanent Output Losses from the Pandemic", Policy Center for the New South, October 2021, https://www.policycenter.ma/opinion/permanent-output-losses-pandemic.

[7] . International Monetary Fund, World Economic Outlook - Countering the Cost-of-Living Crisis (Washington, DC: International Monetary Fund, October 2022), https://www.imf.org/-/media/Files/Publications/WEO/2022/October/English/text.ashx.

Europe, the U.S., Africa, and Latin America itself. Climate change, a plague (pandemic), war, and hunger risks have constituted a 'perfect storm'.

For commodities as a group, 2022 was a very volatile year. After rising dramatically in the first half, because of the shocks mentioned, prices declined in the third quarter, as a reflection of China's growth deceleration,[8] and the U.S. dollar appreciation. The supply shock stemming from the war in Ukraine has been followed by a downward demand shock.

The asymmetric effects of higher commodity prices on the population of the region, harming especially the purchasing power of the bottom of the pyramid, have been—to different degrees—compensated for by social policies of transfers and other types of support. The lack of readily available fiscal space has been a constraint.

Even as Latin American countries continue to deal with the effects of those three previous shocks, a fourth has come with the tightening of global financial conditions. High global inflation in the wake of the previous shocks has been met with tighter monetary policies by central banks in advanced economies.[9]

Growth momentum has surprised positively in most of the region, favored by the return of service sectors and employment to pre-pandemic levels, as well as external conditions that stayed favorable until recently, including still-high commodity prices, still-strong external demand, and remittances, besides the tourism comeback. These explain upward revisions to regional growth forecasts in 2022.

But the tightening of global financial conditions works against this momentum. The availability and costs of domestic finance have become less favorable as major central banks have raised interest rates to tame inflation. Capital inflows to emerging markets have slowed and external borrowing costs have increased. Domestic interest rates in emerging markets have risen as their central banks also hiked rates to curb inflation, and because of the lower risk appetite of investors.

---

8 . Otaviano Canuto, "Whither China's Economic Growth,", Policy Brief, 53/22, Policy Center for the New South, August 2022, https://www.policycenter.ma/sites/default/files/2022-08/PB_53-22%20%28%20CANUTO%20%29.pdf.

9 . Otaviano Canuto, "Whither the Phillips Curve?," Policy Paper, 17/22, Policy Center for the New South, October 2022, https://www.policycenter.ma/sites/default/files/2022-10/PP_17-22_Canuto.pdf.

The region is overall more resilient to a monetary-financial shock than in previous times.[10] Banking systems are healthy and public balance sheets are not in general as fragile as at other times in the past. The cushion in terms of foreign exchange reserves also makes a difference in several cases when favorable commodity prices and trade surpluses led to the piling up of the former. Corporate debt outside the banking system nevertheless deserves attention. Higher domestic interest rates will also stiffen public debt conditions.[11]

After the upward surprises of GDP growth in 2022, the performance expected for next year is weaker. While the IMF and the World Bank, respectively, expect GDP growth rates to reach 3.5% and 3% in 2022, their forecasts drop to 1.7% and 1.6% in 2023. A successful post-perfect-storm recovery in Latin America should not be limited to a simple return to its pre-pandemic 'mediocre' levels of output growth—already unimpressive and vulnerable to shocks—but should represent an inflection point towards more resilient, inclusive, and productive growth patterns.[12]

3. Impact of Tectonic Shifts on Latin America's Economic Relations with China

The global tectonic shifts—labor supply increase, low-cost finance, and natural-resource boom—have had a counterpart in terms of profound changes in the economic relationship between China and Latin America over the past 20 years. In 2001, Latin America's exports to China corresponded to 1.6% of total exports, while in 2020 they had reached 26%. This contrasts with the region's exports to the U.S., which went from 56% of total exports in 2001 to 13% in 2020.[13] Such a radical change was largely due to China's accelerated manufacturing-based growth during this period and its rising

---

10 . Otaviano Canuto, "Will Another Taper Tantrum Hit Emerging Markets?," Project Syndicate, July 14, 2021, https://www.project-syndicate.org/commentary/risks-of-fed-monetary-policy-for-emerging-markets-by-otaviano-canuto-2021-07?barrier=accesspaylog.
11 . Santiago Acosta-Ormaechea et al., "Latin America Faces a Third Shock as Global Financial Conditions Tighten", , The IMF Blog, IMF, October 13, 2022), https://www.imf.org/en/Blogs/Articles/2022/10/13/latin-america-faces-a-third-shock-as-global-financial-conditions-tighten#:~:text=Santiago%20Acosta%2DOrmaechea%2C%20Gustavo%20Adler%2C%20Ilan%20Goldfajn%2C%20Anna%20Ivanova&text=As%20Latin%20American%20countries%20continue,tightening%20of%20global%20financial%20conditions.
12 . Otaviano Canuto and Pepe Zhang, "Global Recovery May Not Be Enough for Latin America," Americas Quarterly, June 3, 2021, https://www.americasquarterly.org/article/global-recovery-may-not-be-enough-for-latin-america/.
13 . Institute of International Finance, China Spotlight: Trade & Investment Ties with Latin America (Washington, DC: Institute of International Finance, May 2021).

demand for raw materials, especially from South American countries such as Peru, Chile, Brazil, Argentina, and Uruguay. Something similar happened in relation to the region's imports of manufactured goods. According to the IIF report, China's total trade with Latin America grew over the past 20 years at a 19% compound annual rate.

The weight of Latin America in China's total imports and exports has also risen. Latin America's share of China's total imports rose from 2.4% two decades ago to 8.1% in 2020: higher than the U.S. and close to Japan's share. China's exports to Latin America, meanwhile, became larger than those to Japan, although remaining smaller than its exports to both the U.S. and the European Union.[14]

China has become the top trading partner for most countries in South America, surpassing the U.S. in all but Colombia, Ecuador, and Paraguay. Mexico, in turn, has strengthened its trade dependence on the U.S. While the tectonic shifts have led to flows of exports of commodities to—and manufacturing imports from—China in South America, the same shifts underlie Mexico's integration into regional manufacturing value chains in North America.

China's investment in Latin America has also undergone a significant evolution, in line with China's rising financial flows that have accompanied its rising trade. Excluding Hong Kong (China), Latin America is the largest destination for Chinese outbound direct investment (ODI), reaching almost 50% of China's total ODI stock.

Since 96% of China's ODI in Latin America went to two offshore financial centers (the Caymans and British Virgin Islands), it is hard to pin down exactly its ultimate destination. China's ODI in those offshore centers is overwhelmingly larger than those of other countries and, if they are excluded, China's ODI in the region is smaller than that of the Netherlands, Canada, Germany, Italy, or Japan, and corresponds to only 5% of the U.S. ODI in Latin America.[15]

The bulk of China's total ODI in the region went to business services (23%), and wholesale and retail (14%), whereas less than 6% was in mining. To some extent, this highlights what could be seen as a 'metamorphosis' in China's financial flows to the region.[16] After becoming a major source

---

14 . Ibid.
15 . Ibid.
16 . Otaviano Canuto, "How Chinese Investment in Latin America Is Changing," Americas Quarterly, March 12, 2019, https://www.americasquarterly.org/article/how-chinese-

of capital flows to Latin America and the Caribbean from 2005 to 2019, a more diverse range of Chinese investors surfaced, interested in more than simply channeling resources toward infrastructure, governments, and state companies.

The profile of Chinese investment in the region has tracked the evolution of China's economy as it has moved to greater reliance on services and domestic consumption (Canuto, 2022a). Lending by the China Development Bank and China's ExIm Bank was until recently directed mostly to infrastructure and the energy sector. Before declining in recent years, China's development lending to Latin America and the Caribbean reached levels larger than lending from the World Bank, Inter-American Development Bank (IDB), and Development Bank of Latin America (CAF) combined.

Of the estimated $140 billion that China lent to Latin America from 2005 to 2018, over 90% went to four countries—Venezuela, Brazil, Argentina, and Ecuador. More than 80% of China's foreign direct investments, either as greenfield investments or through mergers and acquisitions, went to Brazil, Peru, and Argentina, with Mexico also rising as a destination for manufacturing investment more recently.[17]

This shift in focus brought with it the emergence of new investors. Direct investment in the region went from almost nothing in 2005 to likely passing $110 billion by 2018. The initial focus was on the extractive industry (oil, gas, copper, iron ore), but moved to more than half of the flows going to services. The pursuit by Chinese investors of opportunities in transport, finance, electricity generation and transmission, information and communications technology, and alternative energy services catering to local markets, grew rapidly.

China-backed commercial financial institutions and platforms have also established their footprint in the region, engaging actively in private-sector deal-making. As well as co-financing projects and setting up regional investment funds, four major Chinese commercial banks have ramped up operations in the region, many in partnership with international banks. The scale and number of transactions may be smaller than the lending spree led by development banks, but point to a qualitative change in the structure of financing options coming from China.

---

investment-in-latin-america-is-changing/.

[17] . Pepe Zhang and Tatiana Prazeres, "China's Trade with Latin America is Bound to Keep Growing," World Economic Forum, June 17, 2021, https://www.weforum.org/agenda/2021/06/china-trade-latin-america-caribbean/.

Increased participation of non-state investors has introduced new sources of dynamism and diversification to Chinese direct investment in Latin America. Brazil's emerging tech industry, for instance, has successfully and continuously attracted high-profile Chinese investments. Additionally, Chinese participation in mergers and acquisitions into specific value-added sectors reflects new consumption habits in China, ranging from vineyards in Chile to meat-packing plants in Uruguay.[18]

Attention to risk when looking at potential returns has also come to the fore among Chinese investors, particularly after their experience in Venezuela. As domestic regulations and lending caps tighten in China, given concerns with its increased financial fragility, a more stringent look at the country's development lending has followed.

State-owned enterprises are still foremost among Chinese investors in the region, from mining, infrastructure, and oil and gas to hydroelectric plants. China's policy response to the global financial crisis in the form of large-scale stimulus given to infrastructure and housing sectors generated excess domestic capacity in heavy industry and in real estate, while financially boosting industries including construction, retail and wholesale trade, hotels, and restaurants. This overcapacity then went to look for foreign markets.

China's physical integration abroad via the Belt and Road Initiative (BRI) was a vehicle to put its overcapacity in construction and heavy industry to work elsewhere. Nineteen of the 33 Latin American countries have formally signed off on their participation in the BRI, while Brazil and Mexico have not officially done so.

Episodes of contention with Latin American governments around environmental impacts and corruption associated with some previous lending deals, have highlighted the need for China's investment finance to reckon with the risks and fallout from environment and governance issues. Official guidelines have been issued on environment and social policies for Chinese companies investing abroad, signaling the matter has caught the attention of Chinese authorities.

While Chinese deals used to be limited to construction—winning concessions, building projects, then leaving—new equity investments in Latin America indicate longer-term interests and ownership in projects beyond their construction, to include operation, maintenance, and more. This is especially true in port projects.

---

18 . Otaviano Canuto, "How Chinese Investment in Latin America Is Changing."

The speed and intensity of China's growth-cum-structural-change has seemed to a great extent to be matched by the profile and volume of its capital flows to Latin America since 2005. However, the sizable Chinese financial and investment footprint in the region has apparently come close to a halt in the last two years, with a slowdown in reported new flows. In 2020-2021, Chinese policy banks issued no new loans to Latin American governments or state-owned enterprises.[19]

Myers and Ray suggested that the total of combined Chinese finance to Latin America is unlikely to ever approximate the previous peaks of policy bank lending in 2010 and 2015. It remains to be seen if this simply reflects a movement away from big natural resource-based finance to state entities in oil and mining, with Chinese investments eventually returning to positive ground on the services side. Since 2018, financial and investment relations have moved to Chinese companies, backed by Beijing, as investing partners and not only financiers of projects.

4. The U.S.-China Rivalry and China's Economic Extroversion in Latin America

A major consequence of the war in Ukraine has been the exacerbation of the rivalries between major global powers, inevitably encompassing trade and technology policies. The rivalry brings spillovers to Latin America.

Already before the 'perfect storm', such rivalry had escalated with political anti-globalization backlashes in several advanced countries during the last decade. But the pandemic and the invasion of Ukraine mainstreamed geopolitics to government policies and consequently to private-sector corporate strategies.

The U.S.-China rivalry was already evident through U.S. President Trump's trade wars. The pandemic also brought forms of soft-power dispute around vaccines, and the search for reassurance about countries' access to strategic goods (medicines and medical equipment, semiconductors, and others). Russia's invasion of Ukraine and China's apparent alignment took geopolitical tensions to higher levels.

---

[19] . Margaret Myers and Rebecca Ray, "What Role for China's Policy Banks in LAC?," The Dialogue, March 2022, https://thedialogue.wpenginepowered.com/wp-content/uploads/2022/03/Chinas-policy-banks-final-mar22.pdf.

As a justification for his style of trade war, President Trump had alluded to a goal of revitalizing jobs in the U.S. manufacturing industry by protecting it from the unfair trade practices of other countries, particularly China. However, according to a study by two Federal Reserve Bank staff, the effect was just the opposite, i.e. a reduction in U.S. manufacturing employment.[20] President Biden has not reversed Trump's trade measures, but clearly the focus of U.S. actions has shifted predominantly to science and technology, notably in relation to China's access to semiconductors and other high-tech areas.

The war in Ukraine and the pandemic have dovetailed with another reason given as a justification for revisiting the globalization and global value chains that were developed as an outcome of the tectonic shifts. Supply-chain disruptions during the pandemic led to claims that cost optimization attained through global value chains (GVCs) came with reduced resilience in the face of localized shocks that tend to affect entire chains. The war in Ukraine, in turn, raised the profile of geopolitical risks as an additional factor to be reckoned with in the configuration of—and reliance on global value chains.[21]

Such arguments have been raised before, but the pandemic and the war have made them more common and louder. They have been accompanied by calls for re-shoring or near-shoring of global value chains, with 'friend-shoring' to minimize geopolitical risks. National security justifications have reinforced the call in some sectors. The great development of logistics and transport across the world's industrial clusters—as part of one of the tectonic shifts—allowed 'just-in-time' manufacturing to become the main adopted production model. However, to maximize resilience against shocks, this should now move to a 'just-in-case' mode, even if costly, reflecting a trade-off between efficiency and resilience.

So, where does Latin America stand in the middle of such rivalry? Simple calls for alignment of countries in the region will not be effective if not translated into actual advantages, counterbalancing the consequences in terms of losses with whoever is not chosen for such alignment.

---

20 . Aaron Flaaen and Justin Pierce, "Disentangling the Effects of the 2018-2019 Tariffs on a Globally Connected U.S. Manufacturing Sector," Board of Governors of the Federal Reserve System, 2019, https://doi.org/10.17016/FEDS.2019.086.

21 . Otaviano Canuto, Abdelaaziz Ait Ali, Mahmoud Arbouch, "Pandemic, War, and Global Value Chains,"Jean-Monnet Atlantic Network 2.0, October 2022, https://www.policycenter.ma/sites/default/files/2022-10/paper-pcns-pandemic-war-and-global-value-chains-by-otaviano-canuto-abdelaaziz-ait-ali-mahmoud-arbouch.pdf.

As a reaction to the upswing in China's financial and investment flows to Latin America discussed above, the U.S. authorities opted to warn governments in the region about risks of 'debt traps'. Furthermore, China's hands-off approach with respect to environment and governance safeguards—under the guise of respecting local standards and the sovereignty of borrowers—was highlighted as facilitating local corruption and misuse of resources. A typical response from governments in the region was to ask: "what are the alternatives?" Rhetoric around the risks of engaging with China is ineffective.

As remarked by Aragão (2021), historically the predominant U.S. approach to Latin America has been to deal with the region as an "inexhaustible source of problems". the fights against drug trafficking, illegal immigration, and corruption are at the top of the list of U.S. priorities for engagement with the region

In the last decade, U.S. trade agreements have been reached with several countries in the region, though not with the large countries in South America, including MERCOSUR. It is still to be seen if President Biden will come to the region with any trade-boosting plans, while Trump only exercised threats against Mexico and a review of NAFTA that narrowed the scope for Mexico in automobile value chains.

On the finance and investment side, there are obviously the U.S. based private capital flows, but carrying them to bulk infrastructure and risky-asset finance is not straightforward and has not been substantial.[22] Even U.S. President Biden's proposal of an alternative to the Chinese Belt and Road Initiative (BRI) has been shy in terms of resources to be made available with official government support.

Will 'nearshoring' and 'friend-shoring' be used by the U.S. to boost its attractiveness as a partner in the rivalry? For example, recent U.S. initiatives on electric car batteries have sparked a flurry of activity from American and European firms to Canada with proposals of billions in new investments in metals, and more. However, there are reasons to believe that such possibilities cannot be taken for granted. The homework in the region to make it feasible to seize opportunities is a tall order, and direct or indirect subsidies would still be necessary.[23] Not by chance, one may expect

---

[22] . Karim El Aynaoui and Otaviano Canuto, "Bridging Green Infrastructure and Finance," in Scaling Up Sustainable Finance and Investment in the Global South, ed. Dirk Schoenmaker and Ulrich Volz (Geneva: CEPR, 2022), https://cepr.org/system/files/publication-files/175477-scaling_up_sustainable_finance_and_investment_in_the_global_south.pdf.

[23] . Otaviano Canuto, Justin Yifu Lin, Pepe Zhang, "Geopoliticized Industrial Policy Won't Work," Project Syndicate, February 24, 2022, https://www.project-syndicate.org/

deglobalization to remain relative and circumscribed to very high-tech and national security-sensitive sectors.[24]

Soft-power disputes around access to technology, on the other hand, will intensify, in complex ways. In 2020, the communications company Huawei started to distribute 5G kits to Brazilian agribusiness companies, enhancing their connectivity capabilities and searching for their alignment against the Brazilian government following any suggestion by the U.S. to prohibit their participation in 5G auctions as a provider. [25]

The issue is also illustrated by China's donation of thermal cameras to the government of Nicaragua, through which a previously non-existent Nicaraguan dependency on thermal cameras is tentatively being developed. It is likely that, as time passes, the Chinese cameras will not be exchanged for others in Nicaragua, and a market reservation for China in detriment to competitors from the U.S. and Europe may have been created.

The main point here is that—without Trump's unilateral style of trade war, which in the end was counterproductive—the heightened U.S.-China rivalry will have to be exercised mainly through the offer of trade and investment opportunities, and finance to countries of the region.

Is a revival of the pro-active financial and investment stance abroad taken by Brazil between the mid-2000s and mid-2010s, likely after the 2022 Brazilian elections? Probably not, since the former was based on a combination of public debt emissions transferred to the country's National Economic and Social Development Bank (BNDES), including coordination with domestic private companies. The fiscal crisis that erupted in 2015, together with the governance scandals and justice trials that also marked the end of the cycle, have made it politically, fiscally, and practically impossible to replicate.

---

24 . Canuto, Ait Ali, Arbouch "Pandemic, War, and Global Value Chains."
25 . Thiago de Aragao, "The US Still Doesn't Understand China's Strategy in Latin America,",The Diplomat, September 8, 2021, https://thediplomat.com/2021/09/the-us-still-doesnt-understand-chinas-strategy-in-latin-america/.

5. Concluding Remarks

The war in Europe (Ukraine) and the other elements of the 'perfect storm' (pandemic, severe weather phenomenon, hunger, global inflation) have consequences for Latin America. Positive GDP growth surprises in commodity-dependent countries in the region must be weighed against increases in inequality and worsening living conditions for the poor. The scars of the pandemic on health, education, and human capital remain. Except for commodities that are key to the transition to clean energy, the broad picture of their prices ahead is far from that of a new super-cycle. The underlying trend seems to be the mediocre growth performance of the pre-pandemic decade.

The region will have to find new economic growth avenues. A wave of green infrastructure investments looks obvious. It remains to be seen how widely and comprehensively opportunities for nearshoring or friend-shoring will be created by the U.S.-China rivalry and the relative deglobalization.

Apart from specific country cases, there are no clear-cut benefits from aligning automatically to either of the rival powers. Hopefully the rivalry will be exercised through the offer of trade and investment opportunities, rather than via attempts to exclude rivals from the region.

Doubling down efforts around regional integration might finally generate the enjoyment of benefits—regional gains of scale and scope economies—that have so far been blocked by regional fragmentation. The issue was already present before the war in Ukraine because of lack of political will to do what such integration would take. The homework in terms of reforms and joint infrastructure investments, however, will remain substantial. It is not by chance that, exceptions notwithstanding, the region remains relatively commercially closed, including among neighbors.

CHAPTER VII

Global Powers in North and West Africa

Rida Lyammouri & Amine Ghoulidi

North and West Africa are strategic and dynamic regions where global powers seek to outcompete each other and attempt to shape the international order in their favor. The United States, European Union, China, and Russia prize Northwestern Africa as a gateway to the rest of the African continent. The complexities of these countries' local and regional politics, however, do not make for clear or easy alliances for these global and regional powers. This has been further compounded by the war in Ukraine, which has opened up new opportunities for regional, fossil-fuel rich, powers such as Algeria to seek concessions from the global powers in order to shape the regional order in line with their interests. A deteriorating security situation and increased frustration toward Western powers, mainly France, has created an opening for Russia to exploit new partnerships in West Africa. Russia will remain, through the Wagner Group, at least in the short-term a distraction to the efforts of Western global powers in Africa. The U.S. and the EU are unlikely to ignore this distraction, but the focus should be rather on Africa, not on what global rivals such as Russia and China are doing in Africa.

North and West Africa are strategic and dynamic regions for global powers in their efforts to outcompete each other and shape the international order in their favor. The United States, European Union, China, and Russia prize North Africa as a gateway to the rest of the African continent, as well as a strategic access point to Europe—a region with an impact on critical priorities from energy production, to global supply chains, to counterterrorism. Simultaneously, the West African Sahel crisis has become a major source of concern for the international community because of the threat it poses to the rest of West Africa and the rest of the world, especially Europe.

This chapter looks at the relationships of the global powers with the North and West African[1] countries, with a focus on the security and diplomatic cooperation between them and the US, the EU, Russia, China, and Turkey. Then, it critically assesses these relationships from an African perspective in light of the available literature, supplemented by local insights, and suggests ways of making things better for all stakeholders. The first section examines the relationship between global powers and North Africa, while the second focuses on the relationship with West African countries, mainly the Sahel region.

1. North Africa

While North Africa[2] is not the focal point of any of the global powers' geopolitical strategies, all dedicate considerable resources to assert their presence in the region, and prevent the entrenchment of competing powers. Often this is accomplished through the implementation of country-specific developmental, diplomatic, and defense frameworks. While there has been much public focus on development cooperation (foreign direct investment, foreign assistance, among others) and diplomatic engagement, little emphasis has been put on the security-focused efforts of global powers in North Africa.

At the same time, the complexities of the local and regional politics of North African countries do not make for clear alliances for the global powers. Morocco and Algeria view the overtures of global powers through the lens

---

1 . This chapter focuses on Morocco, Algeria, Tunisia, and Libya in North Africa, and Mali, Niger, and Burkina Faso in West Africa. However, other countries, such as Cote d'Ivoire, Benin, Togo, and Ghana, are also mentioned to highlight concrete examples.
2 . For the objectives of this chapter, North Africa refers mainly to Morocco, Algeria, Tunisia, and Libya.

of their own priorities—especially regarding the Sahara issue.[3] Libyan actors both decry foreign influence in their conflict and vie for the legitimacy and military support that such foreign interventions can bring to their side. And Tunisia, focused internally on its precarious economic situation and the mostly self-inflicted institutional fragility, remains vulnerable to regional and global power meddling.

For the best part of the last two decades, U.S. security engagement in North Africa has mainly focused on counterterrorism. The U.S.-led global war against terrorism had significantly raised the geopolitical and security profiles of North Africa in the eye of the U.S.[4] Groups such as Al-Qaeda and ISIS, through local offshoots and allied organizations, entrenched themselves in parts of the vast Sahara desert and staged sometimes spectacular attacks against key regional infrastructure.[5] The region had also seen thousands of its young people join jihadist groups in conflict zones as far away as Iraq and Syria,[6] and was feared to have become a springboard for violent extremism into Europe.[7]

a. Algeria and Morocco: From a Focus on Counterterrorism to the Threat of Military Escalation in the Sahara

Concern about the terrorist threat drove an unprecedented change in U.S. policy towards Algeria, which was traditionally perceived as more aligned with Russia and the so-called 'Axis of Resistance', than with the West. Illustrating this shift in U.S. policy, the Algeria section of the State Department's annual budget justification shifted, evolving from a "cautious and measured approach" in 2001 to seeking to strengthen "a major regional power as it reshapes its post-Cold War orientation" in 2008.[8]

---

3. . The Sahara issue refers to the conflict of the status of Morocco's Southern Provinces. Roughly the size of the United Kingdom, the territory is disputed by a separatist and armed group, the polisario front, based in southwestern Algeria.
4. . Alexis Arieff, "Maghreb Facing New Global Challenges: U.S.-Algerian Security Cooperation and Regional Counterterrorism,"Institut français des relations internationales, July 2011,. https://www.policycenter.ma/sites/default/files/2021-01/IFRI_alexisarieff.pdf
5. . "In Amenas inquest: British victims of Algeria attack," BBC, November 28, 2014, https://www.bbc.com/news/uk-29127935
6. . Aaron Y. Zelin,. "Tunisians of the Iraq Jihad and How That Set the Stage for the Syrian Jihad,: The Washington Institute for Near East Policy, January 29, 2021https://www.washingtoninstitute.org/policy-analysis/tunisians-iraq-jihad-and-how-set-stage-syrian-jihad
7. . Andrea Elliott,. "Where Boys Grew Up to Be Jihadis," New York Times, November 25, 2007, https://www.nytimes.com/2007/11/25/magazine/25tetouan-t.html
8. . Department of State, Foreign Operations, and Related Programs.Congressional Budget Justification, (2023). https://www.usaid.gov/sites/default/files/documents/FY2023-Congressional-Budget-Justification.pdf

However, the keen attempts of the U.S. to upgrade its relationship with Algeria have often been met with skepticism and resistance from Algeria's notoriously fragmented and opaque political and military elite. This is because of Algeria's zero-sum approach to the U.S.'s privileged relationship with neighboring Morocco, but also mainly because of Algeria's fear of upsetting its strategic alliance with Russia, its historical ally and main weapons supplier. In fact, because of rising tensions with Morocco over the status of the Sahara (a territory roughly the size of the United Kingdom), Algeria's desire to establish itself as a great regional power, and the need to secure its vast land borders, Algeria has imported more weapons than the United Kingdom, Israel, and Turkey over the past five years, making the country Russia's third-largest arms importer over the period.[9] Russia accounts for 81% of Algerian arms acquisitions since 2017, with Germany and France respectively in distant second and third places. And with Algeria's unprecedented 130% increase in its 2022 defense budget, accounting for 13% of its annual GDP,[10] the risks of a regional arms race and a potential military conflagration—particularly in the face of mounting escalation in the Sahara—are likely to increase. The war in Ukraine and its ramifications for global energy and food security have upended Algeria's and Morocco's geopolitical positions. Algeria as a major regional natural gas supplier has sought to capitalize on the new global energy reality to extract concessions from countries with influence on the Sahara issue such as Spain and France.[11] Meanwhile Morocco, one of the world's largest exporter of fertilizers, has worked quickly towards the fulfilment of Africa's food security through the provision of inexpensive, critical inputs to the millions of smallholder farmers in Africa.[12]

Undoubtedly mindful of these developments, the White House in its National Security Strategy (NSS), published in October 2022, said that its foreign policy in North Africa and the Middle East will focus on

---

9 . Pieter Wezeman, Alexandra Kuimova, Siemon Wezeman, "Trends in International Arms Transfers, 2021,"Stockholm International Peace Research Institute, March 2022, https://www.sipri.org/sites/default/files/2022-03/fs_2203_at_2021.pdf
10 . "Le budget de l'armée algérienne explose en 2023 (hausse de 130%), " Medias24, October 17, 2022, https://medias24.com/2022/10/17/le-budget-de-larmee-algerienne-explose-en-2023-hausse-de-130/
11 . Inga Kristina Trauthig & Amine Ghoulidi, "Algeria and Libya are unlikely to plug Europe's energy gap," The Conversation, March 16, 2022, https://theconversation.com/algeria-and-libya-are-unlikely-to-plug-europes-energy-gap-178791
12 . Safaa Kasraoui, "Morocco Donates 25,000 Tonnes of Fertilizer to Senegal's Smallholder Farmers,"Morocco World News, October 21, 2022, https://www.moroccoworldnews.com/2022/10/351971/morocco-donates-25-000-tonnes-of-fertilizer-to-senegals-smallholder-farmers

"*de-escalation and integration*".[13] The Biden Administration claims it intends to focus on practical steps to advance U.S. interests and regional stability, rather than defaulting to the "*military-centric policies*" of the past two decades. The NSS also emphasizes security assistance to local partners to improve their capacities, and to deter threats to mutual U.S. and partner interests, including to counter "*external actors' military expansion in the region*".[14] However, this approach has its limitations when pegged against the more pragmatic engagement of countries such as Russia, which have little concern about tipping the military balance in favor of their traditional allies like Algeria. Indeed, a sour issue in U.S.-Moroccan relations has been the U.S.'s reported reluctance to export certain advanced military systems,[15] despite Algeria's astronomical military expenditure and continued acquisition of sophisticated Russian systems, including Su-57 fighter jets or the S-400 missile platform.

Enter China. While the global economic powerhouse has not yet made any significant break into the North African defense market,[16] China appears to be best positioned to take advantage of the expected shortage of Russian arms exports. As Russia, the EU, and the U.S. are increasingly consumed with the war in Ukraine, with its unprecedented arms 'burn rate', China is poised to be the most viable alternative. In fact, there are strong indications that the agnostic Chinese military industrial complex has made recent headways in North Africa with the reported sale of its flagship Wing Loong unmanned aerial vehicle (UAV) to both Algeria[17] and Morocco.[18]

---

13. The White House, National Security Strategy, October, 2022, https://www.whitehouse.gov/wp-content/uploads/2022/10/Biden-Harris-Administrations-National-Security-Strategy-10.2022.pdf
14. Ibid.
15. Mike Stone 3456, Patricia Zengerle, "Exclusive: U.S. nears sale of four sophisticated drones to Morocco – sources," Reuters, December 10, 2020. https://www.reuters.com/article/us-usa-morocco-drones-exclusive-idUSKBN28K2R4
16. Luke Encarnation, "Assessing the Impact of Chinese Arms in Africa," Georgetown Security Studies Review, (April 20, 2021), https://georgetownsecuritystudiesreview.org/2021/04/20/assessing-the-impact-of-chinese-arms-in-africa/
17. Soufiane Sbiti, "Alger renforce ses bases aériennes frontalière avec le Maroc dont celle de Tindouf," LeDesk, October 20, 2022, https://ledesk.ma/enclair/alger-renforce-ses-bases-aeriennes-frontalieres-avec-le-maroc-dont-celle-de-tindouf/
18. Federico Borsari, "Rabat's Secret Drones: Assessing Morocco's Quest for Advanced UAV Capabilities," Italian Institute for International Political Studies, July 22, 2021, https://www.ispionline.it/en/pubblicazione/rabats-secret-drones-assessing-moroccos-quest-advanced-uav-capabilities-31207

Algeria's unprecedented defense budget for 2022[19] (nearly $23 billion), and the expectation that Morocco's would not lag too far behind (reported to approximate $17 billion), mean North Africa is in the midst of a full-fledged arms race. Both Algeria and Morocco seem to be pursuing foreign investments in their nascent domestic arms industries. And with the Russian entanglement in Ukraine, and American and European reluctance to augment the domestic arms industries of non-NATO allies, China could be eager to fill in the gap. Attesting to the Moroccan appetite to achieve a level of self-sufficiency in critical technology against heightened threats by the polisario front are recent reports[20] on an agreement between Morocco and Israel to build a local UAV manufacturing operation mainly destined for domestic consumption.

Turkey, like China, appears to have adopted a more agnostic approach to Moroccan-Algerian rivalry, and has reportedly sold its Bayraktar drones to both countries.[21] [22] It is also feared that other third-party country drones, possibly Iranian, may have found their way into the hands of the polisario militant group,[23] one of the leaders of which threatened in October 2022 their deployment against Moroccan forces.[24] Therefore, there appears to be ample demand for sophisticated arms and weapon systems in North Africa, a ripe opportunity for China should it decide to pursue it.

b. Tunisia and Libya: Countries in Crisis Vulnerable to Encroachment by Regional and Global Powers

Tunisia, the tortured cradle of the so-called Arab Spring, does not appear to occupy an important space within the global powers' strategies for the continent. However, by virtue of its geographic location and its structural

---

19 . Salah Slimani, "Algeria Sees Gas-Export Windfall Boosting Army, Jobless Spending," Bloomberg, October 20, 2022, https://www.bloomberg.com/news/articles/2022-10-20/algeria-sees-gas-export-windfall-boosting-army-jobless-spending
20 . "With the help of Israel, Morocco is the first African country to enter the drone manufacturers club," Middle East Monitor, October 15, 2022, https://www.middleeastmonitor.com/20221015-with-the-help-of-israel-morocco-is-the-first-african-country-to-enter-the-drone-manufacturers-club//
21 . Ragip Soylu, "Algeria nears deal with Turkey to buy Anka drones," Middle East Eye, October 19, 2022, https://www.middleeasteye.net/news/algeria-turkey-anka-drones-nears-deal
22 . Borsari, "Rabat's Secret Drones: Assessing Morocco's Quest for Advanced UAV Capabilities."
23 . The polisario front is an armed insurgent group based in southwestern Algeria claiming to be working for the independence of the Sahara.
24 . Aya Benazizi, "polisario Threatens to Use Drones Against Morocco's Royal Armed Forces," Morocco World News, October 4, 2022, https://www.moroccoworldnews.com/2022/10/351668/polisario-threatens-to-use-drones-against-moroccos-royal-armed-forces

propensity to socio-economic unrest, the country is often seen as a major source of irregular migrants and, to a lesser extent, violent extremism into the neighboring European Union. The EU and its countries therefore engage with Tunisia through the framework of proactive social containment; that is a prosperous, stable, and democratic neighbor is a reliable (and less harmful) one.[25] [26] However, ever since its 2011 revolution, the country has undergone tumultuous years that have left many of its young people highly disenfranchised, disillusioned by the political and economic promises of the revolution.

Mindful of Tunisia's structural inefficiencies in the face of organized crime, and more importantly, terrorist group rooted in neighboring Libya and Algeria, the U.S. and EU have sought to augment the capabilities of Tunisia's military and security apparatuses. Since 2011, the U.S. alone committed $1.4 billion to support Tunisia's democratic transition[27], $225 million of which was security assistance to bolster the country's capacity to *"counter internal and regional threats and terrorism"*.[28] However, Tunisian President Kais Saied's democratic backsliding since his election on July 25, 2021, has led some U.S. officials and policymakers to call for a suspension of all U.S. aid to the country.[29]

The growing European and American lack of confidence in the notoriously intransigent president's willingness to walk back some of his most problematic policies has left him isolated, but also vulnerable to the encroachment of opportunistic regional powers, such as Algeria. Sensing a historic opportunity to shift a longstanding neutral Tunisian policy on the Sahara, Algeria reportedly transferred $300 million into Tunisian coffers in December 2021, ahead of an Algerian presidential visit to Tunis.[30] This, among other generous decisions by Algeria towards its neighbor, including in the energy sector, ultimately led Tunisian President Saied to receive the Secretary General of the polisario front in August 2022 in Tunis, in what was

---

25. "European Neighborhood Policy and Enlargement Negotiations: Tunisia,". European Commission, https://neighbourhood-enlargement.ec.europa.eu/european-neighbourhood-policy/countries-region/tunisia_en
26. Benjamin Fox, "EU to maintain Tunisia funding despite slide towards autocracy," Euractiv, March 31, 2022, https://www.euractiv.com/section/global-europe/news/eu-to-maintain-tunisia-funding-despite-slide-towards-autocracy/
27. U.S. Department of State, U.S. Relations With Tunisia,(June 2022), https://www.state.gov/u-s-relations-with-tunisia/
28. "Fact Sheet: Enduring U.S.-Tunisian Relations," U.S. Embassy in Tunisia, https://tn.usembassy.gov/our-relationship/fact-sheet-enduring-u-s-tunisian-relations/
29. Gordon Gray, "Focus Assistance to Tunisia—Don't Suspend It," September 18, 2022, https://www.americanprogress.org/article/focus-assistance-to-tunisia-dont-suspend-it/
30. "Algeria provides $300 mln loan to Tunisia," Reuters, December 14, 2021, https://www.reuters.com/markets/rates-bonds/algeria-provides-300-mln-loan-tunisia-2021-12-14/

perceived as a shift in Tunisian neutrality on the Sahara issue.[31]

Russian and Chinese engagement in Tunisia is mostly of an economic nature. Russian security cooperation with Tunisia remains limited. In 2016, Russia reportedly began sharing satellite imagery of terrorist groups with their Tunisian counterparts: *"a gesture that Tunisian officials later credited with helping them thwart several attacks linked to smuggling networks along the Libyan border"*.[32] Russia had also pledged to supply Tunisian armed forces with various military gear, *"although it remains unclear whether these supplies have been delivered"*.[33] Chinese commercial investments in Tunisia, however, have raised concerns about their potential national security implications. In 2009, China's Huawei Marine Networks deployed the undersea 'Hannibal' cable communications system linking Tunisia to Italy.[34] China also invested in satellite infrastructure in Tunisia, opening there its first overseas center for its GPS alternative, the Beidou Navigation Satellite System, in April 2018.[35]

Of the four North African countries, Libya is front and center of the global powers' strategies because of the ongoing Libyan civil conflict and its spillover effects in terms of terrorism, migration, and energy. The U.S., EU, and Russia have been hands-on diplomatically in engaging actors across the Libyan political and military spectrum. While the U.S. and the EU have thrown their weight behind the thus-far ineffective UN process, both also partner with security actors—more often those based in Libya's west, who have also received substantial military support from Turkey—to pursue counterterrorism and counter-migration goals. In contrast, Russia, early on, tried to tip the scales in favor of the Eastern coalition led by General Khalifa Hafter, including by deploying Wagner forces to train, equip, and support his forces. China appears to have stayed away from actively soliciting partnerships with Libyan security partners, although it remains open to future opportunities for engagement. With no end in sight to the

---

31 . Simon Speakman Cordall, "Is Tunisia Abandoning Morocco for Algeria?," Foreign Policy, September 19, 2022, https://foreignpolicy.com/2022/09/19/is-tunisia-abandoning-morocco-for-algeria/

32 . Sarah Feuer &Anna Borshchevskaya, "Russia Makes Inroads in North Africa,". The Washington Institute for Near East Policy, November 2, 2017, https://www.washingtoninstitute.org/policy-analysis/russia-makes-inroads-north-africa

33 . Ibid.

34 . Delivering a submarine cable system in Tunisia," Communications Africa, December 10, 2009, https://communicationsafrica.com/internet/delivering-a-submarine-cable-system-in-tunisia

35 . Stephaner R. Alrivy, "China's Increasing Influence in Tunisia: Implications for U.S. National Security" (Master's thesis, Faculty of the U.S. Army Command and General Staff College, June 2019, https://apps.dtic.mil/sti/pdfs/AD1124432.pdf

Libyan conflict, it is unclear how far the global powers are willing to go to influence the outcomes, and whether they will seek to remain entrenched in the hopes influencing post-conflict Libya.

2. West Africa

Two decades after the end of the Cold War, Africa has become again the center of geopolitical competition between great powers and there is a new scramble for Africa.[36] The U.S., EU led by France, together with Russia, China, and Turkey, regularly convene summits with African heads of state to explore ways of advancing their respective interests.

a. France in West Africa: A Former Colonial Master Threatened by New Competitors

Beyond its economic interests, France seems to seek more to preserve its influence and prestige of global power in West Africa against competitors including China and Russia, to defend Western values, and to contain the security threats from state fragility, organized crime, and terrorism. In 2013, France, at the request of the Malian government and with the authorization of the United Nations Security Council, deployed its security forces to Mali to counter the threat of violent extremist organizations (VEOs). While initially France's intervention was celebrated in Mali and the region, that is not the case today. France faces increased unprecedented widespread anti-French sentiment in West Africa, and needs to review its strategy in terms of its military and diplomatic engagements, and rethink its military presence in the region.[37] As the traditional partner and former colonial power of most West African countries, France has established military bases in the region, and has defense accords with French-speaking West African states that date back to the 1960s. But some of these accords are more and more challenged by the new generations, including political leaders and political parties who denounce the subjection of France-Africa relationships to French interests, and who wish to renegotiate them.[38]

---

[36] . The new scramble for Africa, The Economist, March 7, 2019, https://link.gale.com/apps/doc/A577449160
[37] . Ibid.
[38] . Alex Thurston, "Who Are France's Sahelian Critics, and What Are They Saying?," Africa Up Close, July 6, 2022, https://africaupclose.wilsoncenter.org/frances-sahelian-critics/

b. Protecting Europe From Security Threats From the Sahel

The EU's Sahel strategy, inspired by the security-development nexus framework, has consisted of projects that aim to address the political, economic, and social drivers of the Sahel crisis, and of various contributions in the military domain.[39] Encouraged by France, which champions multilateralism in international relations, the EU initiated military cooperation programs with Mali and other Sahel states to counter the jihadist wave. Along with irregular migration, terrorism has been perceived as a threat to Europe, rather than an opportunity to focus on the core issues driving the Sahel crisis and threatening coastal states. This perception has motivated Europe's engagements in the Sahel and the focus on defense and security policy.[40] In addition to the military operation Barkhane, led by France and supported by the U.S., EU has deployed since 2013 multiple military training missions in the Sahel, including the European Union Capacity Building Mission (EUCAP) and European Union Training Mission.[41] Simultaneously, Germany, the Netherlands, Sweden, and the United Kingdom are currently contributing, or have contributed, troops to the United Nations Multidimensional Integrated Stabilization Mission in Mali (MINUSMA).

However, as the situation has continued to deteriorate in the region, despite these security efforts for almost a decade, the EU and France in particularface unprecedented skepticism. As a result, France was forced to withdraw its Barkhane forces, in addition to an EU Task Force, while the MINUSMA peacekeeping mission is finding it difficult to carry out its mission under new restrictions established by the Malian authorities. To sum up how damaged the relationship is between France and Mali, Mali's foreign minister, speaking at the UNSC, accused France of providing arms to terrorist organizations operating in the region, and requested special meetings to provide evidence.[42] Anti-French sentiment is not limited to Mali, but has also been apparent in the last two years in Burkina Faso and Niger,

---

39. Norman Sempijja & Eyita-Okon Ekeminiabasi, "Examining the Effectiveness of the EU Security-Development Strategy in Tackling Instability in the Sahel: The Case for an Alternative Strategy?," South African Journal of International Affairs 29, no.2 (2022), https://doi.org/10.1080/10220461.2022.2089727.
40. Denis M. Tull, "France and the Rest: Testing Alliances in Europe by Providing Security in the Sahel," in Sahel: 10 Years of Instability: Local, Regional and International Dynamics, ed. Giovanni Carbone & Camillo Casola. (Milan: Ledizioni LediPublishing .2022),https://www.ispionline.it/sites/default/files/10_years_instability_sahel_report.ispi_.2022_0.pdf
41. Nabons Laafi Diallo. Le terrorisme au Sahel: dynamique de l'extrémisme violent et lutte anti-terroriste : un regard à partir du Burkina Faso (Paris: L'Harmattan, 2020),.
42. "Mali's Foreign Minister Accuses France of 'Espionage and Destabilising Acts' at UN," Radio France Internationale, October 19, 2022, https://www.rfi.fr/en/africa/20221019-mali-s-foreign-minister-accuses-france-of-espionage-and-destabilising-acts-at-un

where Barkhane convoys have been blocked by civilian protestors.[43] With France, and to some extent the EU, abandoning their military engagements in Mali, efforts have now shifted to Niger, and increasingly to coastal states including Benin, Togo, Guinea, and Cote d'Ivoire, where crisis spillover is a major concern.

EU efforts in West Africa and the Sahel, led by France and Germany, do not appear to be impacted by the war in Ukraine. Instead programs and forces have been shifted to neighboring countries because of Mali's growing collaboration with Russia through the Wagner Group. There were expectations that these efforts would be impacted by the COVID-19 pandemic in 2020. However, military operations, training, and peacekeeping missions continued, though were adjusted and adapted to health measures to prevent further spread of COVID-19.[44] The impact instead came in September 2021, when first reports emerged of the deployment of the Russian private military Wagner Group into Mali, which eventually led to the cutting of diplomatic ties and France withdrawing its forces from Mali, to MINUSMA's mission becoming hindered by restrictions imposed by the Malian government, and to some EU programs being suspended, with concerns over Russian interference.[45]

c. The U.S. in West Africa: A Light Footprint in Support of Allies and Partners

The U.S. has engaged for two decades in training and equipping its African partners, including West African states, to counter the rise of violent extremism and organized crime.[46] The U.S. engagements have consisted of an indirect, light-footprint military intervention, and of various non-military efforts. Since the early 2000s, the U.S. has launched multiple security initiatives

---

43 . "French Military Convoy Blocked in Burkina Faso by Protestors," Reuters, November 20, 2021, https://www.reuters.com/world/africa/french-military-convoy-blocked-burkina-faso-by-protesters-2021-11-19/ ; "At Least Two Killed, 18 Wounded as French Military Convoy Clashes with Protesters in Niger," Voice of America, November 16, 2021, https://www.voanews.com/a/french-convoy-faces-new-protests-crossing-into-niger-from-burkina-faso/6330215.html

44 . Rida Lyammouri, Nihal El Mquirmi, "Impact of Covid-19 in Central Sahel: Niger, Mali, and Burkina Faso,"Policy Brief, 20-67, Policy Center for the New South, August 2020, https://www.policycenter.ma/publications/impact-covid-19-central-sahel-niger-mali-and-burkina-faso

45 . "EU Ends Part of Mali Training Mission, Fearing Russian Interference, Borrell Says," Reuters, April 12, 2022, https://www.reuters.com/world/eu-ends-part-mali-training-mission-fearing-russian-interference-borrell-says-2022-04-11/

46 . Rida Lyammouri, "Unpacking US Foreign Policy in West Africa and the Sahel,". Policy Center for the New South, November 2022, https://www.policycenter.ma/index.php/publications/rapport-annuel-sur-la-geopolitique-de-lafrique-2022

to contain threats to the U.S. and its allies in the region, under the banner of the global war terrorism.[47] These initiatives focused on collaborating with regional partners to prevent violent extremist organizations (VEOs) and criminal networks from making parts of West Africa their safe haven. However, the results achieved by the U.S. remain unclear, as the Sahel region from 2012 to 2022 witnessed its worse decade in terms of political instability, violence, humanitarian situation, and VEO expansion. Simultaneously, the crisis is gradually making its way into the northern regions of the coastal states of Benin, Ghana, Cote d'Ivoire, and Togo.

A combination of military intervention and training missions led by the EU, France, the U.S., and UN has not brought the stability these global powers and their local partners hoped for. This was mainly a result of a disconnect between foreign powers strategies and the reality on the ground, in addition to a lack of political will and responsibility on the part of local and regional partners. The security situation in West Africa is worse than it was a decade or two decades ago. Countries in the region continue to witness regular coups d'états, while national and regional security forces have failed to halt the rise and expansion of jihadist groups. While jihadist groups initially were limited to southern Algeria and northern Mali, today they have a presence and operate in almost all West Africa. The Pentagon has expressed dissatisfaction about the objectives achieved by the U.S., despite efforts led in at least 22 African countries.[48] As a result, West African partners are growing frustrated and are not afraid to blame Western global powers, while failing to take responsibility as part of their populism campaigns to maintain domestic support when seeking new partnerships, even with Russia.[49]

d. Russia: Pushing for Business and Greater Influence Through the Wagner Group

Russia is not a newcomer in West Africa. Some states under socialist regimes, such as Mali, Burkina Faso under Thomas Sankara, Ghana under Jerry Rawlings, Benin under Mathieu Kérékou, and Guinea under Sékou

---

[47] . Stephen Burgess, "Military Intervention in Africa: French and US Approaches Compared", The Air Force Journal of European, Middle Eastern, and African Affairs, . (Spring 2019), https://www.airuniversity.af.edu/Portals/10/JEMEAA/Journals/Volume-01_Issue-1/JEMEAA_01_1_burgess.pdf

[48] . Nick Turse, "The U.S. is Losing Yet Another 'War on Terror," Rolling Stone. October 17, 2022, https://www.rollingstone.com/politics/politics-features/war-or-terror-africa-sahel-niger-pentagon-1234612083/

[49] . Author's discussions with different stakeholders during 2021 visits to West African countries, and during ongoing virtual (messenger applications) exchanges and debates.

Touré, established strong diplomatic ties and even defense accords with the Soviet Union. Some ruling parties and insurgent movements ideologically affiliated with the Soviet Union were also directly or indirectly involved in the proxy wars between the liberal and communist blocs.

In West Africa, as in the Central African Republic, Libya, and Mozambique, Russia is back through the Wagner Group, signing lucrative contracts to provide military support, equipment, and training. Through these contracts, Russia provides counter-insurgency and counter-protest services to governments, in return for mining concessions and cash payments for Wagner mercenaries (though Mali's authorities and the Kremlin deny the existence of any contract with Wagner[50]). According to a Reuters report, the deal between the Malian military junta and the Wagner Group would allow Wagner to get, in return for its military services and the deployment of about 1,000 mercenaries in Mali, access to three gold and magnesium mines, and around $10.8 million per month, along with the protection of senior government officials, the strengthening of diplomatic ties, and military cooperation with Russia.[51] Eighteen of the 28 countries that have signed contracts with Wagner are in Africa.[52] The Kremlin sees in this type of deal an opportunity to extend its influence in Africa and to advance its global prestige in response to Western powers' sanctions and attempts to isolate it after its invasion of Ukraine.[53]

For example, 15 African states, including Mali, Guinea, and Burkina Faso, chose to refrain from participating in the vote on the UN resolution demanding that *"Russia immediately cease the use of force against Ukraine"*.[54] Moreover, the contracts with African states allow Russia to sell arms. Russia is now the first arms provider to Africa, with 49% of arms sales reported on the continent, far ahead of the U.S. (14%), China (14%), and France (6%).[55]

---

50. Danielle Paquette, "Russian mercenaries have landed in West Africa, pushing Putin's goals as Kremlin is increasingly isolated," The Washington Post, March 9, 2022, https://www.washingtonpost.com/world/2022/03/09/mali-russia-wagner/
51. John Irish & David Lewis, "Exclusive Deal allowing Russian mercenaries into Mali is close—Sources," Reuters, September 13, 2021., https://www.reuters.com/world/africa/exclusive-deal-allowing-russian-mercenaries-into-mali-is-close-sources-2021-09-13/
52. Ibid.
53. Jean.-Baptiste Ronzon, "Russie/Afrique : une relation ancienne mise en lumière par l'intervention du groupe Wagner au Mali, » Fondation Jean Jaurès, February 9, 2022. https://www.jean-jaures.org/publication/russie-afrique-une-relation-ancienne-mise-en-lumiere-par-lintervention-du-groupe-wagner-au-mali/
54. Jean-Michel Bos, "En Afrique, le commerce des armes russes se porte bien," Deutsche Welle, March 25, 2022, https://www.dw.com/fr/guerre-en-ukraine-russie-livraisons-darmes-afrique-pays-africains-non-alignement-onu/a-61254723
55. Babacar Ndiaye& Pathé Dieye "The Role of Foreign Actors in the Sahel Crisis: Russia, China, and Turkey," in Sahel: 10 Years of Instability: Local, Regional and International Dynamics, https://www.ispionline.it/sites/default/files/10_years_instability_sahel_report.

Western powers, especially the U.S. and France, which see Russia as a rival and are critical of the human rights abuses by the Wagner mercenaries, argue that Russia is only concerned with making profit and increasing influence, without any regard for human rights, peace, and democracy.[56] As Milton Sands, head of Special Operations at Africa Command (AFRICOM), told *The Washington Post*, *"Wagner comes in, further destabilizes the country, ravages the mineral resources and makes as much money as they can before they choose to leave. The country is left poorer, weaker and less secure. Every time"*.[57] There is partial truth to this, since the group has established a reputation for human rights violations and exploitation of natural resources in Africa.[58] This has not changed in Mali, where Wagner has been linked to massacres of civilians and falsified graves to blame and damage French forces image, following Wagner's arrival in late 2021.[59]

In addition to the rivalry with Russia and its illegal invasion of Ukraine, this very negative perception of Wagner in the West explains why Western powers usually withdraw their cooperation from countries that partner with Wagner. But African countries find it difficult to endorse Western powers' condemnations of Russia, for Russia is a supplier not only of military services and equipment to many African countries, but also, along with Ukraine, of wheat and fertilizers to some of them. Not surprisingly, the African Union in May 2022 pleaded for a cease-fire between Russia and Ukraine, and for Russia to facilitate African imports of wheat and fertilizer from Ukraine, to avoid widespread famine in African countries that are already struggling

---

ispi_.2022_0.pdf

56 . Danielle Paquette, "Russian mercenaries have landed in West Africa, pushing Putin's goals as Kremlin is increasingly isolated," The Washington Post, March 9, 2022, https://www.washingtonpost.com/world/2022/03/09/mali-russia-wagner/; See also Intellivoire, "Des Mercenaires Russes de Wagner Détruisent le Mali, Prévient la Délégation Américaine en Afrique," Intellivoire, October 24, 2022, https://intellivoire.net/des-mercenaires-russes-de-wagner-detruisent-le-mali-previent-la-delegation-americaine-en-afrique/

57 . Paquette, "Russian mercenaries have landed in West Africa, pushing Putin's goals as Kremlin is increasingly isolated."
Seth G. Jones et al., Russia's Corporate Soldiers: The Global Expansion of Russia's Private Military Companies (Lanham: Rowman Littlefield, Chapter 06, p. 51-70, 2021). https://csis-website-prod.s3.amazonaws.com/s3fs-public/publication/210721_Jones_Russia%27s_Corporate_Soldiers.pdf?7fy3TGV3HqDtRKoe8vDq2J2GGVz7N586#page=56

58 . Center for Strategic and International Studies. Russia's Corporate Soldiers: The Global Expansion of Russia's Private Military Companies. (2021). https://csis-website-prod.s3.amazonaws.com/s3fs-public/publication/210721_Jones_Russia%27s_Corporate_Soldiers.pdf?7fy3TGV3HqDtRKoe8vDq2J2GGVz7N586#page=56

59 . Catrina Doxesee & Jared Thomson, "Massacres, Executions, and Falsified Graves: The Wagner Group's Mounting Humanitarian Cost in Mali," (Center for Strategic and International Studies, May 11, 2022). https://www.csis.org/analysis/massacres-executions-and-falsified-graves-wagner-groups-mounting-humanitarian-cost-mali#:~:text=From%20the%20time%20Wagner%20arrived,increasingly%20involved%20in%20combat%20operations.

with soaring food prices and the consequences of COVID-19. The World Food Program highlighted that the number of people suffering from hunger in West and Central Africa rose from 10.7 million in 2019 to 41 million in 2022.[60] Thus, Africa needs Russia (and Ukraine) to ensure its military and food security, as much as the EU needs Russia to ensure its energy security. This partly explains why African countries find it difficult to endorse all Western positions on Russia. Likewise, many African countries owe a lot to China, and are reluctant to go against it when it comes to voting on UN resolutions.

e. China: First Commercial Partner of Africa and Donor Without Conditionality

Along with the increase in its investments, and of the number of Chinese immigrants and workers in Africa, especially since the launch of the Belt and Road Initiative in 2013, China has increased its military presence on the continent, for example by augmenting its contributions in terms of finance and troops to UN peacekeeping missions, including MINUSMA in Mali.[61] According to one analysis, *"China's involvement in the Sahel as a security provider has been primarily driven by the need to defend its growing economic interests on the continent. Indeed, it is an apparatus deployed to defend Chinese workers, as, according to some estimates, there are more than 10,000 Chinese companies in Africa, one million Chinese immigrants and approximately 260,000 workers in the 'One Belt One Road' programme alone"*.[62] China also established its first overseas naval base in the horn of Africa a few years ago.

For instance, in Burkina Faso, China recorded a diplomatic success by isolating Taiwan and establishing an embassy in this Sahelian country where it had been absent for years. China also contributes financially, and military equipment and training, to the G5 Sahel countries.[63] Lastly, from 2000 to 2017, West African governments received a total of $18.2 billion in loans from China, according to estimates by the Organization for Economic Co-operation and Development (OECD) Sahel and West Africa Club.[64] And

---

60. "Hunger in West Africa Reaches Record High in a Decade as the Region Faces an Unprecedented Crisis Exacerbated by Russia-Ukraine Conflict." Word Food Program, April 8, 2022, https://www.wfp.org/news/hunger-west-africa-reaches-record-high-decade-region-faces-unprecedented-crisis-exacerbated
61. Ndiaye& Dieye, "The Role of Foreign Actors in the Sahel Crisis: Russia, China, and Turkey."
62. Ibid., 122.
63. Ibid.
64. "Maps & Facts: Chinese Loans to West African Governments," Sahel & West Africa Club, no. 72, September 2018, https://www.oecd.org/swac/maps/72-chinese-loans.pdf

China has provided enormous debt relief and write=offs to several African countries. Thus, one can understand why China's rivals have difficulty securing loyalty from impoverished countries that are struggling to survive and that owe so much to China. Willing to choose and diversify their partners, several African countries have been striking deals not only with Russia, but increasingly also with Turkey.

f. Turkey in Northern and West Africa: Islamic Diplomacy and Business

Turkey under President Tayyip Erdogan has deliberately increased its influence in Africa through an intensification of its diplomatic engagement, military support, and economic cooperation. A few figures illustrate this trend. Turkey's foreign direct investment in Africa skyrocketed from $100 million in 2003 to $6.5 billion in 2017, and its arms exports to Africa from $83 million in 2020 to $288 million in 2021.[65] In 2018, Turkey donated $5 million to the G5 Sahel Force to contribute to the fight against terrorism. Turkey has also been leading a diplomatic offensive for the last two decades in Africa, with the number of Turkish embassies in Africa increasing to 43, while multiplying official visits to African countries, especially the Sahel and West Africa, where Turkey has signed defense agreements with governments, built mosques and hospitals, and is reportedly seeking to establish a military base near Libya.[66]

In recent years, Togo, Niger, Mali, and Burkina Faso have all purchased drones and other military equipment from Turkey, and have signed various cooperation contracts.[67] In 2021, in Niger, Turkish companies won several contracts, including a €152 million contract to modernize Niamey airport, and a €38 million contract for the new headquarters of the new Ministry of Finance.[68]

---

65 . "Turkey's Expansion in the Sahel, the Sahara and West Africa: Motivations and Ramifications," Emirates Policy Center, 23 August,2020,https://epc.ae/en/details/featured/turkeys-expansion-in-the-sahel-the-sahara-and-west-africa-motivations-and-ramifications
66 . Ibid. See also Ndiaye & Dieye, "The Role of Foreign Actors in the Sahel Crisis: Russia, China, and Turkey."
67 . Khalid Chegraoui, Rida Lyammouri, Maha Skah, "Emerging Powers in Africa: Key Drivers, Differing Interests, and Future Perspectives," The Policy Center for The New South, November 10, 2020, https://www.policycenter.ma/sites/default/files/2021-01/Report%20-%20Emerging%20powers%20in%20Africa.pdf .; See also Nosmot Gbadamosi, "Turkey's Newest African Ally: Anakara's Arms Sales to Niger Could Make the Country the Center of Counterterrorism Efforts in the Sahel. Foreign Policy," Foreign Policy, June 8, 2022, https://foreignpolicy.com/2022/06/08/turkey-niger-arms-drone-sale-counterterrorism-sahel/; See also Ekene Lionel, "Togo Acquires Bayraktar TB2 Drone," Military Africa, August 31, 2022, https://www.military.africa/2022/08/togo-acquires-bayraktar-tb2-drone/
68 . Anne Andlauer, "Le Niger va acheter du matériel militaire à la Turquie, notamment

g. Critical Evaluation and Way Forward

Foreign powers do not intervene the same way in Africa. In West Africa and the Sahel, France has military bases and tends to favor direct military interventions where its interests are attacked or are under imminent threat, whereas the U.S. has favored indirect military intervention by providing financial, logistical, and military support to African armed forces, or to partner forces, in the fight against Al-Qaeda and ISIS-affiliated terrorist groups.[69]

Likewise, the international actors are not perceived and welcomed the same way by Africans. Western powers like France, which have a colonial legacy and are accused of neo-colonialism both by some Africans and by their Chinese and Russian rivals, have often made their cooperation with African states conditional on the latter's compliance with the demands of democracy and human rights. In contrast, Russia, China, and Turkey not only do not impose such conditionalities, but they also have no colonial history in Africa, and they talk about equal partnership with African states, which makes them more attractive in the eyes of some African dictators and/or military regimes. As Babacar Ndiaye and Pathe Dieye wrote, *"By asserting their 'soft power' and using new narratives based on a balanced and 'non-paternalistic' bilateral relationship, these new actors are more likely to be embraced by public opinion in Sahelian countries"*.[70]

Nonetheless, one should note that Turkey has been accused of contributing to the training and arming of jihadist groups in Africa.[71] Some Africans are also becoming critical of Russia's focus on mineral extraction in Africa, and of Wagner's covert operations and human rights abuses against civilians, while others doubt that Russian mercenaries can solve Africa's security challenges.[72]

---

des drones," Radio France Internationale, November 11, 2021, https://www.rfi.fr/fr/afrique/20211121-le-niger-va-acheter-du-matériel-militaire-à-la-turquie-notamment-des-drones.; See also "Mali: étape finale de la tournée africaine du président turc Erdogan," Radio France Internationale, March 3, 2021, https://www.rfi.fr/fr/afrique/20180303-mali-tournee-africaine-presiden-turc-recep-tayyip-erdogan-boubacar-keita-attaques-o

69 . Burgess, Stephen Burgess, "Military Intervention in Africa: French and US Approaches Compared."
70 . Ndiaye & Dieye, "The Role of Foreign Actors in the Sahel Crisis: Russia, China, and Turkey."
71 . "Turkey's Expansion in the Sahel, the Sahara and West Africa: Motivations and Ramifications."
72 . Peter Fabricius, "En Afrique, le groupe Wagner sert d'intermédiaire pour cibler les civils," Institut D'Etudes de Sécurité (ISS), September 16, 2022), https://issafrica.org/fr/iss-today/en-afrique-le-groupe-wagner-sert-dintermediaire-pour-cibler-les-civils

It should be noted that all these global powers, engaged in a geopolitical competition for greater influence and presence in West Africa and the rest of the continent, try to discredit each other, to win the hearts and minds of young people—most often via social media campaigns—and position themselves as the best partners for Africans.[73]

h. The Comparative Advantage of the U.S. Over Non-Western Rivals in Africa

The 2022 US national security strategy about Africa indicates a decision of the Biden Administration to emphasize cooperation in tackling shared global challenges, such as terrorism and climate change, while shifting from a strategy that is *"U.S.-led, partner-enabled"* to one that is *"partner-led, U.S.-enabled"*. The new strategy takes a positive and optimistic look at Africa, which it depicts as a *"major geopolitical force, one that will play a crucial role in solving global challenges in the coming decade"*. It sees in Africa some opportunities for U.S. business investments, but also emphasizes that the U.S. will continue to press African states to do more on promoting democracy, protecting human rights, and fighting corruption, while working with them to tackle enduring challenges, especially food security, clean energy, health security, and job creation.[74] Such a foreign policy approach towards Africa shows clearly that the U.S. is not only concerned about its interests and geopolitical positioning in Africa, but also cares for the wellbeing of the African people. It will not necessarily please dictators who would prefer China, Russia, and Turkey, which help them crush insurgencies and do not require from them any effort to comply with the demands of democracy, human rights, and transparent management of public finances. If enough resources are committed to the implementation of the U.S. strategy, it will greatly benefit both the American and African peoples, and will further strengthen the positive image that most Africans have of the U.S.

---

73 . Adama Ndiaye, "Nous ne pouvons pas continuellement être les pions des autres," Seneplus, October 10, 2022, https://www.seneplus.com/politique/nous-ne-pouvons-pas-continuellement-etre-les-pions-des-autres
74 The White House, "National Security Strategy."

3. Conclusion

A new scramble for Africa has generated a competition between major global players on the continent, including in North and West Africa. Beyond commercial interests—Africa as a whole represents barely 2% of international trade—traditional Western partners such as the U.S. now have to compete with new actors, such as Russia, which seek to increase their influence and military presence, and strengthen diplomatic ties especially through murky security cooperation. Western countries also have to engage with China, which has become Africa's first commercial partner with its so-called 'debt-trap' and its opaque mining and infrastructure deals with an African elite prone to capture.

In the Sahel region, France's failure to impose the security conditions it promised has opened new opportunities for Russia, which appears to be working methodically in uprooting French historical influence in the region. Even though France and the U.S. remain key partners of most West African countries, they face growing competition from Russia, China, and Turkey. Growing popular dissatisfaction with the perceived underperformance of French forces in the fight against terrorism has led many citizens and political leaders to call for a diversification of partnerships, which often means turning to Russia for protection.

The timing of the war in Ukraine came at a critical time for Africa in general, and West Africa in particular. The region had just started to recover from the COVID-19 pandemic, while seeing unprecedented levels of violence, a dire humanitarian crisis, the multiple *coup d'états* in Mali and Burkina Faso, and all-time low diplomatic ties with the EU and France caused by Russia's interference. People in some African countries might see Russia and the Wagner Group as a solution to defeat al-Qaeda and Islamic State affiliated groups and other security issues. However, soon they will realize Russia has no interest in humanitarian, development, and economic struggles. This will become even more challenging for Russia after the Ukraine war, even if the length and outcome of the war remain unclear. Instead, Russia will remain, through the Wagner Group, at least in the short-term a distraction from Western global powers' efforts in Africa. The U.S. and the EU are unlikely to ignore this distraction, but the focus should be rather on Africa, not what global rivals such as Russia and China are doing in Africa.

CHAPTER VIII

African Debt Management in a Time of Pandemic and War

Abdelaaziz Aït Ali & Badr Mandri

The Russian-Ukrainian conflict has placed additional stress on developing economies and adds to the previous economic shock affecting the global economy, including Africa. On one hand, the COVID-19 pandemic has fostered national demands for stronger welfare states and has spurred a rising consciousness among citizens of the role the state should play to provide decent and resilient livelihoods. On the other hand, resources are not particularly abundant or affordable, and financial distress is back as several developing—and even developed—countries experience difficult times. A new debt wave has been building and is heading towards African economies. It could have detrimental effects on the future of every African nation. While the international community should take decisive action to alleviate the potential consequences of such a shock, the bulk of the burden rests on African domestic authorities. They should break with previous paradigms and work on a new approach to making economic policy management.

1. African countries are now more exposed to a debt crisis

Debt and Africa have a long and painful history. It started in the 1980s when the public finance situation in most developing countries deteriorated following the two oil shocks, which necessitated the implementation of structural adjustment plans under the aegis of the International Monetary Fund and the World Bank. Several African countries experienced two decades of austerity, and the issue at stake were the debt relief initiatives, Heavily Indebted Poor Countries (HIPC) and Multilateral Debt Relief Initiative (MDRI), in 2005. As a result of those two initiatives, the average debt-to-GDP ratio in Africa fell from over 65.9% in 2000 to 32.6% in 2010 (Figure 1). In the sub-Saharan region, the IMF estimated a reduction in the debt stock of nearly $100 billion during this period.[1] This was breathing space that allowed African countries to maintain their current and future debt levels and promote development spending in the region.

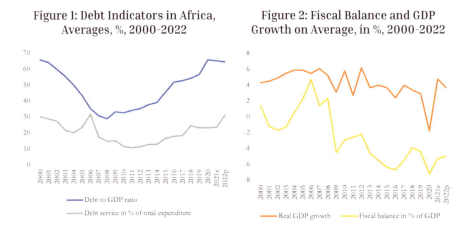

Figure 1: Debt Indicators in Africa, Averages, %, 2000-2022

Figure 2: Fiscal Balance and GDP Growth on Average, in %, 2000-2022

Source: World Economic Outlook (IMF), and AFDB Socio Economic Database (African Development Bank).

In this context, and given their greater fiscal space, African countries have allowed themselves a certain amount of fiscal laxity, which has favored the re-accumulation of debt since 2011. This was also underpinned by more widespread access to international financial markets with affordable

---

[1] . International Monetary Fund, Heavily Indebted Poor Countries (HIPC) Initiative and Multilateral Debt Relief Initiative (MDRI)—Statistical Update, (2019).

interest rates. However, this accumulation was more considerable after 2013 and the commodity price shock. Typically, such situations cause exchange rate volatility and subsidy inflation, which in turn have deteriorated the macroeconomic conditions of African countries in different ways. In fact, between 2012 and 2017, average real GDP growth in Africa fell from 6.2% to 4%, while the average fiscal deficit widened from 2.1% of GDP to 5.5% (Figure 2). As a result, more than two-thirds of countries in the sub-Saharan region saw their public debts as a share of GDP increase by more than 10 percentage points, while one-third of countries experienced an increase in the debt-to-GDP ratio of more than 20 percentage points.[2]

These higher debt levels across Africa have begun to raise fears of a return to unsustainable debt levels, particularly considering the limited capacity of countries to generate the fiscal resources needed to keep pace with rapid debt evolution. The IMF in its April 2019 *Regional Economic Outlook* report sounded the alarm by stating that the debt levels of some African countries are approaching pre-HIPC ratios, and that signs of debt distress are especially strong on the continent. In 2019, seven African countries were debt distressed and another nine were considered at high risk of debt distress, figures that had doubled since 2014.[3] The health crisis of 2020, which caused great damage to the public finances of the continent's countries, has made the situation worse. The African Development Bank estimates that pandemic-related expenditures had increased the debt-to-GDP ratio by an average of 10 percentage points by the end of 2020.[4] Average debt in Africa is now estimated at 65% of GDP. However, this level is still far from that recorded in other regions of the world at the end of 2020. So why all the concern? The answer to this question refers to the African debt profile and not to debt levels.

The international community is concerned about the debt situation because of the change in the debt structure, which makes fragile countries even more exposed to the risks of a possible debt crisis. In fact, Africa does not have to deal with the same creditors as before. At the turn of the century, most of Africa's public debt was owed to multilateral institutions and some bilateral creditors of the Paris Club. As explained earlier, as a result of debt-relief initiatives, these countries had been able to rebuild their debt capacity, which has given them better access to market-based

---

[2] . The World Bank, Africa's Pulse: An analysis of issues shaping Africa's economic future, no. 17, (April 2018).
[3] . International Monetary Fund, Sub-Saharan Africa Regional Economic Outlook: Recovery Amid Elevated Uncertainty, (April 2019).
[4] . African Development Bank, African Economic Outlook, (2018).

debt instruments. Hence, after the global financial crisis of 2008, some 15 African countries entered the Eurobond market, taking advantage of the prolonged period of low interest rates that followed, and the strong demand from private investors. Private investors, seeking alternative low rates from developed countries, were attracted by the yield prospects offered by African sovereign bonds. This interest in commercial debt increased the share of private creditors from 20% in 2010 to more than 40% in 2020.[5]

Along with the increase in private creditors in Africa, the profile of bilateral creditors has also changed. The share of debt held by traditional Paris Club members declined by 8% between 2010 and 2017, while China has strengthened its position as the largest lender to Africa.[6] According to data from the China-Africa Research Initiative (CARI), China loaned about $160 billion to African countries between 2000 and 2020. This lending has accelerated since 2010, from an average of $2.5 billion between 2000 and 2009 to about $12.3 billion per year over the past decade. In 2018, it was estimated that 20% of the total external debt of the sub-Saharan region is owed to China.[7]

This change in the creditor map, according to the international financial institutions, could jeopardize the debt sustainability of some African countries, as they will be more exposed to the risks of exchange-rate volatility and rising interest rates on international financial markets. In addition, the multitude of private creditors and the presence of China make debt restructuring negotiations difficult. These types of obstacles prevailed notably when the G20 launched its Debt Service Suspension Initiative (DSSI). This mechanism, set up in May 2020 as an emergency measure to deal with the COVID-19 crisis, has not been as successful as hoped, mainly because of the difficulty of getting all the stakeholders to the same negotiating table.

---

5 . Badr Mandri & Lotfi El jai, Debt Sustainability and Development Financing in Sub-Saharan Africa: Recent Dynamics, Policy Brief 19-28, Policy Center fot the new South, 2019, https://www.policycenter.ma/publications/debt-sustainability-and-development-financing-sub-saharan-africa-recent-dynamics?page=108
6 . World Bank, Africa's Pulse : An Analysis of Issues Shaping Africa's Economic Future, No. 19, (April 2019)
7 . Jubilee Debt Campaign, Africa's growing debt crisis: Who is the debt owed to?, (October, 2018).

2. The war in Ukraine puts African countries' debt sustainability at further risk

The war in Ukraine comes at a time when African countries are still struggling to recover from the impact of the global COVID-19 pandemic, which caused a deep economic decline and huge macroeconomic imbalances. The debt problem is now much more serious for several reasons. The war has caused disruptions in the commodity market and, as a result, unprecedented widespread inflation. These factors have direct and indirect effects on public finances and the debt situation in African countries.

The Ukrainian crisis has accelerated already-rising inflation in Africa. Higher international commodity prices (mainly food and fuel) are the main factors behind accelerating overall inflation. Food and fuel account for more than one-third of the consumer price index in most African countries. In 2022, the average inflation rate in the continent is expected to reach 16%, up from 9.1% in 2019, a level not seen since 1996.

Beyond the social consequences that this inflationary spiral could cause, public finances are expected to take a hit through subsidy spending on energy and food, especially for in countries that are not rich in natural resources. Commodity exporting countries are expected to see the increase in fiscal revenues from commodity prices offset the remarkable increase in subsidy spending, and the impact on the overall fiscal balance will be limited. However, for other African countries, the impact is expected to be significant, and consequently public debt will increase. This is, in fact, the first direct effect of the war on the fiscal situation of African states.

The second channel through which the fiscal situation of African countries is expected to be impacted is interest rates. The inflationary context has led advanced countries to tighten their monetary policies by raising their policy rates. This is bad news for African countries. They have benefited from favorable financing conditions during the last decades by resorting increasingly to international financial markets, and will now see their risk premiums increase, and consequently widening of sovereign spreads. This issue is all the more significant because of the need to borrow to support economic recovery, and, most importantly to roll-over debts that will mature in the coming years (Table 1).

Table 1: African Sovereigns, Principal Debt Maturities by Year

	2022	2023	2024	2025	2026	2027	2028	2029	2030	2031	2032
Egypt		1.8	3.3	3.1	2.7	3.1	2.6	1.8	2.8	2.9	2.8
South Africa	1.0	1.0	1.5	2.0	1.8	1.0	2.0	2.0	1.4		1.4
Nigeria	0.3	0.3		1.1		1.5	1.3	1.3	1.3	1.0	1.5
Ghana					1.0	2.0		2.0	1.0		1.3
Morocco	1.5	1.5	1.1		0.6	0.8			0.6	1.1	1.0
Angola				0.9			1.8	1.8			1.8
Cote d'Ivoire			0.1	0.3			0.8		1.0	1.0	2.4
Kenya			2.0			0.9	1.0				1.2
Tunisia			1.0	1.0	0.8	0.2					
Zambia	0.8	0.8	1.0			1.3					
Gabon			0.1	0.7						1.8	
Senegal			0.2								
Ethiopia			1.0								
Benin						0.2					0.8
Cameroon				0.2							0.8
Mozambique									0.9		
Namibia				0.8							
Rwanda										0.6	
Rep. of the Congo							0.2				

■ Less than $1 billion   ■ $1 billion-$2 billion   ■ More than $2 billion

Source: Moody's (June 2022).[8]

These disruptions in financial markets are not limited to higher interest rates, but also intensify uncertainty and increase risk aversion. This situation favors capital flight, as with more profitable U.S. and European sovereigns, investors tend to lean towards these safer assets than those in Africa. This would lead to currency depreciation and higher debt service costs.

3. What is the international community offering Africa to avoid another debt crisis?

Since the COVID-19 outbreak, multilateral institutions and bilateral lenders have announced support for economies in deep financial distress and have directed all the necessary means to fight the pandemic. Indeed, the IMF's director stated in the Russian annual Gaidar economic forum, "*starting in March, I would go out and I would say: 'please spend'. Spend as much as*

---

[8] . Moody's Investors Service, Rollover risk increases amid tighter financial conditions and upcoming maturity wall, (June 28, 2022).

you can and then spend a little bit more".[9] The declaration marked a new paradigm in the international financial institution's position when dealing with economic shocks. The scale of the unprecedented COVID-19 shock, and the uncertainties surrounding its duration and implications, explains this—temporary—shift towards unorthodox economic policy.

The international institutions' responses have including providing funding options to most vulnerable countries, providing debt-relief programs to free-up resources to meet the exceptional health and social expenditures, and granting policy advice and assistance programs.

On the funding side, the Bretton Woods institutions extended financial resources to the most vulnerable countries to mitigate the crisis, either on the macro-side, notably the balance of payments crisis, or the social side. For instance, the IMF deployed various financial assistance programs, such as the Rapid Credit Facility and the Rapid Financing Instrument. As mentioned by the Fund, these programs are more flexible in terms of implementation and responding to several financial issues facing developing countries, unlike the classical fully-fledged IMF programs. African countries have been among the main beneficiaries of the financial assistance programs. Africa accounts for 50% of country beneficiaries globally. Of the $170 billion made available by the fund, Africa received 15.2% of the total (Table 2).

The beneficiaries are diverse and comprise low and middle-income, and resource and non-resource intensive countries. The smallest economies were the keenest to ask for the assistance and the financial mobilization was significant. Seychelles, one of Africa's hard-hit economies of the continent, requested over 11% of GDP, while the fiscal deficit hovered around 17% of GDP. Sudan also mobilized over 9% of GDP, in a difficult economic situation because of the COVID-19 shock and because of structural issues. It's worth mentioning that the continent's largest economies, including Nigeria, South Africa, and Egypt, have solicited from programs amounts ranging from 0.8% to 2.2% of GDP.

On October 5, 2022, the IMF raised by 50% the cap for the funding it provides under the emergency liquidity program. This 'Food Shock Window' has been designed specially to mitigate the implications of the mounting inflation pressures, hitting mainly food, energy, and fertilizers, and hurting the most vulnerable countries. The other Bretton Woods institution mobilized $98.8 billion for the public to weather the COVID-19 impacts.

---

[9]. Reuters, 'Spend as much as you can,' IMF head urges governments worldwide," January 15, 2021, https://www.reuters.com/article/us-russia-imf-idUSKBN29K1XJ

Over one third of this historic amount goes to sub-Saharan Africa, and $6.2 billion to MENA region. The program is more oriented to alleviate the social impact of COVID-19, by "*saving lives, protecting the poor and vulnerable, supporting business growth and job creation, and rebuilding in better ways*", as stated by the institution. In response to the current context, the World Bank has extended a new funding line of $170 billion to support countries in their fight against the compounded crisis environment. In the same vein, the African Development Bank (AfDB) deployed around $10 billion as a Rapid Response Facility. The program was launched in the early phases of the pandemic and entails loans to the public and private sector.[10]

Table 2: IMF COVID-19 Financial Assistance and Debt Service Relief

African Countries	Financial assistance in % of 2020 GDP	debt relief in % of 2020 GDP	2020 fiscal balance in % of GDP
Angola	1.4	-	-1.9
Benin	1.8	0.2	-4.7
Burkina Faso	0.6	0.3	-5.7
Burundi	2.7	0.9	-6.6
Cabo Verde	1.9	-	-9.1
Cameroon	2.6	-	-3.2
Central African Republic	1.6	0.8	-3.4
Chad	7.0	0.1	2.1
Comoros	1.0	0.4	-0.5
Congo, Dem. Rep.	3.9	0.1	-1.4
Côte d'Ivoire	1.4	-	-5.6
Djibouti	1.4	0.3	-1.6
Egypt	2.2	-	-7.8
Equatorial Guinea	0.7	-	-1.7
Eswatini	2.8	-	-5.4
Ethiopia	0.4	0.02	-2.8
Gabon	5.6	-	-2.2
Gambia, The	5.3	0.6	-2.2
Ghana	1.4	-	-15.6
nGuinea	1.0	0.7	-2.9

---

10 . For a global and regional overview for funding mechanism, refer to "UN, Funding mechanisms for COVID-19 response, 2020."

Guinea-Bissau	1.4	0.4	-10.0
Kenya	3.1	-	-8.1
Lesotho	2.2	-	0.3
Liberia	1.6	-	-3.8
Madagascar	4.9	0.2	-4.0
Malawi	1.6	0.4	-8.2
Mali	1.1	0.2	-5.4
Mauritania	2.0	-	2.9
Mozambique	2.2	0.4	-5.1
Namibia	2.6	-	-8.2
Niger	2.8	0.3	-5.3
Nigeria	0.8	-	-5.7
Rwanda	2.2	0.7	-9.4
Sao Tome and Principe	3.0	0.2	5.9
Senegal	4.5	-	-6.4
Seychelles	11.4	-	-17.4
Sierra Leone	4.8	2.0	-5.8
Somalia	5.7	-	0.4
South Africa	1.3	-	-9.7
South Sudan	-	-	6.7
Sudan	9.2	-	-5.9
Tanzania	1.5	0.04	-2.5
Togo	1.3	0.1	-6.9
Tunisia	1.8	-	-9.1
Uganda	4.0	-	-7.5

Source: IMF COVID-19 Financial Assistance and Debt Service Relief Tracker, accessed October 20, 2022, and author's calculations.

One of the most prominent actions has been the $650 billion Special Drawings Rights (SDR)[11] allocation. SDR allocations are distributed in proportion to countries' participation in the IMF capital, which in turn reflects the size of their economies. Africa's share is around 4.5%, which is still above the contribution of Africa to global wealth creation. According to the IMF, the largest SDR allocation in the history of the IMF in a time of unprecedented crisis, was to provide additional liquidity to the global

---

11 . The SDRs is an international reserve asset created by the IMF to supplement the official reserves of its member countries, although it is not a currency. SDR are a potential claim on the freely usable currencies of IMF members. As such, SDRs can provide a country with liquidity.

economy, especially for highly distressed economies. For Africa, it represents up to 4.5% of external debt, and it may cover up to 10% of country-level GDP, as is the case of Liberia. Indeed, for 21 countries, the share covers above 2% of GDP, and the spending of this resource is defined by local authorities, which offers freedom to better channel the resources according to domestic priorities.

Table 3: SDR allocation for African economies in % of GDP.

African Countries	Share of GDP in %
Liberia	10.4
Burundi	6.8
Zambia	6.6
Sierra Leone	6.2
Central African Republic	5.9
Zimbabwe	4.8
Gambia, The	4.2
Sao Tome and Principe	3.8
Lesotho	3.8
Libya	3.7
Somalia	2.9
Sudan	2.9
Congo, Dem. Rep.	2.7
Guinea-Bissau	2.4
Eswatini	2.4
Togo	2.4
Seychelles	2.3
Madagascar	2.3
Namibia	2.2
Mauritania	2.0
Mozambique	2.0
Rwanda	1.9
Congo, Rep.	1.9
Guinea	1.8
Comoros	1.8
Gabon	1.7
Cabo Verde	1.7
Algeria	1.7
Senegal	1.6

Botswana	1.6
Chad	1.6
Mauritius	1.6
Tunisia	1.6
Malawi	1.4
Mali	1.3
Cote d'Ivoire	1.3
Ghana	1.3
Djibouti	1.2
Uganda	1.2
Niger	1.2
South Africa	1.1
Benin	1.0
Morocco	1.0
Cameroon	0.8
Burkina Faso	0.8
Tanzania	0.8
Nigeria	0.7
Egypt, Arab Rep.	0.7
Kenya	0.7
Ethiopia	0.3
Total	$29.2 Billion

Source: IMF 2021 SDR allocations Finance Department, accessed October 20, 2022, and author's calculations.

Debt relief programs were also set on track to alleviate the debt burden. The IMF made accessible to developing economies the Catastrophe Containment and Relief Trust. Since March 2020, the program has been adapted to grant immediate debt service relief to its most vulnerable and poorest members hit by natural catastrophes, including public-health disasters. Becoming eligible for the program is not straightforward, and countries should have access initially to *"concessional borrowing through the Poverty Reduction and Growth Trust (PRGT)"*, if they have GDP per capita below the International Development Association's (IDA) threshold, or are small states with fewer than 1.5 million people, but are above the IDA's cutoff.[12] The program covers only debt owed to the IMF, and thus its

---
12 . These programs are dedicated to poor countries. Thus, eligibility for IDA support depends first and foremost on a country's relative poverty, defined as gross National Income (GNI) per capita below an established threshold and updated annually ($1,255 in the fiscal year 2023).

impact doesn't seem to be decisive for most African countries, though it would be for Sierra Leone for instance, where the program freed up 2% of GDP. Other African countries that opted for this window mobilized in the best-case scenario less than 1% of GDP (table 2). Nevertheless, Africa stands at the top of the beneficiaries from this program.

At the top of the debt relief programs comes the Debt Service Suspension Initiative (DSSI), convening multilateral and some bilateral lenders. In May 2020, the G20 opened a temporary window for low-income[13] countries to pause debt repayment for Paris Club members and non-members. The program provided a relief package of $13 billion. Africa accounted most of the countries that participated in the program. By the end of 2020, $2.5 billion in debt repayment had been postponed, representing for Somalia around 14.3% of GDP. For the rest of eligible African countries, the suspension freed an average of 0.2% of GDP in 2020 (Figure 3), which was not a significant amount for a continent in deep need of financial resources to fight COVID-19 and support the recovery. Indeed, six out of the 38 eligible countries did request to participate in this program, by February 2022. It is feared that participation in this program could lead to increases in borrowing costs, as participation signals that countries face issues in fulfilling their commitments. The window closed at the end of 2021, as Africans and developing economies navigated through new challenges, including rising inflation, tightening financial conditions, and weak global economic growth.

---

13 . The World Bank annually classifies economies following their GNI into several classes. For the current 2023 fiscal year, low-income economies are defined as those with a GNI per capita, of $1,085 or less in 2021.

Figure 3: DSSI Savings Per African Country, in % of GDP

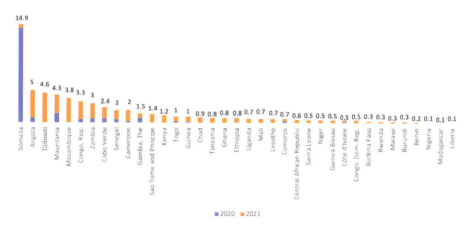

Source: *World Bank Debt Service Suspension Initiative Brief; estimates are current as of February 28, 2022.*

Beyond this program, the G20 established a debt-treatment mechanism to address the insolvency wave likely to hit developing economies. Participation in this program enables the IMF and MDBs to extend their provision of financial support. The debtor country willing to restructure its debt should trigger the process, and the restructuring will be founded on IMF-WBG Debt Sustainability Analyses (DSA). The process requires, on one side, strong coordination among creditors, and on the other side, full commitment by the debtor country to provide information on debt to Bretton Woods institutions and creditors participating in the program. Broadly, the mechanism has not reached its objectives, for various reasons addressed below.

4. How can the international community improve the mechanism of debt relief restructuring?

It is difficult to assess at this stage the response of the international community to the overlapping nature of the shocks affecting the global economy, including Africa. However, the Bretton Woods and multilateral institutions such as the G20 have reacted swiftly to the ongoing situation to avert a social and economic disaster. They have mobilized unprecedented financial assistance under flexible terms. The SDR allocation couldn't have come at better time, granting around $29 billion to Africa, and strengthening the foreign reserves of the continent. The DSSI was meant to free up resources to let African countries fight back against the pandemic, instead of worrying about debt repayment at a critical moment. The new common framework for debt restructuring aspires to create a viable and an inclusive platform to countries in debt distress. But these programs have limits. Some have argued that they might require re-engineering to better fit the current circumstances and the challenges facing the developing world and the African continent.

a. Striking the Balance in Loan Conditionality

The terms of the loans provided by the Bretton Woods institutions did not go unnoticed. The IMF has been criticized for its massive use of conditionality throughout its history.[14] Since the financial crisis hit emerging countries in the 1990s, the IMF has imposed more stringent conditions on its loans and has required implementation of reforms that go far beyond the ambit of the IMF. The World Bank does not escape these criticisms, as *"conditions have increased both in number and in the degree of intervention in the internal affairs of member countries"*.[15] As COVID-19 struck the global economy, and countries were left on their own, the IMF and the World Bank launched their rapid funding programs, with the common aim of flexibility and less conditionality. Once an economy is eligible, it could benefit from financial support at an affordable cost. At the top of these initiative comes the new SDR allocation, which creates no debt for the recipient countries. It therefore marks a shift in the relationship between developing economies and multilateral international institutions. The advocates for a more symmetrical relationship between the IMF, in this case, and developing countries have criticized this movement,[16] even qualifying the IMF as a new 'aid agency' and calling for it to stick to its core mandate. The challenge is to strike the balance between conditionality and flexibility in the programs. For African countries, unfortunately, quality of governance still poses several issues for the growth model; unless African countries can fight corruption and put in place accountable institutions, a situation of 'no conditionality' is a double-edged sword. It could provide more room for

---

14 . Andreas F. Lowenfeld, "The International Monetary System and the Erosion of Sovereignty: Essay in Honor of Cynthia Lichtenstein," Boston College International and Comparative. Law Review 25, no. 2 (2002), http://lawdigitalcommons.bc.edu/iclr/vol25/iss2/6.
15 . Carlos Santiso, "Good Governance and Aid Effectiveness: The World Bank and Conditionality," The Georgetown Public Policy Review 7, no. 1 (2021), https://www.researchgate.net/publication/228959367.
16 . Kenneth Rogoff, "Why Is the IMF Trying to Be an Aid Agency?," Project Syndicate, January 3, 2022, https://www.project-syndicate.org/commentary/imf-acting-like-aid-agency-risks-embarrassment-by-kenneth-rogoff-2022-01?barrier=accesspaylog.

economic policy design domestically, but it could also leave countries to slide into precarious situations if the appropriate decisions are not taken.

b. Debt Relief and Restructuring Programs Should be Redesigned to Better Account for the Changing Nature of Bilateral Creditors

The main loan providers across the world to developing economies have changed dramatically in the last decades. Low and middle-income economies owe most of their debt to commercial creditors, accounting for 83% of the total.[17] This shift brings the challenge of coming up with an inclusive platform for debt treatment. The DSSI couldn't mobilize private lenders, with only one lender willing to participate in the program. The debt moratorium benefited mostly private lenders, as debt repayment still flowed to them, and not to bilateral and multilateral lenders under the umbrella of the G20. As shown earlier, this initiative did not provide adequate relief to African countries, with an average saving for 2020 of 0.2% of GDP.

In addition, developing countries, including in Africa, have contracted an increasing share of variable rate loans, reaching 31% by the end of 2020, compared to 15% in the 1990s. This fact means African economies face tightening financial conditions seen at global scale. The dramatic surge in interest rates will burden their public finances.

On the debt restructuring side, the contribution of the private sector is still missing to complete the picture. Furthermore, the enthusiasm of countries in debt distress to the Common Framework for Debt Restructuring is losing momentum for several reasons. Only three African countries—Chad, Zambia, and Ethiopia—have requested a restructuring process under this mechanism. The IMF and the World Bank—institutions in charge of the follow up—are urging improvements. The process suffers from slow treatment, compromising its usefulness and sending the wrong signals to countries that might be willing to enter the program. An important signal is also sent to the market for countries requiring the assistance. Their access to financial markets and private funds has been undermined by the 'debt restructuring' step, meaning the country will face extreme barriers to fund its needs, and the private sector will doubt its capacity to meet its commitments. Indeed, downgrade fears have likely deterred countries from

---

17 . Marcello Estevão, "Are we ready for the coming spate of debt crises?," World Bank Blogs, The World Bank, March 28, 2022, https://blogs.worldbank.org/voices/are-we-ready-coming-spate-debt-crises.

seeking such mechanisms, and have therefore cast doubt over the scope of the program.[18] For example, Moody's downgraded Ethiopia in May 2022. According to the agency *"The passage of time since Ethiopia's application to the Common Framework for Debt Treatment suggests a relatively complex decision by the Common Framework's creditor committee, which in turn indicates that an outcome that does not impose any losses on private sector creditors is less likely"*.[19] Historically, the private sector has always been reluctant to participate, because of low financial returns and the absence of a unified private creditor committee.[20]

c. **African Countries Should be More Transparent About Their Liabilities to Foster the Involvement of All Stakeholders; Although Criticisms are Well-founded, They Should Not be Instrumentalized to Hamper the Access of Africans to Alternative Funding, Notably Chinese**

Developing economies, especially African economies, have also been criticized. Greater transparency to creditors should frame the relations between debtors and creditors, and enhance coordination between private lenders. According to the World Bank, almost 40% of low-income economies do not publish their debt data and, when they do, data lacks exhaustive coverage. It is not easy to cover all the dimensions of debt, ranging from local government to state-owned enterprises, and borrowers and lenders—in some cases—may not see the advantages of full transparency. Greater debt transparency has benefits. Studies argue that debt transparency contributes to lower borrowing costs and improved credit ratings.[21] Transparency also makes local government more accountable, and enables citizen, civil society, and researchers to actively monitor fiscal policy, and to contribute to the sound design and implementation of economic policy in general.

---

18 . Karin Strohecker, "Downgrade fears will deter countries from joining G20 debt relief framework -World Bank," Reuters, February 23, 2021, https://www.reuters.com/world/asia-pacific/downgrade-fears-will-deter-countries-joining-g20-debt-relief-framework-world-2021-02-23/.

19 . Moody's Rating Agency, "Moody's downgrades Ethiopia's rating to Caa2; outlook negative," October 20, 2021, https://www.african-markets.com/en/news/east-africa/ethiopia/moody-s-downgrades-ethiopia-s-rating-to-caa2-outlook-negative.

20 . Kathrin Berensmann, et al, Resolving Debt Crises In Developing Countries: How Can The G20 Contribute To Operationalising The Common Framework?, Policy Brief, G20 Insights, August 30, 2022, https://www.g20-insights.org/policy_briefs/resolving-debt-crises-in-developing-countries-how-can-the-g20-contribute-to-operationalising-the-common-framework/

21 . World Bank, "Why One African Country Opted for Full Disclosure on Debt," July 10, 2022. https://www.worldbank.org/en/news/feature/2022/07/10/why-one-african-country-opted-for-full-disclosure-on-debt.

Africa is one of the regions where debt transparency is weak.[22] However, one African country stands out for its debt transparency strategy. The World Bank has praised Burkina Faso for converging on debt transparency standards by meeting the 'full disclosure' criteria.[23]

The call for greater transparency could be interpreted as targeting Chinese involvement in Africa, which is surrounded with opacity. U.S. and Western officials have claimed in some cases that China seeks, through loans to African countries, to gain political leverage and gain control of key assets and commodities, when the states default.[24] Some argues that the propaganda around the Chinese debt trap diplomacy started to spread in 2017.

Although loan agreements between African countries with China should be disclosed, China has brought a new economic model and considerable financial resources to Africa. Since 2010, China has become the largest lender to the continent, exceeding western powers. While the main providers of financial assistance have either shifted their interest or maintained their funding stable, China has fostered its development assistance to the continent. In 2016, the amount of Chinese loans to the continent exceeded the combined total of U.S., United Kingdom, French, and German funding.[25]

More recently, the European Union has reinvigorated its economic partnership with Africa. The EU Global Gateway is bringing extra financial resources to the continent, tackling the green and digital transitions, decent job creation, and human capital (health systems and education). The program has mobilized around $150 billion. The program was framed, according to some analysts, as a competitor to China's Belt and Road Initiative in Africa. It's worth considering deeply the positive implications of such a program, and its implications for Africa, but China has been a committed partner for the continent and has delivered in the past decades. With the war in Europe and the attention it has drawn, Europe could be mostly focusing on resolving domestic issues.[26] The bottom line is that Africa was and is

---

22 . H. Morsy, Debt Transparency, Accountability and Reporting in Africa, AfDB, (2020).
23 . World Bank, "Why One African Country Opted for Full Disclosure on Debt."
24 . Alex Vines, "Climbing out of the Chinese debt trap," Chatham House, August 3, 2022, https://www.chathamhouse.org/publications/the-world-today/2022-08/climbing-out-chinese-debt-trap.
25 . Zainab Usman, "What Do We Know About Chinese Lending in Africa?," Carnegie Endowment for International Peace, 02 June, 2021, https://carnegieendowment.org/2021/06/02/what-do-we-know-about-chinese-lending-in-africa-pub-84648
26 . Chloé Farand, "As EU seeks to rival China's infrastructure offer, Africans are sceptical," Euractiv, December 20, 2021, https://www.euractiv.com/section/energy-environment/news/as-eu-seeks-to-rival-chinas-infrastructure-offer-africans-are-sceptical/.

still demanding significant financial resources to fund its growth model and close its infrastructure gap, and China is a global power that could bring resources, technology, and new options to Africa as it moves up the development ladder. Africans should seize the huge opportunity of global powers seeking consolidate their footprints in Africa and turn it into a lever to foster their economic transformation.

5. No Matter What the International Community Does, Africa Still Needs to Rely on Africa to Address Debt Issues

Critics of the international community and the mechanisms deployed to prevent a new systemic debt crisis in developing countries, including those in Africa, might sound as if they are seeking to divert blame from Africans. Debt distress is still a result of mismanagement of financial resources at the domestic level. Some countries have been engaged in debt accumulation, expecting it would feed the economic system and lead eventually to unleashing of the growth potential of the country. Africa is urged to mark a new paradigm in its governance model and, in this case, its economic policy design.

Meanwhile, Africa should foster its ties with commercial lenders, bilateral funders, and the multilateral institutions, in order to tap into foreign savings, which will always be an option to complement domestic resources. Indeed, the recurrence of debt waves in Africa should not lead us to definitively exclude the option of external financing and debt accumulation. Debt is not per se the issue, but how borrowed money it spent.

We argue that the newly announced African Mechanism for Financial Stability can facilitate the coordination with the G20 to accelerate the implementation of the Common framework for Debt Restructuring, while supporting better macroeconomic management. It goes without saying that sound macroeconomic policies can contribute better to averting debt problems. Addressing sovereign debt problems can only happen with structural reforms. The development of deep domestic capital markets is the bedrock for the mobilization of dormant domestic savings and can reduce the 'addiction' to foreign funding. Broadening tax bases and reassessing the effectiveness of public expenditures in Africa is a must for the continent. The African diaspora can also contribute to the mobilization of financial resources in foreign currencies, while setting a mechanism to pay back in local currency.

a. **The Starting Point for African Countries is to Conduct a Sound Macroeconomic Policy with Proper Use of Capital Flow Management to Limit Side Effects.**

Fiscal and monetary policies should play their roles fully in mitigating the implications of the global financial cycle, the fluctuation of commodity prices, and the domestic shocks affecting the African economy. For resource-intensive economies, managing the flow of related export revenues will enable them to shield their growth from commodity prices volatility. Although those classic recommendations have been documented, this challenge remains on top of the agenda for the continent. On the monetary policy side, central-bank independence will allow the institution to set its objective and prevent any intervention in its mandate that could lead eventually to the undermining of its fiscal policy orientation. The World Bank assessment of macroeconomic management in Africa comes with no surprises, pointing out low performance in the region compared to the rest of the world (Figure 4). The macroeconomic management toolkit includes also macroprudential policies. They can indeed insulate the economy, or at least attenuate the disruptive consequences of capital flow volatility on the financial stability of the country. The IMF has updated its view on the utilization of capital controls to better manage the situation.[27] This shift has been justified by the external debt build-up and the risk it entails for economic stability.

---

27 . Tobias Adrian, et al. "Why the IMF is Updating its View on Capital Flow," IMF Blog, International Monetary Fund, March 30, 2022, https://www.imf.org/en/Blogs/Articles/2022/03/30/blog033122-why-the-imf-is-updating-its-view-on-capital-flows.

Figure 4: Performance of Macroeconomic Management for International Development Association (IDA)-Eligible Countries in 2020*

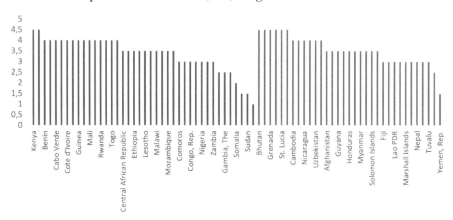

Source: World Bank Country Policy and Institutional Assessment (CPIA).
* rating (1=low to 6=high), african countries in green.

b. The African Financial Stability Mechanism (AFSM) Governed by the African Development Bank (AfDB) Could be an Anchor for Better Macroeconomic Management and a Bridge Between Countries in Distress and the Common Framework

In March 2021, the president of the AfDB announced the institution's intention to create an African Financial Stability Mechanism. The mechanism's objectives are broad and ambitious. The pan-African platform aims to support countries in their cyclical macroeconomic management, funding countries in deep stress to prevent defaults, providing a platform to restructure debt, and mitigating further complications and side effects of a sovereign default.[28] The mechanism seeks to complement the existing African Monetary Fund. Therefore, the platform seeks not only to help with the clean up when an African economy fails to meet its obligations, but also to prevent such scenarios in the first place, by committing to support countries in their macro-management and handle the fluctuation along the cycle. Accelerating the implementation of the platform will further consolidate the toolkit to combat the various shocks threatening the financial stability of the

---

28. African Development Bank Group, "Address to the African Union's F15 Group of Ministers of Finance by Dr. Akinwumi A. Adesina President, African Development Bank Group Washington DC, April 21, 2022," speech, April 22, 2022, https://www.afdb.org/en/news-and-events/speeches/address-african-unions-f15-group-ministers-finance-dr-akinwumi-adesina-president-african-development-bank-group-washington-dc-april-21-2022-51161.

continent.[29] The Common Framework for Debt Restructuring should seek synergies with this regional platform to increase efficiency and credibility among African nations. The AfDB, which champions this initiative, is a well-established institution across the continent, and the stigma associated with soliciting foreign powers to address domestic issues in Africa can be overcome through more involvement of the AFSM. An African platform established by African nations will be more acceptable when intervening in local government decisions and ensuring countries' macroeconomic policies are on track.

c. Development of Deep and Liquid Local Currency Sovereign Debt Markets in Africa is Essential and Could Boost Involvement of the Diaspora in Closing the Funding Gap

A well-established sovereign bond market will enable African countries to mobilize extra financial resources for their increasing social and economic needs. The current context, marked by tightening financial conditions, especially for developing countries, has shown how favorable it would be to leverage a domestic and deep local-currency sovereign debt market. Beyond the role of the market in catalyzing the development of the capital market in general, especially the fixed-income compartment, it will add a new funding option for countries and improve their bargaining power in international financial markets. The steps needed to create or deepen the market have been widely documented.[30] They include coordination among market regulators, such as central banks and finance ministries, and the creation of the market infrastructure and a central securities depository. An enabling, comprehensive, and transparent legal framework will give the system the credibility it requires to attract foreign and domestic investors. The African diaspora can see through these actions a call for their commitment to support their countries. The World Bank estimated 11 years ago that the accumulated savings of the African diaspora were $53 billion a year,[31] representing almost one third of the continent's infrastructure financing needs. In addition, the African Union has in 2021 endorsed the African Diaspora Finance Corporation (ADFC).

---

29 . T-20 Indonesia, For an African Stability Mechanism, Policy Brief, 2022, https://www.t20indonesia.org/wp-content/uploads/2022/10/TF7_Proposal-for-the-Long-Due-African-Stability-Mechanism.pdf.

30 . Asian Development Bank, Good Practices for Developing a Local Currency Bond Market: Lessons from the ASEAN+3 Asian Bond Markets Initiative.» May 2019, http://dx.doi.org/10.22617/TCS190146-2.

31 . World Bank, "Harnessing the Diaspora's Resources to Boost African Development," June 16, 2011, https://www.worldbank.org/en/news/feature/2011/06/16/harnessing-the-diasporas-resources-to-boost-african-development

d. Tax Policy Should Strike a Balance Between Mobilizing Financial Resources and Broadening the Tax Base Without Suffocating Economic Activity

African economies, especially low-income and resource-intensive economies, have among the lowest tax-to-GDP ratios in the world. While the OECD average is 34%, and Latin America and the Caribbean hovers around 23%, in Africa this ratio was 16.6% in 2019.[32] Unless Africa adopts an ambitions tax policy, enabling authorities to raise the due amount of tax, the funding issue will remain unresolved. Indeed, tax revenues are more stable and predictable than external funding or revenues related to commodity exports.[33] Increasing tax collection should not come at expense of economic activity, and should not weigh down economic growth on the continent. Tax administration should strike the right balance between collecting the due tax revenues and catalyzing economic growth. The informal sector issue is complex and requires a thoughtful and fully-fledged approach instead of a unique tax policy focus. Tax reform also brings into the spotlight tax expenditures policies in Africa. In African countries, estimates report that tax incentives on average amount to 2.8% of GDP and 17.8% of total tax revenue. These can take the form of allowances, exemptions, rate relief, tax deferral, or even credits. In general, they represent postponed revenues for a set of sectors or economic agents relative to a benchmark tax. They are especially high in Senegal (7.8%), and Mauritania (58.4%).[34] A systemic impact analysis to assess the effectiveness of those measures is crucial for the orientation of fiscal and tax policies. Empirical analysis suggests that tax expenditures often don't achieve their main objectives and end up disrupting the economic system and feeding into economic inequality, or even exacerbating climate change.[35] Phasing out ineffective tax incentives is the right measure to limit the disruption and enable the tax administration to design the appropriate economic policy in the medium and long run.

---

[32] . The African Tax Administration Forum (ATAF), "The African Union Commission (AUC) and the Organization for Economic Co-operation and Development (OECD), 2021, Revenue Statistics in Africa, 2021
[33] . Agutin Redonda, Christian von Haldenwang, and Flurim Aliu, eds., "Tax expenditure reporting and domestic revenue mobilization in Africa," in Taxation, International Cooperation and the 2030 Sustainable Development Agenda, (Springer, 2011), https://doi.org/10.1007/978-3-030-64857-2.
[34] . Ibid.
[35] . Ibid.

6. Conclusion

Africa's debt problems have come to the fore in recent years. The rapid accumulation of debt, especially after the recent shocks, and the changing profile of creditors, are the main reasons why African debt sustainability is at risk. To avoid a possible debt crisis in Africa, the international community has proposed initiatives in favor of the most-indebted countries. In this context, Bretton Woods institutions and multilateral banks have mobilized different mechanisms to provide fragile countries with the appropriate cushions to withstand the successive waves. For instance, the IMF 'granted' about $29 billion to African countries within the new SDR allocation, which amounted worldwide to $650 billion. The G20 has also launched the DSSI to defer debt repayments and thereby free up resources for Africans to fight the pandemic. Also, a common framework for debt restructuring has been put in place. Nevertheless, these programs have several limitations, in terms of their scale, implementation, and the involvement of different stakeholders. On one front, we argue that they may need to be re-engineered and scaled-up to adapt to the current circumstances and challenges facing the developing world and the African continent. On the other, we believe firmly that in the face of these constraints, Africa is more than ever called on to adopt a new paradigm in its governance model, that of improving its fiscal policy and setting the stage for the adoption of a pan-African mechanism for debt resolution. The African Mechanism for Financial Stability, for example, under the auspices of the African Development Bank, could be the initiator of this new paradigm.

CHAPTER IX

A World on the Brink: Implications for Global Supply Chains and Food Security for the Global South

Isabelle Tsakok

Russia's invasion of Ukraine on February 24, 2022 darkened global prospects for a strong recovery from the devastating assault of the COVID-19 pandemic. The whole world is now on the brink. Already burdened by the stiff challenges of underdevelopment, violent conflict, and recurrent, life-threatening climate events, will the Global South seek not only short-term recovery but also long-term transformation to become food secure and resilient?

Indeed, what should be its vision? Its vision should be of building food systems to achieve food security for all. In so doing, the Global South will remove a major source of its vulnerability to recurrent shocks, thus giving a major boost to the prospects and the wellbeing of its peoples.

What paths promise at least survival in the short term while expanding the options for a food secure and resilient future? This chapter explores two promising scenarios. Both scenarios advocate expanding and deepening economic integration through regional trade, on the African continent, and among Global South countries. To date, worldwide experience in major trading blocks, including the EU, USMCA (formerly, NAFTA-North America and Mexico), the ASEAN, and the PACIFIC ALLIANCE, clearly show that regional trade integration has been a historic path to transformation. The Global South should not miss this golden opportunity to "recover together and recover stronger".

Introduction

These are perilous times as crisis follows crisis within a few years.[1] Now, more than ever, the stakes are high. Which road must the Global South (GS) choose? This chapter focuses on the main implications of these multiple crises for value/supply chains and food security and the need for the GS to identify paths to take that will expand its options and assets.

1. The Terrible Trio: COVID-19, Conflict, Climate Change

Continuing crises inflict inflation and hardship, and disrupt fragile recoveries: It is not that our world has not known shocks but this time, COVID-19 has introduced a new dimension—a global health shock that has triggered global demand collapses and global value/supply chain dislocations. With high inequality globally and within countries, the negative impact has been felt most severely by the vulnerable in all countries, rich and poor. These multiple crises have been quickly followed by Putin's war on Ukraine, which began on February 24, 2022. All this has happened in the context of the slow but accelerating wreck, climate change, which is increasing the numbers of climate refugees. Sub-Saharan Africa is one of the most-threatened regions as it is home to six of the ten most affected countries.[2]

A snapshot of disasters impacting Africa: Africa has been beset with major disasters in recent decades. Between 2000 and 2019, it was hit by 1,143 natural disasters (e.g., droughts, floods, storms), affecting 337 million

---

1. For example, the locust invasion since 2019 in the Horn of Africa, Arabian Peninsula and Indian subcontinent; the global COVID-19 pandemic in 2020; ever more frequent catastrophic climate events (e.g. drought, wild fires, and floods in the western United States; heat waves, drought, and wild fires in the United Kingdom and Western Europe; severe climate events in Russia; drought, floods, and fires in Africa, Australia, Asia and the Pacific); and the continuing Russia-Ukraine War since February 24, 2022.
2. "10 of the countries most affected by climate change," Concern, July 04, 2022. The other four non-African countries are: Afghanistan, Bangladesh, Haiti, and Pakistan. The six African countries are: Chad, Kenya, Malawi, Niger, Somalia, and Sudan. The original data comes from the Notre Dame Global Adaptation Initiative (ND-GAIN) and the Germanwatch's Climate Risk Index. https://www.concern.net/news/countries-most-affected-by-climate-change. The ND-GAIN Country Index summarises a country's vulnerability to climate change and other global challenges in combination with its readiness to improve resilience. According to the ND GAIN Country Index Rankings (2020), the bottom five countries are: Dem. Rep. of Congo (DRC); Eritrea; Guinea-Bissau; Central African Republic (CAR); and Chad. https://gain.nd.edu/our-work/country-index/.

people, and resulting in over 46,000 deaths.³ A record number of 4.3 million people in sub-Saharan Africa were displaced in 2020 by extreme weather events and conflict. According to the International Organization of Migration, over 89,000 crossed the Sahara Desert in Northern Niger, on their way to, or coming from, Algeria and Libya, the well-known path into Europe.⁴ It has been challenging on the economic front as well. Although Africa's trade as a whole with either Russia or Ukraine is insignificant, some countries⁵ rely on these two countries for critical imports of wheat, fertilizers, and steel. Imported inflation spiked in several countries between February and April 2022: e.g., in Kenya at 34%; Namibia at 20%; and Cameroon at 26%.⁶ At the same time, the pandemic and the war have reduced taxation revenues, while governments have to spend more on social safety nets. Prior to 2020, African countries were some of the fastest growing economies in the world, but COVID-19 reversed decades of hard-won developmental gains—macroeconomic, socio-economic, and governance. Fragile growth recovery in sub-Saharan Africa is projected to decelerate from 4.2% in 2021 to 3.7% in 2022.⁷

Uncertainty prevails: How long these major upheavals last depends in part on both the pandemic and the war, the duration and severity of both being uncertain. So far, the conflict of Russia versus Ukraine and the West shows no sign of a speedy resolution. The havoc wrecked by climate change will intensify unless the world community is on a path to reach net-zero carbon emissions by 2050. This increased uncertainty in turn dampens

---

3 . "Disasters in Africa: Twenty Years in Review (2000-2019)," no. 56, CRED CRUNCH, November 2019, https://reliefweb.int/report/world/cred-crunch-newsletter-issue-no-56-november-2019-disasters-africa-20-year-review-2000#:~:text=As%20seen%20in%20Figure%203,not%20prominent%20types%20of%20disastershttps://reliefweb.int/report/world/cred-crunch-newsletter-issue-no-56-november-2019-disasters-africa-20-year-review-2000#:~:text=As%20seen%20in%20Figure%203,not%20prominent%20types%20of%20disasters.

4 . Antony Sguazzin, Katarina Hoije, and Maya Averbuch,. "Rich Nations' Toxic Habits Bring African Refugees to Their Doors," Bloomberg , June 1, 2022, https://www.bloomberg.com/news/features/2022-06-01/rich-nations-toxic-habits-bring-african-refugees-to-their-doors#:~:text=A%20record%204.3%20million%20people,conflict%20with%20communities%20already%20there.

5 . For example, Kenya imported 30% of its wheat from Russia and Ukraine in 2021; Cameroon imported 44% of its fertilizers from Russia in 2021; Ghana imported 60% of its steel and iron ore imports from Ukraine. https://www.usip.org/publications/2022/06/russias-war-ukraine-taking-toll-africa#:~:text=Russia's%20war%20in%20Ukraine%20has,continent%2C%20said%20United%20Nations%20Assistant .

6 . Ashish Kumar Sen,. "Russia's war on Ukraine is Taking a Toll on Africa," United States Institute of Peace, June 15, 2022, https://www.usip.org/publications/2022/06/russias-war-ukraine-taking-toll-africa#:~:text=Russia's%20war%20in%20Ukraine%20has,continent%2C%20said%20United%20Nations%20Assistant .

7 . World Bank, Global Economic Prospects (Washington D.C: World Bank Group, 2022): 130. https://openknowledge.worldbank.org/handle/10986/37224 .

potentially productivity-increasing investment and trade, and therefore growth. Pervasive uncertainty by itself has become a major problem.

2. The Global South Under Increased Stress – Continuing Policy Uncertainty, Global Value/Supply Chain Dislocations, and Rising Inflation

The Global South—concept and selected features: The GS comprises most but not all countries south of the equator. It is a development-cum-geopolitical concept rather than a geographical category; thus, Australia and New Zealand are in the tropics but they are not considered part of the GS, whereas the People's Republic of China and India are included in the GS. The group is heterogeneous in terms of political ideologies, governance philosophies and practice, progress in socio-economic development, and per-capita income levels.[8] The concept typically refers to developing countries which face similar challenges of underdevelopment,[9] as shown by the following common features: (i) they are not high-income, industrialized economies; (ii) they were previously colonies or near colonies of countries from the 'Global North'; (iii) agriculture is still a major sector (10% or more of GDP); (iv) they experience extensive poverty and cannot ensure food security for millions of their people even during peace times; (v) many are highly indebted especially because of the COVID-19 pandemic; and (vi) they are trade- (as commodity exporters and/or as importers of food and manufactured inputs) and aid-dependent. The majority of the world's population live in the GS, including the surging sub-Saharan African youth (age 15-35) population.[10]

---

8 . The term "Global South" encompasses multiple characteristics. The term was first coined by the social activist Carl Oglesby in 1969; https://worldpopulationreview.com/country-rankings/global-south-countries.
There are pros and cons with this concept. Much depends on the purpose of the categorization and inquiry. The World Bank does not use this concept, but classifies countries according to income level, GNI per capita. Thus, it has four groups: low, lower middle-, upper middle-, and upper income countries. Its latest (July1, 2022) classification is available at https://blogs.worldbank.org/opendata/new-world-bank-country-classifications-income-level-2022-2023.

9 . The concept of developing or underdeveloped countries is unifying but it is not accepted by all parties. For example, the Kingdom of Saudi Arabia is definitely high income—GNI/cap: $22,270 (2020. Current USD. Atlas method. World Bank), but the IMF classifies it as developing because of its lower economic performance, and the United Nations classifies it as developed because it has a Human Development Index (HDI) of 0.853, but the WTO does not accept it.
https://worldpopulationreview.com/country-rankings/developing-countries.

10 . According to the IMF, around 85% of the world's population live in 152 developing countries. If the total world population is estimated at nearly 8 billion (Nov 2022), then total population in developing countries is around (.85x8) = 6.8 billion. https://www.

The Global South under increased market and geo-political stress—A snapshot: The growth of global value chains (GVCs) was rapid in the 1990s. Thus, by 2020, they accounted for around 50% of world trade. Such growth was beneficial as it promoted unprecedented convergence of poor countries towards rich countries; that is, the GDP of the former grew faster than the latter, and poverty fell sharply. Unfortunately, the pandemic accelerated the slowdown in the growth of GVCs, a trend that was already ongoing since the financial and food crisis of 2007-08. Global value/supply chain disruptions, however, increased during COVID-19. Other key causal factors include increasing geopolitical tensions among large countries, rising nationalism, trade protectionism, policy uncertainty, and internal structural issues of GVC operations. Thus:

- An important case is the U.S.-China trade dispute, which has been ongoing for decades but flared up in 2017 under former President Trump. In 2018, the Trump Administration imposed special tariffs on more than 50% of imports from almost every sector in China. U.S. 'new special tariffs' rose from an average of less than 3% to over 12%. China retaliated on more than 70% of US imports into China. By the end of 2018, China's anti-U.S. tariffs had risen from less than 10% to over 18%.[11]

- Global supply chain dislocations were first triggered by the U.S.-China trade dispute as it injected much policy uncertainty and volatility which made companies rush to build inventories in anticipation of higher trade barriers. This unexpected shift in world trade increased stress on global logistics. Then came COVID-19, triggering a collapse in demand in early 2020, which was followed by a demand surge starting in summer 2020 because of the substantial fiscal stimulus of the Biden Administration. Companies however, had already retrenched; e.g., they had canceled sailings by ocean carriers, cut manufacturing capacity, and laid off staff. The global economic machine had to be turned back on again, but it could not cope with the demand surge in the immediate term because predictability and advance planning are essential for the smooth functioning of a highly complex, interlinked, and just-in-time global production process. Inflation surged on a wide range of intermediate and final goods, showing clearly that a chain is as strong as its weakest

---

worlddata.info/developing-countries.php#:~:text=According%20to%20the%20IMF%20definition,and%20numerous%20other%20island%20states.

11 . Chad P. Bown, "The 2018 US-China Trade Conflict After 40 years of Special Protection" Peterson Institute of International Economics, Working Paper 19-7, April 2019, 6-11, https://www.piie.com/system/files/documents/wp19-7.pdf .

link—and there was more than one weak link.[12]

- The gains from GVCs were not equally shared across and within countries. Large corporations which outsourced parts and tasks to developing countries have seen rising markups and profits, while the same markups for producers in developing countries were declining (e.g., markups in garment firms). Within countries, there was a growing premium for skilled workers while wages were stagnant for unskilled workers, in particular, for women.[13] Such unequal distribution of benefits has undermined political support for out-sourcing, GVCs, and trade openness, contributing to the rise of protectionism and the U.S.-China trade war.

- The inflation caused by the breakdowns in global value/supply chains is not just because of the pandemic, the U.S.-China trade dispute, and the Russia-Ukraine War. There are also internal structural issues of non-competitive behavior that exacerbate the price hikes. The 2007-08 global recession showed clearly the increasing market concentration of GVCs—geographically and organizationally—as major multinational enterprises sought to streamline their supply chains to focus on smaller numbers of large, more capable, and more strategically located suppliers near dynamic GVCs. An important example is mobile phone production, which is clustered in several Asian countries, notably China, South Korea, and Vietnam. The five leading firms account for more than 50% of global markets in mobile phones. Two leading firms, Apple and Samsung, enjoy oligopolistic market power and control a big portion of the market segments for mobile phones, smartphones, contract manufacturing, and smartphone operating systems.[14]

---

12 . Garth Friesen,. "No End in Sight for the COVID-Led Global Supply Chain Disruption,". Forbes, , September 03, 2021, https://www.forbes.com/sites/garthfriesen/2021/09/03/no-end-in-sight-for-the-covid-led-global-supply-chain-disruption/?sh=155
13 . World Development Report 2020: Trading for Development in the Age of Global Value Chains. A World Bank Group Flagship Report, Overview, 1-4. http://hdl.handle.net/10986/32437.
14 . Joon Koo Lee and Gary Gereffi, "Global value chains, rising power firms, and economic and social upgrading," Critical Perspectives on International Business 11, no. .3/4, (2015): 326-327, DOI 10.1108/cpoib-03-2014-0018.

3. Impact on Hunger, Malnutrition, and Food Insecurity in the Global South

A global food-security crisis as millions more plunge deeper into hunger: By June 2022, an estimated 345 million people in 82 countries had been plunged into acute hunger, according to the World Food Program (WFP).[15] Even pre-COVID-19, since 2014-15, global hunger and malnutrition had been on the rise. By 2021, some 3 billion people were not able to afford nutritious diets at all times. With COVID-19, 720 million to 811 million faced hunger, raising the prevalence of undernourishment from 8.4% in 2019 to 9.9% in 2020.[16] The explosion of the Russia-Ukraine war created a perfect storm. With the substantial support Ukraine receives from NATO, the U.S., and other western democracies (including in the form of wide-ranging sanctions on Russia), the war is having multiple ripple effects, disrupting interlinked food, fuel, and fertilizer markets.

What is food security? "Food security exists when all people, at all times, have physical and economic access to sufficient safe and nutritious food that meets their dietary needs and food preferences for an active and healthy life" (FAO, 1996). This holistic concept of food security (FSH) specifies four pillars which jointly constitute food security: availability, access, utilization, and stability. It is different from the concept of food self-sufficiency (FSS) which equates national self-sufficiency—no dependence on imports—as food security. It is also different from the concept of food sovereignty (FSY) which specifies that the country should be in control of its basic food supplies and the approach taken to acquire them.

The many facets and high cost of food insecurity: Food insecurity has been increasing in the Middle East and well beyond, resulting from successive waves of refugees fleeing war, persecution, gang violence, violation of human rights, and famine, reaching over 100 million for the first time on record, by June 20, 2022, World Refugee Day.[17] So much hunger

---

15 . World Bank, "Joint Statement by the Heads of the Food and Agriculture Organization, International Monetary Fund, World Bank Group, World Food Programme, and World Trade Organization on the Global Food Security Crisis," July 15, 2022, https://www.worldbank.org/en/news/statement/2022/07/15/joint-statement-by-the-heads-of-the-food-and-agriculture-organization-international-monetary-fund-world-bank-group-world.
16 . FAO- Food and Agriculture Organization of the United Nations, The State of Food Security and Nutrition in the World 2021:, The World is at a Critical Juncture (2022), https://www.fao.org/state-of-food-security-nutrition/2021/en.
17 . World Health Organization (WHO), "20 June is World Refugee Day", June 20, 2022, https://www.who.int/news-room/events/detail/2022/06/20/default-calendar/world-refugee-day#:~:text=20%20June%20marks%20World%20Refugee,the%20first%20time%20on%20record.

and malnutrition leave deep, durable scars, especially on women and children. Globally, 29.9% of women between 15-49 years old suffer from anemia. These estimates are pre-COVID-19.[18] As expected, the situation has considerably worsened, given COVID-19 and other crises. For example, in 2020, some 22% of children under five years old were stunted (nearly 150 million); 6.7% were suffering from wasting (45.4 million); and 5.7% were affected by being overweight (38.9 million).[19] Most of these children live in Africa and Asia. The Global Report on Food Crises (2022) estimates that the population in crisis has risen from 135 million (2019) to 193 million (2021), spread out in 53 countries.[20] Hunger is being compounded by a debt crisis on top of layers of overlapping crises. This situation primarily afflicts some of the world's poorest countries, but some middle-income countries too are being impacted. The pandemic has forced many countries to increase their social safety net expenditures, just when their economies and therefore government revenues were collapsing. Many of the poorest African countries were highly indebted even before COVID-19 struck. By the end of 2020, the public and publicly-guaranteed debt owed to foreign creditors amounted to a record of US $123.8 billion, a 75% increase from the 2010 level, with debt service payments constituting nearly 10% of the export earnings of the poorest African economies. [21]

4. Rebuilding Food Systems and Food Security in Turbulent Times: What Opportunities Should the Global South Pursue? A Scenario Analysis

Introduction: Winston Churchill is credited for having said: "*Never let a crisis go to waste*". To do so, what bold, forward-looking actions should the GS undertake to lay the foundations of a food-secure and resilient future? In this section, we assume a global environment in 2022-23 characterized by the following: (i) The nine-month-old Ukraine war continues to be a major burden on the entire world economy in 2022 and likely into 2023, in

---

18 . FAO, The State of Food Security and Nutrition in the World 2021, 2.2. https://www.fao.org/3/cb4474en/online/cb4474en.html#chapter-2_2.
19 . FAO, The State of Food Security and Nutrition in the World 2021, 2.2, Fig. 7. https://www.fao.org/3/cb4474en/online/cb4474en.html#chapter-2_2.
20 . WFP et al, 2022 Global Report on Food Crises, Food Security Information Network, https://docs.wfp.org/api/documents/WFP-0000138913/download/?_ga=2.23642482.99605424.1661024574-594572009.1661024574.
21 . Marcello Estavão. "For poor countries already facing debt distress, a food crisis looms," World Bank Blogs, July 18, 2022, https://blogs.worldbank.org/voices/poor-countries-already-facing-debt-distress-food-crisis-looms.

particular with respect to reduced official (developmental) foreign aid for the Global South; (ii) Tightening of fiscal space for many governments in the GS; (iii) Continued inflation of the cost of basic consumption items; (iv) Increased business uncertainty contributing to retrenchment in expansion plans; and (v) Continued global warming and acceleration in the climate crisis.

Within this global environment, we explore two scenarios which are complementary and synergistic:

- The global economy is divided into regional blocs. The major regional blocs are: the EU, USMCA (formerly, NAFTA), MERCOSUR, the PACIFIC ALLIANCE, ASEAN, and ASEAN+3 (ASEAN PLUS THREE, APT).[22] In this scenario, Africa should focus on investing in the African Continental Free Trade Area (AfCFTA). Regional integration has been a historic path to transformation not to be missed.

- South-South regional market integration. The regional blocs within the Global South increase trade, investment, and financing links among them, while cooperating on public health, and investing in digital transformation and energy transition, all required to achieve food security and resilience to shocks in a world of climate change.

a. Scenario One—Africa invests in regional market integration while protecting the poor and vulnerable from price and health shocks

Make continental trade the engine of sustainable and inclusive growth: The first steps in that journey *"of a thousand miles"*[23] include reductions in non-tariff barriers on goods and services, and improvements in trade facilitation services.[24] These measures account for 66% of total estimated

---

[22] . "Overview of ASEAN Plus Three Cooperation," ASEAN Plus Three, July 06, 2022, https://aseanplusthree.asean.org/wp-content/uploads/2022/07/Overview-of-APT-Cooperation-6-July-2022.pdf

[23] . The proper reference is: "A journey of a thousand miles begins with a single step", ancient Chinese philosopher Laozi in Dao de Jing. The Chinese phrase: 千里之行，始於足下; pinyin: Qian li zhi xíng, shi yú zú xià; literally: "A journey of a thousand li starts beneath one's feet", has been variously translated. One popular translation is: A journey of a thousand miles starts with the first step. https://www.setquotes.com/the-journey-of-a-thousand-miles-begins-with-one-step/

[24] . Roberto Echandi, Maryla, Maliszewska, ; Victor Steenbergen,. Making the Most of the African Continental Free Trade Area: Leveraging Trade and Foreign Direct Investment to Boost Growth and Reduce Poverty (World Bank Group, 2022), https://openknowledge.worldbank.org/handle/10986/37623.

potential gains of $450 billion. If African governments invest in their own economies to integrate their domestic markets of 1.3 billion people with a combined GDP of $3.4 trillion, such investment is likely to attract foreign direct investment (FDI) also.

Where to get the funds? Reallocate and mobilize funds to invest in Africa: The prevalence of undernourishment in sub-Saharan Africa is high today—20%—but that is not because the region is resource poor.[25] Quite the contrary. Africa is well known as a resource-rich continent.[26] In addition, it can tap financial resources from at least six main sources: (a) The recently replenished International Development Association (IDA)—3 year, $93 billion;[27] (b) The Sovereign Wealth Funds—US$ 300 billion (2020);[28] (c) Stemming or eliminating illicit financial flows (IFFs) in Africa. Africa loses $50 billion a year in IFF (2015);[29] *The Economic Governance Report I* (2021) correctly notes this is "*conservatively estimated*" and that "*Stemming those outflows could shrink the continent's infrastructure gap considerably, and strengthen its productive capacities…*".[30] According to UNCTAD (2020) Africa loses $88.6 billion every year in IFFs, equivalent to 3.7% of its GDP;[31] (d) Impact investing, which is an approach of private business to invest in

---

25. World Bank group, "Prevalence of undernourishment (% of population) of sub-Saharan Africa," https://data.worldbank.org/indicator/SN.ITK.DEFC.ZS?locations=ZG.
26. Ivailo Izvorski, Souleymane Coulibaly, Djeneba Doumbia, Assert in their book: Reinvigorating Growth in Resource Rich Sub-Saharan Africa, that "resource-rich Africa accounts for a dominant part of SSA's GDP, though Africa is not as rich as is usually believed, for in aggregate and in per-capita terms, its natural resources are slightly higher than the South Asia Region and lag all other developing regions." - Ivailo Izvorski, Souleymane Coulibaly, Djeneba Doumbia, Reinvigorating Growth in Resource Rich Sub-Saharan Africa (World Bank Group, 2018): 1, https://openknowledge.worldbank.org/bitstream/handle/10986/30399/5-9-2018-17-9-2-SSAGrowthforweb.pdf?sequence=1&isAllowed=y.
27. Axel van Trotsenburg, "Will the International Community Stand with Africa in the Latest Crises?," World Bank, https://www.worldbank.org/en/news/opinion/2022/07/04/will-the-international-community-stand-with-africa-in-the-latest-crises.
28. Issa Faye, "The impact that sovereign wealth funds can make," World Bank, https://blogs.worldbank.org/africacan/impact-sovereign-wealth-funds-can-make-africa.
29. UNECA- United Nations Economic Commission for Africa. "Economic Governance Report I: Institutional Architecture to Address Illicit Financial Flows," 2021, https://repository.uneca.org/bitstream/handle/10855/46555/b11997643.pdf?sequence=5&isAllowed=y.
30. According to the Economic Governance Report I, cited above, "IFFs mainly come from: tax fraud, trade mis-invoicing, corruption, and money laundering. Reducing and eliminating them would require major institutional coordination and overhaul. It will also require collaboration between Africa and countries receiving the IFFs", https://repository.uneca.org/bitstream/handle/10855/46555/b11997643.pdf?sequence=5&isAllowed=y.
31. African Union., "The African Union Commission to fight Illicit Financial Flows (IFFs) out of Africa and to harmonize continental tax policy on tax incentives," April 19, 2022, https://au.int/en/pressreleases/20220419/african-union-commission-fight-illicit-financial-flows-iffs-out-africa-and#:~:text=Press%20releases-,The%20African%20Union%20Commission%20to%20fight%20Illicit%20Financial%20Flows%20(IFFs,tax%20policy%20on%20tax%20Incentives&text=The%20global%20economy%20has%20plummeted,the%20world%20in%20early%202020.

order to "*contribute to the achievement of positive social and environmental impacts*".³² It is estimated that "*globally that the appetite for impact investing is …up to US $ 26 trillion or about 10% of global capital markets*"; (e) African diaspora funds;³³ and (f) Transact and obtain financing from China's Cross Border Interbank Payment System (CIPS)³⁴ (which was launched in 2015).³⁵ Since the existence of potential financial resources does not always translate into access to actual financial resources, the African Union rightly emphasizes the importance for Africa of developing a harmonized continental tax policy, and of combating IFFs to generate resources for the successful implementation of its transformational programs. In other words, Africa should increasingly rely on generating its own financial resources.³⁶

AfCFTA's development potential is great but so are the challenges of full implementation: Full implementation at country, sub-regional, and continental levels is essential if Africa is to realize the promise of AfCFTA over the coming decades. This may sound like a tautology, but world-wide experience of economic integration shows that sound implementation is a decisive factor in success. And implementation is challenging. Attempts at regional economic integration are not new to Africa as it already has eight Regional Economic Communities (RECs).³⁷ However, intra-African exports, though they have grown from 10% (1995) to 17% (2017) of total African exports, remain low compared to levels in Asia at 59%, Europe at 69%, and North America at 31%.³⁸ Why? And what insights can be obtained

---

32. IFC- International Finance Cooperation, "Impact investing at IFC." https://www.ifc.org/wps/wcm/connect/Topics_Ext_Content/IFC_External_Corporate_Site/Development+Impact/Principles/.
33. Dilip Ratha and Sonia Plaza. "Harnessing Diasporas,". Finance and Development 8, no. 3, Sept. 2011., IMF. https://www.imf.org/external/pubs/ft/fandd/2011/09/ratha.htm.
34. Huileng Tan, "China and Russia are working on home-grown alternatives to the SWIFT system Here's what they would mean for the US dollar," Business Insider, April 28, 2022, https://www.businessinsider.com/china-russia-alternative-swift-payment-cips-spfs-yuan-ruble-dollar-2022-4.
35. Barry Eigengreen, "Sanctions, SWIFT, and China's Cross Border Interbank Payments System," Center for Strategic and International Studies, May 20, 2022, https://www.csis.org/analysis/sanctions-swift-and-chinas-cross-border-interbank-payments-system.
36. African Union/Economic Commission for Africa, "Report of the High Panel on Illicit Financial Flows from Africa," July 08, 2021, 13-14, https://au.int/sites/default/files/documents/40545-doc-IFFs_REPORT.pdf.
37. The eight RECs are: 1. AMU – Arab Maghreb Union; 2. CEN-SAD- The Community of Sahel-Saharan States; 3. COMESA-Common Market for Eastern and Southern Africa; 4. EAC: East African Community; 5. ECCAS- Economic Community of Central African States; 6. ECOWAS- Economic Community of West African States; 7. IGAD- Intergovernmental Authority on Development; and 8. SACU/SADC-South African Customs Union/Southern African Development Community. African Union. https://au.int/en/organs/recs.
38. Vera Songwe, "Intra-African trade: A path to economic diversification and inclusion," Brookings, January 11, 2019, https://www.brookings.edu/research/intra-african-trade-a-path-to-economic-diversification-and-inclusion/.

from various attempts—not only Africa's RECs, but also the EU, the ASEAN, MERCOSUR, and USMCA at economic integration that sheds light on the nature of the challenges? Some key factors which have driven or derailed economic integration include[39]:

- A 'crucial' reason regional African trade is small is because most African economies are not transformed. Most imports into Africa are finished or manufactured goods, which few economies in the region produce in sufficiently large scale. African economies remain heavily dependent on finished goods produced in other regions of the world. Thus, one cannot separate the low level of trade in Africa from its lack of transformation. Therefore, there is a vicious circle between low level of trade and low level of economic transformation.[40]

- Strong private sector support is critical for driving economic integration. In the EU, it was not until the 1980s—25 years after the Treaty of Rome was signed in 1957—that leaders from some of Europe's major companies intensified lobbying pressure on governments to integrate, e.g. ,by companies such as Phillips, Siemens, Shell, Unilever, and Volvo. Governments' efforts to integrate were not enough.[41]

- Regional integration of agriculture is undermined by difficulties in agricultural production itself, such as problems of land ownership and tenure, poor use of inputs, and threats of expropriation.[42]

- Government leadership in implementation from at least one country is important, because regional integration agreements require many diverse measures of inter-governmental coordination, and there are winners and losers in integration, at least in the early period. Implementation is more likely to succeed if at least one government in the region takes the lead in pushing integration. An example is Germany, which is the largest economy of Europe: it took the lead and was able to do so effectively because large parts of its private sector supported integration.[43] In Africa, Kenya has been eager to take a leadership role in the East African Community (EAC).

---

39 . Paul Brenton, & Barak Hoffman (eds.) Political Economy of Regional Integration in Sub-Saharan Africa. (World Bank Group, 2016): https://openknowledge.worldbank.org/bitstream/handle/10986/24767/Political0econ0n0sub0Saharan0Africa.pdf?sequence=1&isAllowed=y.
40 . Ibid, 8.
41 . Ibid, 3.
42 . Ibid, 5.
43 . Ibid,5.

- Since economic integration typically generates winners and losers, especially in the short term, the equalization of the benefits of economic integration is a critical supportive political economy move. The backlash against globalization is in part due to the fact that the gains have not been equally shared. A major example of backlash is the United States, where the American public, which used to support international trade, now associates it with job insecurity and job losses. The discontent has been building up in the manufacturing sector concentrated in the U.S. Mid-West and parts of the South. At the same time, globalization is associated with increased income inequality which has benefited the top 10%, or 1% of American society, while leaving behind the middle and working classes.[44]

The above are some key factors that show how implementation is a complex and long-term process that requires an 'all hands-on deck' approach to succeed. In fact, Africa has given considerable thought already to the range of challenging issues which the implementation of AfCFTA must address. These include: (a) loss of government revenue due to tariff liberalization; (b) lack of harmonization of standards at national and sub-regional levels; (c) disparities in economic development levels under AfCFTA; (d) loss of jobs arising from short-term adjustment costs in the less-competitive sectors; and (e) socio-political instability in some regions.[45] From past experiences, what is clear is that governance-cum-leadership writ large will be one determining factor. The World Bank has pointed out that *"implementing the AfCFTA will usher in the kinds of deep reforms necessary to enhance long-term growth in African countries"*.[46]

Synergistic interaction between food security and economic transformation: Rebuilding food systems for food security requires the transformation of agriculture, which in turn promotes economy-wide structural transformation. As Timmer has pointed out: *"Food security and economic growth interact in a mutually reinforcing process over the course of economic development ... no country has sustained rapid economic*

---

[44] . Jeffry Frieden, "The backlash against globalization and the future of the international economic order.", 6-9. Harvard University, February 2018, https://scholar.harvard.edu/files/jfrieden/files/frieden_future_feb2018.pdf
[45] . Francis Mangeni & Joseph Atta-Mensah. Existential Priorities for the African Continental Free Trade Area (UNECA, 2022); 59. https://repository.uneca.org/bitstream/handle/10855/47860/b12015659.pdf?sequence=3&isAllowed=y.
[46] . World Bank. The African Continent Free Trade Area," July 27, 2020, https://www.worldbank.org/en/topic/trade/publication/the-african-continental-free-trade-area.

growth without first achieving food security at the macro level".⁴⁷ Also: "*No country has succeeded in its industrial revolution without a prior (or at least simultaneous) agricultural revolution. Neglecting agriculture in the early stages of development is neglecting development*".⁴⁸ Africa's structural transformation both requires and promotes agricultural transformation. It has already started this transformative process. The implementation period for AfCFTA is expected to last at least until 2035-40. The ongoing Phase Two negotiations on key issues include competition policy, investment protection, and intellectual property rights. Rules governing trade on digital platforms are scheduled to conclude at the end of 2022.⁴⁹ Phase three on e-commerce will start immediately after.

b. Scenario Two: South-South regional market integration to achieve food security and increase resilience to shocks in a world of climate change

South-South regional market integration a promising way forward: As the Global North is reshoring for whatever reason (e.g., rise of protectionism and nationalism; geo-political tensions intensified by the Ukraine war), the GS should expand South-South regional market integration as the major driver of transformative, poverty-reducing growth among developing countries. In pursuing expanded regional trade, GS countries should give top priority to removing their major vulnerability: their inability to build food systems that enable millions of their people to enjoy food security most of the time, and to be resilient to shocks. Resilience will increasingly require geographical diversification of risks spread over large areas throughout the GS. Food security should not be confused with national food self-sufficiency which is not only more costly but more perilous, as it restricts a country's supply options to its national borders.

---

47 . Peter Timmer, "Food Security and Economic Growth: An Asian Perspective,". Working Paper, no. 51, Center for Global Development, December 2004, pp 1-24. https://www.cgdev.org/sites/default/files/2738_file_WP_51_Food_Security.pdf.
This paper was delivered as the H.W. Arndt Memorial Lecture at Australian National University, Canberra, on November 22, 2004.

48 . Peter Timmer, Food security and Scarcity: Why Ending Hunger is So Hard, (Philadelphia: University of Pennsylvania Press, 2015).

49 . Baker-McKenzie, "Africa: AfCFTA Update- the streamlining of intra-African trade gathers momentum, " Baker-McKenzie Insight Plus, February 14, 2022, https://insightplus.bakermckenzie.com/bm/international-commercial-trade/africa-afcfta-update-the-streamlining-of-intra-african-trade-gathers-momentum#:~:text=Phase%20two%20of%20AfCFTA%20negotiations,by%20the%20end%20of%202022.

Expanded regional South-South trade in agri-food needed as countries experience increasing urbanization—a low-hanging fruit for the GS? Access to expanded regional markets can accelerate the transformation of agri-food into high productivity systems; transformation needed to generate the surplus demanded by growing populations, especially in urban centers. Some 68% of world population is expected to live in urban areas by 2050, with most of the increase expected in Asia and Africa.[50] A key consideration in increasing agri-food productivity is the development of and access to agricultural research, extension, and education services. For millions of smallholders, this support is a must for enabling smart adaptation, mitigation, and survival in a world with a changing climate. The three pillars of the G20 Summit are particularly important for building smart agriculture that contributes to the global energy transition and uses the power of digitization to reach millions of smallholders throughout the GS.

"Recover together, recover stronger"—a timely focus [51] [52]: The approach advocated by the Indonesian Presidency of the G20 Summit in November 2020 was timely. It is particularly appropriate for lower-income developing countries struggling against major odds, for together they increase their bargaining power and therefore their options. Isolation is no way to face crises. Furthermore, the three priority pillars of the G20 Summit are forward looking and fundamental. They are: (1) Strengthening the global healthcare architecture; (2) Digital transformation; and (3) Energy transition. If the triple challenges of COVID-19, climate change, and conflict have taught us anything, it is that our fates are closely interlinked, for better or for worse, and it is up to us together to make it for the better. The three pillars also respond to the challenges and opportunities of our time. If implemented over the coming decades, they could be transformative. Jointly implemented, they would promote the productivity and inclusiveness of economies and their food systems in the GS. The pandemic has clearly shown that the entire economy grinds to a halt without sound global public

---

50. "68% of the world population projected to live in urban areas, says the U.N." According to the United Nation's Department of Economic and Social Affairs, on May 16, 2018, available at https://www.un.org/development/desa/en/news/population/2018-revision-of-world-urbanization-prospects.html.
51. G 20 Leaders' Summit 2022; Nov 15-16, Bali, Jakarta Raya, Indonesia. The G20 is made up of 19 countries and the European Union. The 19 countries are Argentina, Australia, Brazil, Canada, China, Germany, France, India, Indonesia, Italy, Japan, Mexico, the Russian Federation, Saudi Arabia, South Africa, South Korea, Turkey, the UK, and the U.S. IISD/SDG Knowledge Hub. https://sdg.iisd.org/events/g20-leaders-summit-2022.
52. Ministry of Foreign Affairs of the Republic of Indonesia. "Indonesia promotes spirit to recover together in the 2022 G 20 presidency." https://kemlu.go.id/portal/en/read/3288/berita/indonesia-promotes-spirit-to-recover-together-in-the-2022-g20-presidency.

health, which requires countries to work together. Digital transformation has been essential for the functioning of millions in a pandemic world. Digitization promises to empower smallholders by facilitating access to the latest agricultural research, extension, and education services, and to lucrative markets, two major areas in which smallholders are at a great disadvantage. The energy transition is essential for effectively slowing down global warming. Agriculture and food must contribute to this transition, otherwise they will continue to be major casualties of climate change, unless the global community slows global warming and limits it to 1.5° C. This will require methane emissions to be reduced by about one third; and the peaking of greenhouse gas (GHG) emissions by 2025 at the latest, and their subsequent reduction by 43% by 2030 (in only eight years' time!).[53]

Recovering and thriving despite multiple crises: how to navigate in this emergency situation? Given the amount of GHG emissions the global community must cut by 2030, we seem to be simply running out of time to overcome this existential threat. We in the GS who are still highly dependent on agriculture are staring at a looming disaster. To avert it, governments in the GS must mobilize all the resources they can. These resources include:

- Accessing financial resources (domestic and foreign) while managing financial risks;

- Drawing upon past cases of success in achieving food security, in using regional market integration to drive transformation, and in developing links with regional and global value/supply chains;

- Developing strategic trade partnerships with complementary comparative advantages.

Thus, although there is no proven path on how to navigate successfully an emergency situation, there are potentially promising paths to pursue.

GS must assess and manage inter-related financial risks: A daunting challenge to recovery is how to finance it. Financial turmoil can kill any attempts at recovery. Therefore, for resource-constrained governments of the GS, any sustainable recovery depends on managing and reducing priority inter-related financial risks. In 2020, the average debt burden of low- and middle-income countries increased by roughly 9% of GDP, compared

---

53 . Intergovernmental Panel on Climate Change (IPCC). April 04, 2022. "The evidence is clear: The time for action is now. We can halve emissions by 2030." IPCC press release. 2022/15/PR. https://www.ipcc.ch/site/assets/uploads/2022/04/IPCC_AR6_WGIII_PressRelease_English.pdf (Accessed Sept 8, 2022).

to an average annual increase of 1.9 percentage points over the previous decade. As a result, 51 countries (including 44 emerging economies) had their sovereign credit debt ratings downgraded.[54] Early detection and swift resolution of such risks can determine whether recovery is strong, sustainable, and equitable. Given that financial risks are inter-twined, monetary, fiscal, and financial policies must be well designed to take into account the linkages. Key considerations should include the following: (a) Given the link between the financial health of households, businesses and the overall financial sector, it is essential that debt burdens of households and businesses remain sustainable and they continue to have access to credit for an equitable recovery; (b) Given that the financial sector will be required to extend credit to finance consumption and investment during the recovery phase, it needs to be well capitalized; and (c) Given that governments will have to directly support households and firms, governments need to manage and reduce their high levels of sovereign debt. The critical and complex task of managing finance for recovery is recognized by the global community.

Global initiatives to address this critical financial challenge provide some basis for hope: The G20 Chair's Summary of the Third G20 Finance Ministers and Governors Meeting, Bali, July 15-16, 2022, expressed the need for, and a commitment to, strengthening global financial system resilience and stability.[55] The GS will benefit to the extent their fourth meeting held on Oct 12-13, 2022 in Washington D.C. has resulted in adequately funded, concrete mechanisms to reduce inter-related financial risks and ensure financial stability. These mechanisms include measures to strengthen global financial resilience by (i) welcoming IMF revised Institutional View (IV) to monitor the risks of increased capital volatility; (ii) voluntary channeling of Special Drawing Rights (SDRs) amounting to USD 80.6 b and the voluntary contribution to the IMF Resilience and Sustainability Trust (RST) for the most vulnerable countries; (iii) commitment to implement a historic agreement on a G20/OECD two pillar international tax package. Pillar One deals with the Inclusive Framework on Base Erosion and Profit Shifting (BEPS). Pillar Two deals with the rules of the Global Anti-Base Erosion

---

54 . World Bank Group, World Development Report 2022: Finance for an Equitable Recovery, (Washington D.C: World Bank Group, 2022), https://openknowledge.worldbank.org/bitstream/handle/10986/36883/9781464817304.pdf?sequence=56&isAllowed=y.
55 . "G 20 Chair's Summary: Third G20 Finance Ministers and Central Bank Governors Meeting," Bali, 15-16 July 2022, G 20 Information Center, http://www.g20.utoronto.ca/2022/220716-finance.html

Model.[56] Furthermore, (a) The World Bank Group is making available $30 billion to help countries address food insecurity, and has set up a Pandemic Prevention, Preparedness, and Response (PPR) Financial Intermediary Fund (FIF) to complement efforts in developing countries to strengthen their health systems. This PPRFIF has already received $1.1 billion in financial commitments, with many more countries pledging contributions;[57] and (b) The G20 Blueprint for scaling up Infratech Financing and Development, the development of a framework to best leverage private sector participation, and a compendium of case studies on financing digital infrastructure.[58] Given that even the Global North is facing economic headwinds and tightened fiscal space, the GS must be prepared for shortfalls in pledges.

What can we learn from progress in economic transformation and food security forged during times of crisis? A few examples from the GS: Times of crisis have also been times of transformation in countries with very different natural endowments and historical legacies.

- A striking example is *Rwanda*, a small landlocked and hilly country, famous for its remarkable socio-economic achievements after it was devastated by the genocide against the Tutsis and moderate Hutus in 1994. Land-scarce, low-yielding, rainfed, subsistence agriculture prevailed in the 1990s[59]. Rwanda is still struggling to transform its agriculture. But the progress made is such that the African Union has designated Rwanda as the country that has achieved the most progress against the Malabo Declaration goals and targets for 2025.[60] From a GNI/capita of $150 at the height of the genocide, it is now $850 (2021), with the ambition of achieving middle-income status by 2035, and high-income status by 2050[61]. Poverty substantially declined before COVID-19. Rwanda still has

---

56 . Bank of Indonesia. "At their last meeting in 2022, G20 ministers and central bank governors demonstrates concrete actions to tackle global economic challenges," October 14, 2022, https://www.bi.go.id/en/publikasi/ruang-media/news-release/Pages/sp_2427922.aspx
57 . "Remarks by World Bank Group President David Malpass to G20 Finance Ministers and Central Bank Governors on the Global Economy and Health Agenda," World Bank Group, July 15, 2022, https://openknowledge.worldbank.org/bitstream/handle/10986/37809/IDU09b20a3260a09091b400e6e6dc78f18.pdf?sequence=1&isAllowed=y.
58 . "G20 Chair's Summary," 7-8.
59 . World Bank, "Rwanda Agricultural Strategy Review," May 22, 1991, 3-5, https://documents.worldbank.org/pt/publication/documents-reports/documentdetail/669521468105854094/rwanda-agricultural-strategy-review.
60 . African Union, "Africa Agriculture Transformation Scorecard: the 2017 progress report to the assembly," 2017, https://au.int/sites/default/files/documents/33005-doc-br_report_to_au_summit_draft_stc_eng.pdf.
61 . The sterling achievements of Rwanda are discussed more fully in: Isabelle Tsakok and Tharcisse Guedegbe, "From Asian Green Revolution 1.0 to Sustainable Green Revolution 2.0: Towards a Fertilizer Policy for Smallholder Agriculture in Sub-Saharan Africa, September 2019, Policy Paper, no. 19-16, https://www.policycenter.ma/sites/default/

a long way to go but it has, so far, defied all expectations. Crisis has not crushed it.

- Similarly, *Mauritius* was on the brink of collapse in the early 1980s but is now an upper-middle-income country. At independence (1968), its GNI/capita was $260; now it is $10,860 (2021).[62] Given the high population growth rate—3% per year—of a tiny island nation struggling within a vulnerable, mono-crop economy, the Tittmus and Meade reports (1961) painted a bleak picture of Mauritius' prospects.[63] In the 1980s, Mauritius reeled under several shocks, including a 30% drop in sugar prices (sugar was then the backbone of its economy), the second oil price shock of 1979, and repeated balance-of-payments crises. During these dark days, instead of choosing divisive politics (ethnic and racial tensions can run very high in Mauritius), Mauritius chose to re-orient its sugar-dependent, inward-looking economy into a diversified, trade-oriented, inclusive economy. It had to undertake deep reforms, starting with the vital sugar sector, which took decades.[64] Stiglitz (2011) referred to Mauritius as "*The Mauritius Miracle*".[65]

Vietnam was ravaged by long years of war (from around the mid nineteenth century under French rule), until it was unified under Communist rule in 1975. Following a centralized planning model, by 1986, Vietnam was still an impoverished nation reeling from an annual inflation rate of

---

files/PP%20-%2019-16%20%28TSAKOK%29_0.pdf.
Also, in Isabelle Tsakok, "Regional market integration within AfCFTA to further agri-food and food security—The case of the Republic of Rwanda: Policy Brief, no. 51/22, August 2022, Https://www.policycenter.ma/sites/default/files/2022-08/PB_51-22%20%28%20Tsakok%20%29.pdf.

62. Mauritius' GNI/CAP was US$ 12,840 (Atlas Method, 2020), but it fell following the COVID-19 pandemic to US$ 10, 860 (2021) WDI. https://data.worldbank.org/indicator/NY.GNP.PCAP.CD?locations=MU.

63. The two reports were to the Governor of Mauritius, Sir Colville Montgomery Deverell (Nov 2, 1959 - Jul 10, 1962). They are: Social Policies and Population Growth in Mauritius, by Richard M. Titmuss et al.(1961) London, Methuen; and The Economic and Social Structure of Mauritius by J.E. Meade et al (1961), London, Methuen.
The annual population growth rate in Mauritius has fallen to 0.1% (2018) and 0.0% (2021). WDI. https://data.worldbank.org/indicator/SP.POP.GROW?locations=MU.

64. For more detailed discussions, see Sanjeev K Sobhee, and B. Rajpati, "Rethinking Africa's Agricultural Sector and Rural Transformation in the Global Context: Challenges, Opportunities and Strategic Policy options—The Case of Mauritius," June 2013.; also in Isabelle Tsakok, "Food Security in the Context of COVID-19: The Public Health Challenge—The case of Republic of Mauritius", Policy Brief, no. 37/21, October 2021, .. https://www.policycenter.ma/sites/default/files/PB_37-21_Tsakok.pdf.

65. Joseph E. Stiglitz, "The Mauritius Miracle, " Project Syndicate, March 07, 2011. https://www.project-syndicate.org/commentary/the-mauritius-miracle-2011-03 Also, Joseph Stiglitz, "The Mauritius Miracle or how to make a big success of a small economy," The Guardian, March 7, 2011. https://www.theguardian.com/commentisfree/2011/mar/07/mauritius-healthcare-education_.

more than 400%, with food in short supply, and the budget chronically short of resources.⁶⁶ Doi Moi (economic renovation) was the response to this dire situation. Launched in 1986, it was a return to private smallholder agriculture widespread in Asia, with the Land Law of 1988 mandating the break-up of agricultural collectives. Vietnam managed successfully the gradual transition from a centralized and isolated economy to a market-oriented economy integrated into the global economy. From roughly 1990 to 2016, its growth rate of GDP *per capita* averaged 5.5% per year, and extreme poverty was virtually eliminated except for minority groups. Once, a low-income country—GDP/capita (at 2015 US$) at $481 in 1986; it reached lower middle-income US$2,655 in 2020—Vietnam now aspires to be a high-income industrialized country by 2045.⁶⁷

While very different, these countries share three features: (i) visionary leadership; (ii) good governance of mission-oriented governments; and (iii) a skillful mix of private markets in open economies, public direction and support, and foreign assistance. These few cases clearly show that crisis need not be the end of the road, but can be the beginning of a better road. Their experiences also show that while failure is not permanent, nor is success. Their struggle continues.

---

66 . World Bank Group & the Minister of Planning and Investment in Vietnam, Vietnam 2035: Towards Prosperity, Creativity, Equity, and Democracy—An Overview (Washington D.C: World Bank Group, 2016) 3-4, https://openknowledge.worldbank.org/bitstream/handle/10986/23724/VN2035English.pdf?sequence=11&isAllowed=y.
67 . World Bank Group & Australian Aid. From the Last Mile to the Next Mile: Vietnam Poverty and Equity Assessment (Washington D.C: World Bank Group, 2022): 1-2, https://documents1.worldbank.org/curated/en/099115004242216918/pdf/P176261055e180087097d60965ce02eb562.pdf.

5. Conclusion

We live in turbulent times. Lest we become overwhelmed by these multiple crises, we should remind ourselves of successes in the GS during tough times, the main one being the Green Revolution in wheat and rice in the mid-1960s. Its spread was a giant leap for agriculture and food security, enabling densely populated Asia to avert mass famine. Scientists, governments, farmers, private business, and markets worked together. The Green Revolution highlighted key factors for success. Of course, there is still much more to do as we learn from and build on the Green Revolution. As Snowden (2020) stated for global health: *"Scientific research, enhanced healthcare infrastructures, close international collaboration, health education, protection of biodiversity, and ample funding will all need to be deployed around the globe if we are to secure our civilization"*.[68] We should do no less to build a food secure and resilient Global South.

---

[68] . Frank M Snowden, Epidemics and Society: From the Black Death to the Present, (Yale University Press, 2019); https://doi.org/10.2307/j.ctvqc6gg5

CHAPTER X

Sanctions and Energy Supplies: Challenges and Opportunities for the Global South

Rim Berahab

Over the past two decades, the global energy system has undergone a profound transformation, driven by the urgent need to reduce carbon emissions. The system now appears to be at another inflection point caused by a succession of economic and geopolitical crises that disrupted the energy markets in 2022, and have brought energy-security concerns to the forefront. These crises will spread beyond energy prices, and lead to structural changes in energy flows, investments, and consumption patterns, which will have a lasting impact on the sector and alter the geopolitical balances in the process. The crises also have major implications for the Global South and its energy strategies. On the one hand, the urgent need for Europe to diversify away from Russian oil and gas could open new avenues for some African and Latin American export markets. Yet, this risks locking them into fossil-fuel industries at a time when the world, and Europe in particular, is preparing to phase out such energy. On the other hand, many countries of the South are contenders in terms of renewable energy and critical minerals for the energy transition, but face structural challenges they must overcome first. This conjuncture highlights the divide between the developed and developing world over energy policy, climate action, and energy transition. In particular, countries of the Global South must manage the trilemma of economic development, energy security, and energy transition. Their responses will depend on national priorities, as well as the types of energy and financial resources available. This highlights significant complementarities that, if properly exploited, can increase energy cooperation in the region. But for this, countries of the Global South need to better define their strategies in light of broader social, economic, and geopolitical priorities, including the ability to decarbonize their energy systems, and address the lack of energy access and poverty.

Introduction

The Russia-Ukraine war has caused an overwhelming cascade of events in a global economy already weakened by the COVID-19 crisis and the consequences of climate change. Its fallouts are reshaping the contours of economic and international relations, leading to severe repercussions for the Global South. Ukraine and Russia are both significant producers of crucial commodities: they supply about *"30% of the world's wheat and barley production, one-fifth of the world's corn, and more than half of the world's sunflower oil"*,[1] while Russia is among the world's largest producers and exporters of oil and natural gas. Consequently, commodity prices have peaked in all areas. The agricultural and fertilizer price indices increased by 25% and 10%, respectively, in the first quarter of 2022 compared to the same period in 2021. The price of Brent crude oil increased by about 55% between December 2021 and March 2022, while European natural gas prices were almost seven times higher in March 2022 than in March 2021.[2]

Besides the economic impacts, the war in Ukraine, along with the gas market volatility that started in 2021, has disrupted the geopolitics of energy. Now more than ever, energy security is at the forefront. While oil has been the main driver of global politics and international relations over the past century, the future of oil, and that of fossil fuels more generally, is seemingly challenged by the advent of renewable energy and the recent global wave of decarbonization. However, Russia's invasion of Ukraine has shattered this idea, at least in the short term, leading to significant repercussions for the primary energy players. Consequently, more fossil fuels will be needed in the short term to mitigate strategic exposure to record prices. In contrast, in the longer term, momentum for renewables seems to continue to emerge as a policy trend.

---

1 . United Nations, "Global Impact of War in Ukraine on Food, Energy and Finance Systems: A Three-Dimensional Crisis," Brief no. 1, April 13, 2022, 3-5, https://news.un.org/pages/wp-content/uploads/2022/04/UN-GCRG-Brief-1.pdf.
2 . World Bank Group, Commodity Markets Outlook: The Impact of the War in Ukraine on Commodity Markets, April 2022 (Washington DC, 2022), P. 29-44, http://hdl.handle.net/10986/37223.

Although not directly affected by the war, countries in the Global South will feel the brunt of its consequences. The restructuring of Russia's oil export flows to China and India has direct implications for Middle Eastern players, which may perceive Russia as a competitor in their market. In addition, African oil and gas producers, given their proximity to Europe, and some Latin American countries, such as Venezuela, may see an opportunity to substitute for Russian oil and gas, although already facing structural challenges in production and export capacity. On the other hand, countries of the South that are forerunners in the energy transition or have vast mineral resources could benefit from an acceleration of the energy transition, thus capitalizing on the European Union's ambition to diversify and decarbonize its energy mix by 2050.

The unpredictable nature of the energy crisis may lead to contrasting responses, notably because of the different priorities of countries in the South. One wonders whether the war will lead to a bifurcation of the world's energy supply systems. Indeed, developing countries seem to want to remain in both camps: the partisans of fossil fuels versus the forerunners of the energy transition. However, a return to the pre-pandemic economy model is not an option, given the urgency of the climate crisis. This implies a transformation of the energy landscape. Hence the importance of a well-defined energy strategy at national level, which takes into account short-term uncertainties as well as the long-term vision, and efficient cooperation at regional level to improve synergies and foster positive externalities.

This chapter analyzes the short-term economic and geopolitical implications of the energy sanctions against Russia on countries of the South, in a context of transforming energy geopolitics. It also explores the longer-term prospects of the evolution of energy strategies of countries of the South, focusing on Africa.

1. A Snapshot of Recent Changes in The Geopolitics of Energy: From Oil and Gas to Renewables

Fossil fuels have long underpinned the global energy system, economic growth, and modern lifestyles. The control of oil and gas supplies has been a critical factor in international relations, and has often been intertwined with political and military developments worldwide, with trends influenced by events such as the wars in the Middle East, the Asian and subprime crises, and political upheavals in oil- and gas-producing regions. The geopolitics of oil and gas can therefore be seen as the result of the balance between supply and demand, affecting, among other things, energy prices, the power dynamics between energy exporters and importers, and their energy security.[3]

A few key players stand out in this complex system. As one of the world's most resource-rich countries, Russia's oil resources constitute an economic lever, while its abundant natural gas remains politically relevant in the European and global sphere.[4] In 2021, it was the largest exporter of natural gas (via pipelines), and the second largest producer of crude oil after the United States (Table 1). Saudi Arabia is another important player. It was the world's largest crude oil exporter and third-largest producer after the U.S. and Russia in 2021.[5] Its unique position allows it to influence the global economy and politics significantly. Saudi Arabia, along with other producers including Kuwait and the United Arab Emirates, has the financial ability to voluntarily cut oil production. In contrast, other Organization of the Petroleum Exporting Countries (OPEC) members—Nigeria, Libya, Algeria, Iran, Iraq, and Venezuela—rely on maximum production and high prices to finance their budgets.[6] The U.S., while a significant oil and gas producer, is also a large consumer and is therefore not immune to oil price fluctuations.

Table 1: Top 5 Crude Oil Producers, and Crude Oil and Natural Gas Exporters, 2021

Crude oil production		Crude oil exports		Total natural gas exports	
Thousands of barrels per day		Million tons		Billion cubic meters	
US	11188	Saudi Arabia	323	Russia	241
Russia	10455	Russia	264	US	179
Saudi Arabia	9394	Canada	197	Middle East	143
Canada	4748	West Africa	187	OECD Asia	108
Iraq	4032	Iraq	176	Africa	97

Source: British Petroleum, Statistical Review of World Energy (2022).

---

3 . Aymeric Bricout et al., "From the geopolitics of oil and gas to the geopolitics of the energy transition: Is there a role for European supermajors?," Energy Research & Social Science 88 (2022), https://www.sciencedirect.com/science/article/abs/pii/S2214629622001384.
4 . Fred B. Olayele, "The Geopolitics of Oil and Gas," International Association for Energy Economics, (2015).
5 . British Petroleum, Statistical Review of World Energy (2022).
6 . Fred B. Olayele, "The Geopolitics of Oil and Gas."

In recent years, the prospect of peak oil demand in the not-too-distant future has become a topic of debate in energy circles. This 'peak demand' will have significant geopolitical and geo-economic consequences for oil-producing and importing countries alike.[7] Thus, in the context of an increased alignment of climate policies, the geopolitics of oil and gas seems to be progressively shifting to the geopolitics of the energy transition, partly because of impressive technological advances in renewable energy and their declining technological costs. The dominant literature on the geopolitics of the energy transition argues that the shift from fossil to renewable energy technologies could lead to geopolitical and strategic reshaping, including *"the emergence of new winners and losers, increased competition for critical materials (e.g., lithium, cobalt, copper), the re-emergence of the resource curse among countries rich in critical materials and/or with large exportable surpluses of renewable energy, the risk that interstate power outages will become an important foreign policy tool and an increased level of vulnerability to cyberattacks on power grids"*.[8]

This view of the geopolitical challenges of the energy transition, however, has been criticized on the grounds that *"the risk of geopolitical competition over critical materials for renewables is limited; the resource curse as we know it in the oil sector will not necessarily reappear in many countries with respect to renewables; cross-border power outages will generally not be able to be used as a geopolitical weapon, and it is not clear that the increasing use of renewables will exacerbate cybersecurity risks"*.[9] Altogether, multiple issues related to the geopolitics of the energy transition remain contested in the literature.

Despite this, the energy transition and increasingly ambitious decarbonization policies worldwide will have undeniable economic consequences for oil and gas-producing countries. These countries have still not diversified their economies and are highly dependent on oil revenues for most of their budgets. Declines in revenues can, thus, have a destabilizing effect, particularly on countries with fragile political institutions, such as Venezuela, Iran, and Nigeria, or that are marked by political, cultural, or economic fractures, such as Libya and Iraq. Conversely, countries deprived

---

7 . Robert J. Johnston, "Shifting Gears: Geopolitics of the Global Energy Transition," Atlantic Council, June 10, 2021, https://www.atlanticcouncil.org/in-depth-research-reports/report/shifting-gears-geopolitics-of-the-global-energy-transition/.
8 . Bricout. et al., "The geopolitics of the energy transition.".
9 . Ibid.

of oil and gas, but which have significant renewable energy resources, such as Morocco, can benefit from this transformation by capitalizing on clean technologies. In this context, the war between Russia and Ukraine has exacerbated the significant disruptions in the energy markets that have been observed since the end of 2021.[10] It has also brought the concept of energy security back to the forefront, and has provided another source of uncertainty and instability within the geopolitics of energy.

2. Energy Sanctions Against Russia and Resulting Challenges: Crossed Economic and Geopolitical Insights

As the war between Russia and Ukraine unfolds, sanctions against the former are multiplying so rapidly that it is proving challenging to monitor their evolution. Measures taken so far include sanctions against individuals, economic sanctions, restrictions on state media, and diplomatic measures. In the case of the European Union (EU), these sanctions add to existing measures imposed on Russia since 2014, following the annexation of Crimea and the non-implementation of the Minsk agreements.

Russia is thought to have earned nearly $100 billion from oil and gas exports during the first 100 days of the war.[11] To limit Russia's energy export revenues, the EU adopted its eighth major sanctions package in October 2022. This included the implementation of a price cap on Russian oil, as agreed with the G7 and announced on September 2, 2022. While the ban on the EU importing Russian crude oil by sea remains in place in its entirety (with a temporary exception for certain crudes delivered by pipeline), this price cap, once implemented, *"would allow European operators to undertake and support the transportation of Russian oil to third countries, provided that its price remains below a pre-determined cap"*.[12] The aim of this sanction is to reduce Russia's revenues, while maintaining the stability of global energy markets through continuous supply. This measure, closely coordinated with G7 partners, would take effect after December 5, 2022,

---

10 . These disruptions lie in a lack of investment in hydrocarbon production, combined with the low level of natural gas storage in Europe and a rapid increase in the demand for hydrocarbons in the main world markets.
11 . Leggett Theo, "Ukraine war: Russia earns $97bn on energy exports since invasion," BBC, June 13, 2022, https://www.bbc.com/news/business-61785111.
12 . European Commission, "Ukraine: EU agrees on eighth package of sanctions against Russia"), Press release, October 6, 2022, https://ec.europa.eu/commission/presscorner/detail/en/ip_22_5989.

for crude oil, and February 5, 2023, for refined petroleum products, after a further EU decision. The EU also announced it would halt Russian coal imports by August, but is less keen to impose sanctions on Russian gas because it relies on Russia for about 45% of its gas needs.

In the U.S., the Biden Administration, despite the sharp increase in energy prices, issued an Executive Order in March 2022 banning imports of Russian oil, liquefied natural gas, and coal, and in April 2022, signed the Ending Importation of Russian Oil Act into law. However, it should be noted that the U.S. is not highly dependent on Russia for its energy supplies, as Russian crude oil represents only 3% of total U.S. crude imports, according to the American Fuel and Petrochemical Manufacturers (AFPM) trade association.[13] The United Kingdom announced it would phase out imports of Russian oil over the rest of 2022, while Australia banned imports of Russian oil and coal.[14]

a. Economic Implications: Towards Tighter Monetary Policy to Curb Inflationary Pressures

From an economic perspective, several mechanisms can be distinguished through which sanctions against Russia, particularly energy sanctions, are being transmitted to the global economy. Among the most important are changes in commodity prices, disruption of commodity supply chains, and tightening of monetary policies.[15] At first glance, the escalating Russia-Ukraine conflict has pushed Brent and West Texas Intermediate (WTI) crude oil prices to their highest levels since 2014 (Figure 1). This comes in the context of global energy markets being under strain since late 2021 because of a combination of supply and demand factors, in particular a booming demand for oil and natural gas related to the rapid post-COVID-19 economic recovery, and a decline in stocks and inventories. Adding to this global tension, oil and gas supply has not kept pace with strong demand, and OPEC production has fallen short of its targets, with Angola and Nigeria unable to meet their quotas.

---

13. "Russia-Ukraine war: Biden bans US imports of Russian oil and gas," Al Jazeera, March 8, 2022, https://www.aljazeera.com/news/2022/3/8/russia-ukraine-war-biden-bans-us-imports-of-russian-oil-and-gas#:~:text=The%20US%20is%20not%20highly,Manufacturers%20(AFPM)%20trade%20association.
14. Chad P. Bown, "Russia's war on Ukraine: A sanctions timeline," Peterson Institute for International Economics, August 15, 2022, https://www.piie.com/blogs/realtime-economic-issues-watch/russias-war-ukraine-sanctions-timeline.
15. Ira Kalish, "How sanctions impact Russia and the global economy," Deloitte Insights, March 15, 2022, https://www2.deloitte.com/us/en/insights/economy/global-economic-impact-of-sanctions-on-russia.html.

Figure 1: Price Volatility in Energy Markets: Crude Oil and Gas (Price index, base = 1 October 2021)

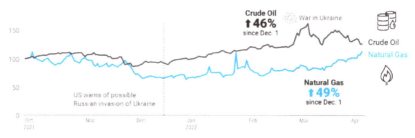

Source: UN ECA based on Bloomberg & MarketWatch data, up to 7 April 2022.

Adding to this price pressure are the risks associated with supply-chain disruptions. Even before the start of the Russia-Ukraine war, freight costs were multiples of their historical averages, complicating re-routing efforts and increasing consumer prices and import costs.[16] Since the start of the war, many container shippers, fearing sanctions imposed by Western governments, have halted all freight bookings to and from Russia, except for food and medicine shipments. Moreover, European and Russian aircraft are banned from entering each other's airspace.

As a result, soaring prices for commodities and disruptions of supply chains have led to high and prolonged inflation in many economies (Figure 2). Global inflation is expected to reach 7.4% in 2022 and approach 5% in 2023, compared to average annual global inflation of 3.8% from 2001 to 2019[17]. In emerging markets and developing economies (EMDEs), inflation has reached its highest level since 2011. As a result, half of the inflation-targeting central banks in developing economies now face rates above their target ranges.[18] Inflation forecasts vary by region. Still, there is an upward trend (Figure 3), particularly for Central and South Asia, Latin America, and the Caribbean, where inflation is associated with currency depreciation, and political instability in some countries, as well as the recovery of domestic demand.

---

16 . United Nations, Global Impact of war in Ukraine, (2022).
17 . IMF, "World Economic Outlook Database," IMF, April 2022, https://www.imf.org/en/Publications/WEO/weo-database/2022/April.
18 . Indermit Gill, "Developing economies face a rough ride as global interest rates rise," World Bank Blog, March 03, 2022, https://blogs.worldbank.org/voices/developing-economies-face-rough-ride-global-interest-rates-rise.

Figure 2: Consumer Price Inflation, Year-on-Year

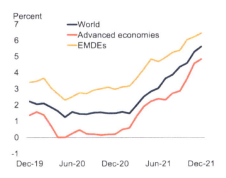

Figure 3: Changes in Inflation Expectations

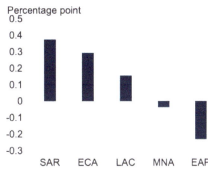

Figure 4: Shifts in Monetary Policies in EMDEs

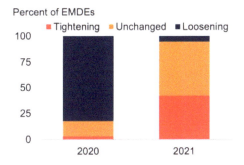

Source: Consensus Economics; Haver Analytics; IMF Annual Report on Exchange Arrangements and Exchange Restrictions; World Bank. EMDEs = emerging market and developing economies, EAP = East Asia and Pacific, ECA = Europe and Central Asia, LAC = Latin America and the Caribbean, MNA = Middle East and North Africa, SAR = South Asia.

To prevent the possibility of more sustained inflationary pressures, many central banks in advanced economies have tightened their monetary policies by signaling earlier-than-expected increases in interest rates, which may result in higher debt-servicing costs for developing countries. This is especially true since the COVID-19 crisis has left many developing economies with limited monetary and fiscal space. Furthermore, central banks in several emerging markets have taken their cue from their advanced economy counterparts. About 40% of emerging and developing country central banks, at time of writing, have already raised their key interest rates in the last year.[19] Admittedly, monetary policy alone cannot solve the remaining bottlenecks

---

19 . Ibid.

related to the pandemic; however, it can slow aggregate demand to deal with demand-driven inflationary pressures.

Therefore, given the high levels of socio-economic stress in countries of the South as a result of the COVID-19 crisis and the effects of climate change, the Russia-Ukraine war has further exacerbated their economic vulnerabilities. Indeed, according to the 2022 *Report on Financing for Sustainable Development*, "60% of least developed countries and other low-income countries are already at high risk of debt distress or are in debt distress because of the war".[20] These countries are also far more affected by shortages of essential goods and electricity, even at a time when the focus is mostly on Europe's dependence on Russian energy. Countries that would fare best are likely to be those that have more robust economic diplomacy networks and the ability to substitute more local imports.[21]

b. Geopolitical Implications: A Restructuring of Export Flows That Could Disrupt the Current Power Balances

The shock inflicted by the Russia-Ukraine war has major short-term implications for energy geopolitics. Chief among these is the restructuring of export flows in the global energy market. On the one hand, Europe has begun a race to find alternative oil suppliers to Russia, mainly in the Atlantic basin. This region exported just under 3 million barrels per day (b/d) to Europe in 2020, including 1.1 million b/d from the U.S. The latter was expected to increase its crude production by more than 1 million b/d between March and December 2022.[22] Much of this increase is likely to come from light sweet oil, which is not a direct substitute for the medium sour Ural oil blend Russia exports to Europe. U.S. shale oil appears to be another alternative, but it alone cannot substitute for Russian oil, especially since U.S. shale production is declining.[23] Canadian crude oil production, the best alternative in terms of substitution, is growing, but there are capacity constraints on export infrastructures. Some Latin American oil production

---

20 . United Nations, Global Impact of war in Ukraine, (2022).
21 . Jonathan Hackenbroich & Abhinav Chugh, "What do sanctions help achieve? An expert explains," World Economic Forum, March 22, 2022, https://www.weforum.org/agenda/2022/03/what-do-sanctions-help-achieve-an-expert-explains/.
22 . Kaushik Deb & Abhiram Rajendran, "How Sanctions on Russian Crude Oil Could Impact Market Share for Major Regional Suppliers," Columbia SIPA, Center on Global Energy Policy, May 26, 2022, https://www.energypolicy.columbia.edu/research/commentary/how-sanctions-russian-crude-oil-could-impact-market-share-major-regional-suppliers.
23 . Helen Thompson, "What does the war in Ukraine mean for the geopolitics of energy prices?" Economics Observatory,26 May, 2022, https://www.economicsobservatory.com/what-does-the-war-in-ukraine-mean-for-the-geopolitics-of-energy-prices.

is also closer to Urals oil. However, these producers are either very small (Ecuador, Colombia, Cuba), or face structural problems affecting their production, as in Venezuela. West African crude production, meanwhile, appears to be in structural decline, with a drop of almost 1.8 million b/d between 2010 and 2020. It is, therefore, unlikely to be able to supply high volumes to the EU in the short term.[24] This leaves OPEC's Middle Eastern members to play a key role. Among the EU's major crude suppliers before Russia's war in Ukraine were Saudi Arabia and Iraq, both of which exported about 0.8 million to 0.9 million b/d to Europe. However, so far, OPEC has stuck to its July 2021 quota agreement, promising incremental increases of 400,000 barrels per month, but delivering much less because of production constraints.[25]

Conversely, Russia is also looking for alternative markets in order to adjust to the various energy sanctions and compensate for the European market share it stands to lose in the coming years. Asia offers a promising outlet, as it has seen significant growth in energy demand over the past few years. India has become the main buyer of additional volumes of Russian oil. Its imports increased from almost zero in February 2022 to 0.9 million b/d in May 2022. By comparison, its average imports did not exceed 0.2 million b/d in previous years.[26] China quickly followed India's lead. In April and May 2022, Russian offshore oil deliveries to China reached their highest levels since March 2020, exceeding 1 million b/d, compared to an average of 0.8 million b/d in 2021. Demand for Russian oil is not limited to China and India, as Indonesia and Sri Lanka also show interest. Several factors underpin the growth of Russian oil supply to Asia. The most prominent is the unprecedented discount that Russian producers offer their customers to offset the potential risks and costs of buying politically sensitive oil. According to various estimates, this discount could be as high as $25 to $35 per barrel. In addition, considering the new geopolitical realities, Russian oil flow into Asia has been facilitated by several techniques previously used to circumvent sanctions to purchase Iranian oil.

---

24 . Deb & Rajendran, "How Sanctions on Russian Crude Oil Could Impact Market Share for Major Regional Suppliers."
25 . Raad Alkadiri, "Ukraine war reshapes energy geopolitics and decarbonization." Energy and Commodities Outlook, ReedSmith, 2022, https://www.reedsmith.com/en/perspectives/energy-commodities-outlook-2022/2022/04/ukraine-war-reshapes-energy-geopolitics-and-decarbonization.
26 . Nikolay Kozhanov, "The war in Ukraine and the new reality in Asian oil markets," Middle East Institute, June 01, 2022, https://www.mei.edu/publications/war-ukraine-and-new-reality-asian-oil-markets.

The search for alternatives to Russian natural gas is not as straightforward since Europe is much more dependent on Russian gas than oil. Yet, new prospects for liquefied natural gas (LNG) are arising. In recent years, LNG has begun to change the dynamics of the gas market and the politics of this energy commodity. Gas markets have traditionally been regional, constrained by the geography of pipelines. However, the flexibility and marketability of LNG relative to pipeline gas give it a flexibility more akin to crude oil, as flows can now be redirected to meet demand. This offers European consumers and policymakers options to diversify gas supplies they did not have before. Once again, the U.S. has emerged as a promising LNG exporter, but the question is whether sufficient volumes can be imported from the U.S. in the short term. Another constraint for Europe is the lack of infrastructural storage facilities for LNG. This shift is prompting Russia to look for new buyers for its natural gas, with China likely to absorb much of any surplus. However, this will not happen overnight; new pipeline infrastructure will need to be put in place, requiring significant time and funds. More recently, the sabotaging of the Nord Stream 1 and 2 pipelines on September 26, 2022, has raised additional concerns among Europeans. Although the damage to the Nord Stream 1 and 2 pipelines will have only a limited immediate impact on Europe's natural gas supply, as neither pipeline was operational, the incident further clouds the prospects for energy supply and security in Europe, especially as the origin of the attacks remains unknown.

These changes in the supply of energy products, particularly the redirection of Russian oil and gas exports to Asia, will have a direct and significant short-term impact on Middle Eastern players, particularly Gulf oil producers. Iran was one of the first to be affected, as Russia challenged its position on the grey market for sanctioned oil, mainly because the restrictions on Russian oil are not as strict as those on Iranian oil. Moreover, Russian liquefied petroleum gas (LPG) has also become an important competitor to Iranian LPG in Turkey, Pakistan, and Afghanistan. In the Indian market, Russian oil has challenged the positions of other Gulf producers, notably the United Arab Emirates, Saudi Arabia, and especially Iraq. By May 2022, these three countries had lost a significant share of their supply to Moscow. Russian oil may also pose a threat to Saudi interests in the Chinese market, although the volume of Saudi supplies to China has increased steadily so far.[27]

All these factors have caused Gulf countries to reconsider their pricing policies. Iraq was the first to reduce its oil prices in April 2022, and other

---

27 . Ibid.

Gulf producers followed suit in May. However, in October 2022, OPEC+ announced that it would reduce oil production by approximately 2 million b/d, representing a reduction of nearly 2% of global supply. This announcement had an immediate effect on oil and gas markets, driving prices higher, and came at an interesting time, ahead of the November midterm elections in the U.S. While the U.S. has accused Saudi Arabia of aligning itself with Russia to drive up oil prices at a time when much of the world is struggling to manage rising inflation, Saudi Arabia counters that the OPEC+ decisions were based on purely economic considerations and not politically motivated to hurt the U.S.[28] This situation illustrates how politicized oil and gas is, making it difficult to forecast future evolutions in the market. Despite this, Russian prices have proved more influential than other factors affecting the energy market. However, Russia will also be unable to immediately redirect all its oil to Asia and find buyers for it, as shown by the growing volume of Russian oil reserves accumulating in warehouses and tankers. This means that Moscow will have, at least in the medium term, some hydrocarbon reserves that it can use to influence the market balance.

3. What's Next: Towards More Concerted Energy Policies Among the Countries of the South?

Beyond the short-term adjustments dictated by the disruption of energy markets following the sanctions against Russia, it remains paramount that countries of the Global South maintain a long-term vision of energy policy consistent with the goals of development, stability, sustainability, and economic resilience. From an energy perspective, one of the mid- to long-term impacts would be the effect of disruption on the pace of energy transitions, and the divergence between different regions of the world in the speed of decarbonization and emissions reductions. This is an important issue, especially since many countries in the Global South are on the frontlines of the negative effects of climate change. Therefore, a persistent long-term rise in oil and gas prices could have opposite effects. It could redirect investment towards extractive industries and fossil-fuel power generation, at the risk of reversing the decarbonization trend observed over the last five years. But it could also accelerate the transition to alternative energy sources, especially in countries that seek to build energy resilience.

---

28 . Tom Wilson, "OPEC+ oil output cut risks tipping world into recession, warns IEA,". Financial Times, October 13, 2022, https://www.ft.com/content/86254c47-711f-4115-bcec-cefead602b65.

Admittedly, this vision will depend on political leadership and maintaining momentum toward meeting the commitments of the Paris Agreement and the 2030 Agenda. It also has significant implications for countries of the South and their respective energy policies.

a. The EU's Renewed Quest for Oil and Gas: A Short-Term Fix Perpetuating the North-South Divide on Climate Action?

With its partial embargo on Russian oil and its plan to phase out imported Russian natural gas by 2030, the EU is showing a renewed interest in the hydrocarbon industry. Given its proximity to Europe, Africa could benefit. Recent examples include, but are not limited to, German Chancellor Olaf Scholz's visit to Senegal in May 2022 to pursue the development of a gas field scheduled to open next year; talks in April 2022 between EU diplomats and Nigerian officials on developing the country as an alternative gas supplier; and various new agreements by Italy to boost natural gas imports from Algeria, Angola, and the Republic of Congo.[29] However, this renewed interest seems to be at odds with the EU's increasingly ambitious decarbonization policies, as set out in its European Green Deal strategy. It also carries long-term implications for African countries.

While African oil and gas producers may benefit from this interest, mainly in the form of additional revenues, most countries that currently produce oil and gas have limited spare capacity to rapidly increase supply. In addition, the development of future potential projects may be delayed because of operational factors. In Mozambique and Tanzania, for instance, investment decisions on major liquefied natural gas (LNG) projects are unlikely to be made until at least 2024, given safety concerns in the former, and ongoing negotiations and pending project design processes in the latter. This means that significant production is unlikely before 2030. In addition, most of the oil and gas reserves in Mauritania and Senegal will not be developed until later phases of the projects.

Furthermore, rapidly scaling up oil and gas production in Africa will require significant investment. However, in recent years, international oil companies (IOCs) have drastically reduced their financing of hydrocarbon projects in Africa because of growing calls from several European countries

---

29 . Neil Munshi, Paul Burkhardt & William Clowes, "Europe's Rush to Buy Africa's Natural Gas Draws Cries of Hypocrisy," Bloomberg, July 10, 2022, https://www.bloomberg.com/news/features/2022-07-10/europe-s-africa-gas-imports-risk-climate-goals-leave-millions-without-power#xj4y7vzkg.

for a faster energy transition.[30] Thus, while Europe has urged IOCs and African countries to move away from fossil fuels, it has failed to accelerate financing for green projects that could provide alternative energy sources. Consequently, while Africa has abundant sunshine and wind, it has little infrastructure to harness it. It also faces much higher financing costs for green projects, which are considered riskier investments. This has prompted many African leaders to denounce what they see as energy hypocrisy that perpetuates the West's exploitation of the region.

This is occurring at a time when Africa still deals with vital structural challenges in the energy sector. Access to energy is still uneven in most African countries. Sub-Saharan Africa's share of the world's population without access to electricity has increased from 74% before the pandemic to 77% today.[31] And for those with access to electricity, reliability is another issue. The challenge of energy poverty, thus, remains an important energy security issue for Africa, and deserves the same urgency as the energy crisis in Europe. Furthermore, with most African countries seeing increasing domestic energy demand, many governments are now shifting their focus to local markets to meet domestic demand, rather than European and Asian markets.

It can be argued that Europe's renewed interest in oil and gas would be short-lived. However, it is a quick fix to short-term needs but carries long-term consequences. For producers in the South to bring additional oil and gas to market, they must invest today in their future production. However, investment in oil and gas is a capital-intensive business with long payback periods. Investors must be confident that by the time their products reach the market, demand will still be there and will remain there for many years. The problem is that these same governments are not only encouraging developing countries to accelerate their phase-out of fossil fuels, but are also committing to killing demand for these products in the years ahead in their quest for decarbonization. This would risk locking oil- and gas-producing countries into fossil fuels for much longer, leading to stranded assets at a time when the energy transition will progress worldwide. Therefore, countries in the South must carefully assess long-term uncertainties and ensure that sound revenue management frameworks are in place, including

---

30 . International Energy Agency, "Key areas for policy action," in Africa Energy Outlook, World Energy Outlook Special Report (International Energy Agency, 2022), https://iea.blob.core. windows.net/assets/2598fb11-8c7e-4e73-a105-3295954212d4/AfricaEnergyOutlook2022. pdf.
31 . IEA, "Access to electricity, SDG7: Data and Projections: Covid-19 continues to reverse electricity" 2022, IEA. https://www.iea.org/reports/sdg7-data-and-projections/access-to-electricity.

the directing of potential windfall oil and gas revenues toward sustainable development and economic diversification.

b. The Energy Transition Amid Increased Uncertainties: What Opportunities for the South?

Amidst the shock to energy markets caused by the Russia-Ukraine war, the South continues to face a dual structural energy challenge: meeting the needs of millions of people who still lack access to basic modern energy services, while participating in the global transition to clean, low-carbon energy systems. This dilemma raises the question of the pace of the energy transition. It is undeniable that the threat of climate change is imminent and that it must be given the same attention and urgency as other economic or geopolitical crises. Yet, because of their level of economic development, limited financing capacity, and lower responsibility for anthropogenic greenhouse gas emissions,[32] many developing countries argue that the transition, while imperative, must be tailored to their different socio-economic contexts, in order to generate maximum benefits in terms of sustainable growth, job creation, climate resilience, and energy security, while minimizing the risks of energy supply disruptions, stranded assets, and job losses in the fossil-fuel industries.

Therefore, the emerging position in many developing countries is that different energy sources, both fossil and renewable, are needed to ensure socio-economic development objectives. This would imply the coexistence of both types of energy, until the structures are in place to gradually substitute fossil fuels with clean, reliable, viable alternatives. The time this takes will depend on several country-specific factors, including the level of development, energy resources, financing capacity, institutional and regulatory environment, and political will. Studies have also shown that sustainable energy policies are more likely to succeed if they also contribute to other societal and economic development goals.[33] Nevertheless, the energy transition in developing countries will also depend on the level of financing that rich countries are willing to mobilize to accelerate the switch to clean energy.

---

32 . However, the role of some developing countries with high GHG emissions, such as China and India, revives the divide between the North and South on climate action.
33 . Dilip. Ahuja & Marika. Tatsutani, "Sustainable energy for developing countries," Sapiens 2, no. 1, 2022, https://journals.openedition.org/sapiens/823#tocto1n3.

At the same time, developing countries are not helpless. There is significant potential for cross-regional cooperation in the energy transition. For instance, low-carbon technologies cannot be deployed without mining. Minerals including copper, lithium, and cobalt are essential to the energy transition. The EU's commitment to decarbonization thus presents opportunities for African countries that produce the critical minerals needed for these low-carbon technologies. Africa has more than 40% of the world's reserves of cobalt, manganese, and platinum, critical minerals for batteries and hydrogen technologies.[34] South Africa, the Democratic Republic of Congo, and Mozambique currently hold a significant share of world production, but many other countries may have undiscovered deposits. Latin America is not to be outdone. Chile is the world's largest copper producer, but significant investments are needed to maintain current production volumes.

However, the main challenges for the mining sector are how to decarbonize the production of critical minerals, and how to better communicate their crucial role in the energy transition to the public. If these challenges are not addressed, critical minerals risk becoming a bottleneck in the energy transition. The issue of a new mining dependency must also be addressed, to prevent the current dynamics of increased interdependence of oil and gas markets from being transmitted to the critical minerals market. Indeed, in 2019, China alone was responsible for processing and refining 90% of the rare earth elements produced, 50%-70% of lithium and cobalt, and about 35% of nickel production.[35]

---

34 . IEA, Africa Energy Outlook.
35 . IEA, The Role of Critical Minerals in Clean Energy Transitions (Paris: IEA, 2022), https://www.iea.org/reports/the-role-of-critical-minerals-in-clean-energy-transitions, License: CC BY 4.0.

Figure 5: An Expanding Network of Hydrogen Trade Routes, Plans, and Agreements

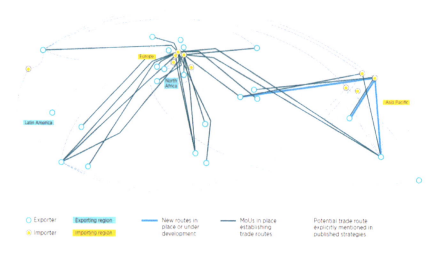

Source: IRENA (2022).

In addition to critical minerals, some countries in the South are among the forerunners in wind and solar technologies. Others have great potential for green-hydrogen production, which is a cornerstone of the EU's REPowerEU energy strategy. Indeed, *"the REPowerEU plan's ambition is to produce 10 million tonnes and import 10 million tonnes of renewable hydrogen in the EU by 2030 – a substantial increase from the 5.6 million tonnes foreseen within the revised Renewable Energy Directive, published in July 2021"*.[36] Hydrogen has, thus, the potential to influence the geography of energy trade, further regionalizing energy relationships. Africa, the Americas, the Middle East, and Oceania have the highest technical potential for green-hydrogen production (Figure 5).[37] However, the ability to produce large volumes of low-cost green hydrogen varies considerably. Moreover, while having access to abundant renewable energy is an asset in the race for clean hydrogen, it may not be enough. Many other factors come into play, including existing infrastructure and the current energy mix, as well as the cost of capital and access to necessary technologies. Realizing the technical

---

36 . European Commission, "Energy: Hydrogen," (2022), https://energy.ec.europa.eu/topics/energy-systems-integration/hydrogen_en#:~:text=Hydrogen%20accelerator,-With%20the%20publication&text=The%20REPowerEU%20plan's%20ambition%20is,Directive%2C%20published%20in%20July%202021.

37 . IRENA- International Renewable Energy Agency, Geopolitics of the Energy Transformation the Hydrogen Factor, (Abu Dhabi: IRENA, 2022), https://www.irena.org/publications/2022/Jan/Geopolitics-of-the-Energy-Transformation-Hydrogen.

potential will also depend on soft factors, including government support, investment climate, and political stability.

The current energy crisis highlights the many reasons why global decarbonization is crucial, not only to combat climate change but also to enhance sustainable economic growth, peace, and security. But it also shows how complicated the energy transition will be, and the inevitable tensions between urgent needs and long-term goals. Achieving a carbon-free global energy system that can meet the needs of all will require treating energy poverty as the crisis it is, abolishing double standards in development finance, and managing the new geopolitical vulnerabilities created by the shift to a low-carbon economy. Ultimately, it requires partnerships between private and public sectors, and the North and South.

4. Conclusion and Policy Recommendations

The geopolitics of energy is now a source of increased instability. The energy sanctions against Russia have led to global repercussions, as shown by the tightening of energy markets, which has caused prices of all fossil fuels to spike. In the Global South, these disruptions have created vicious cycles of rising living costs, falling real incomes, and reduced social protection and safety nets, which can trigger social and political unrest. Developing countries are now increasingly called on to contribute to Europe's energy security, whether by supplying oil and gas, or by tapping into their renewable energy and mineral resources. This has important implications for their own national energy strategies, especially as they face structural economic and energy challenges, and must also ensure their domestic markets are supplied.

The ongoing energy crisis also highlights the disconnect between the developed and developing world on energy policy, climate action, and energy transition. In a region where fossil fuels are still coveted, tensions between urgent needs and long-term objectives are therefore inevitable. In general, countries in the Global South struggle to manage the trilemma of economic development, energy security, and energy transition. Their responses to these challenges will depend on national priorities, the type of energy resources (renewable or fossil), and the financial resources available to them. For oil and gas exporting countries, such as Nigeria, the transition will require trade-offs between fossil fuels and renewables in the short term to maintain an uninterrupted energy supply. This trade-off involves an efficient oil and gas sector, along with increased investment in renewable energy deployment, as well as diversification of their export structure to reduce their economy's dependence on oil and gas revenues. For oil and gas importing countries rich in renewable energies, such as Morocco, the focus should be on the institutional and regulatory environment to further facilitate the deployment of clean energy.

In both cases, government intervention in the energy sector is likely to be enhanced by providing a greater diversity of energy supplies and adequate reserves for emergencies. However, state intervention to strengthen energy security should not be limited to oil and gas, but should also include other commodities such as minerals essential for transition. Nor should it be limited to subsidies, tax breaks, and other incentives, as diplomacy can also help ensure adequate energy supplies in times of crisis. Moreover, the relatively short timeframe for achieving climate goals should encourage countries of the Global South to opt for energy policies that meet today's needs without compromising tomorrow's energy transition. In this sense, governments must be very careful in adopting such policies, as the latter should be limited to hydrocarbon projects deemed necessary to meet short-term energy security needs, while favoring more versatile projects, such as those that can provide clean energy in the medium to long term. One solution would be to ensure that new oil and gas facilities can be adapted to low-carbon technologies, such as carbon capture technology or low-carbon fuels like green hydrogen and ammonia.

Underlying these efforts is the issue of financing the transformation of the energy sector, which remains crucial. Current strategies, capacities, and funding levels are not yet sufficient for a fundamental energy-sector transformation in emerging and developing economies. Annual investments in all parts of the energy sector in developing and emerging markets have fallen by about 20% since 2016, partly because of persistent challenges in raising financing for clean energy projects.[38] The COVID-19 pandemic has weakened corporate balance sheets and consumers' ability to pay, and has put additional pressure on public finances. Public funding will continue to play a critical role, particularly in grid infrastructure and transitions for emissions-intensive sectors, but will not be sufficient by itself. Mobilizing capital on a much larger scale will require a dramatic increase in the role of the private sector. A greater role for international financial and development

---

38 . IEA, "It's time to make clean energy investment in emerging and developing economies a top global priority," June 9, , Press release, June 9, 2021, https://www.iea.org/news/it-s-time-to-make-clean-energy-investment-in-emerging-and-developing-economies-a-top-global-priority.

institutions will be essential to catalyze these investments. Actions by policymakers at home to address challenges and opportunities will not, on their own, generate sufficient momentum. Supportive international commitment and support will be essential to catalyze needed investments in critical areas and to support longer-term reform processes, starting by fulfilling the commitment by developed economies to mobilize $100 billion per year for climate finance.[39]

Therefore, efforts to achieve a real concerted energy strategy among countries of the Global South will remain futile until the interests of countries of the region are aligned. The divergence between these countries on energy policies hides complementarities that, if well exploited, can strengthen regional cooperation with positive externalities for each party. To foster such collaboration, countries of the Global South should better define their strategies in light of broader social, economic, and geopolitical priorities, including the ability to decarbonize their energy systems and address the lack of energy access and poverty.

---

39 . Lorena Gonzales & Joe Thwaites, Julie Bos et al., "Are Countries Providing Enough to the $100 Billion Climate Finance Goal?", World Resource Institute, October 7, 2021, https://www.wri.org/insights/developed-countries-contributions-climate-finance-goal.

CHAPTER XI

The EU Carbon Border Adjustment Mechanism Amid Global Tensions: A Recipe for Disaster

Kevin Verbelen

The Carbon Border Adjustment Mechanism (CBAM) is a draft European Union law that was first presented as part of the 'Fit for 55' package of the European Commission, and which aims at reducing the EU's carbon emissions by 55% by 2030, compared to 1990. The Fit for 55 package comes as the EU sees the need to accelerate the reduction of CO_2 if it wishes to achieve its goal of becoming climate neutral by 2050, in accordance with its European Green Deal. Aware that this target implies drastic economic and industrial change, the bloc is wary of businesses relocating from the EU to environmentally less-ambitious regions, an effect referred to as "carbon leakage". The European Commission therefore determined that more legislation is needed to counter carbon leakage. The Commission, the Council of the EU and the European Parliament are aligned on introducing the CBAM. Even though discussions continue about the nature and effect of this innovative mechanism, little attention is paid to the international reactions to CBAM. Australia and India see it as a protectionist tool. Countries from the Global South worry about their much-needed access to the EU market. Even though the CBAM is promoted as a climate measure, it is seen by others as a trade-restricting measure. Amidst global tensions and the efforts of the world's biggest economies to become strategically autonomous from each other, business is restructuring at a rapid pace towards a local-for-local strategy. This strategy, however, reduces the intra-dependency of countries. It pushes countries into more competitive relationships and widens the gap between those who can keep pace and those who cannot. With a dysfunctional Dispute Settlement Body of the World Trade Organization, and an increasingly more pressing public debt crisis because of the COVID-19 pandemic and the war in Ukraine, CBAM could act as a trigger for global economic disintegration. It is in this regard that the CBAM can be considered a recipe for disaster with implications to the health of Europe's industry and a cause for concern for countries of the Global South.

Introduction

The adoption of the 2015 Paris Agreement under the United Nations Framework Convention on Climate Change (hereinafter UNFCCC) was a historic milestone. For the first time, countries committed to collectively tackling climate change.[1] One hundred and ninety-six parties signed the Paris Agreement, and it contains a panoply of unseen national pledges and efforts aiming at reducing global emissions of carbon dioxide (hereinafter CO_2) and other greenhouse gases, as well as other measures to ensure that the planet's rise in average temperature remains below two degrees Celsius above pre-industrial levels.[2] [3]

The merit of the Paris Agreement lays in the comprehensiveness of the legally binding commitments made by the members to the Agreement. However, the Paris Agreement has led to a mosaic of national action plans that differ in scope, time, and ambition. Following the signing of the Paris Agreement, the European Union (EU) presented the *European Green Deal*. The European Green Deal is a series of legislative packages that aim at making Europe the first climate neutral continent by 2050.[4] In order to obtain this objective, the EU commits to 'greening' its policies in different areas of governance, covering ocean management, industries, agriculture, transport, energy, research and innovation, as well as financial and regional development schemes. The European Green Deal represents the EU's chosen path to the Paris Agreement. Nevertheless, the Agreement

---

1 . Paris Agreement, 29 November 2018, UNFCC, https://unfccc.int/sites/default/files/english_paris_agreement.pdf.
2 . Paris Agreement, Art. 2.1.
3 . Ibid., Art. 4.1.
4 . "Communication From the Commission to the European Parliament, the European Council, the Council – The European Economic and Social Committee and the Committee of the Regions, The European Green Deal," European Commission, December 11, 2019, https://eur-lex.europa.eu/resource.html?uri=cellar:b828d165-1c22-11ea-8c1f-01aa75ed71a1.0002.02/DOC_1&format=PDF.

allows for all signatory countries to present their own plan at the speed they have determined for themselves. It goes without saying that the EU has set ambitious targets as it arguably wishes to lead the world when it comes to climate policy. The consequence is that the cost for de-carbonization and climate mitigation will increase globally, but it will not be the same in different parts of the world. To a certain extent this is a good thing, since many developing countries also have a lesser share in global carbon emissions, or are dealing with the consequences of policies imposed on them in the past. However, the lack of a steady base of rules and regulations at multilateral level in addition to a substantial asymmetry in national policies are resulting in uncertainty, economic concerns, insufficient comparability and a lack of level playing field for industries vulnerable to fast changing climate policies. These adverse effects could easily lead to so called 'carbon leakage', which refers to the moving of industrial activities and investments from a region or country with a more ambitious climate policy to a region or country with less ambitious climate policies. This is especially of concern to regions and nations that have introduced a cost linked to carbon emissions, such as the European Union, Canada, Switzerland, and Norway among others. Given the lack of an international base, regions and nations also investigate national solutions to adapt and mitigate the above-mentioned adverse effects of the Paris Agreement. One such regional legal instrument is the European Union's Carbon Border Adjustment Measure (CBAM).

This chapter will investigate the CBAM as an innovative but complex legal instrument. It will explain the framework in which it was conceived, what it wishes to establish, and what initial and potential scope is envisaged by its creators. This chapter will also discuss the difficulties that can result from the CBAM proposal, and the consequences of the CBAM at a global level. It will finally lay out a conclusion which points out that the implementation of CBAM could lead to the opposite effect to what European lawmakers want to achieve and instead heavily damage Europe's relations with economic and other allies and partners at a time of economic dislocation for many EU partners in the Global South.

1. The Functioning of the CBAM

a. Foundational Principles

After a public consultation on the CBAM in 2020, the European Commission published an Inception Impact Assessment explaining that the CBAM would aim to ensure *"that the price of imports reflect more accurately their carbon content"*.[5] The same assessment determines that any CBAM should only apply to imports entering the EU. The European Parliament adopted a resolution on *"A WTO-compatible EU carbon border adjustment mechanism"* in the beginning of 2021.[6] In it, the European Parliament confirmed its support for the CBAM *"provided that [it] is compatible with WTO rules and EU free trade agreements (FTAs) by not being discriminatory or constituting a disguised restriction on international trade"*.[7] The CBAM *"should be exclusively designed to advance climate objectives and not to be misused as a tool of protectionism, unjustifiable discrimination or restrictions"*.[8] With this support of the European Parliament, in which it created the contours of an acceptable CBAM, the European Commission presented its proposal for a Regulation on the establishment of a Carbon Border Adjustment Mechanism later in 2021.

Within the above-mentioned framework, the European Commission wants to introduce a cost related to the carbon content of imported products. The CBAM is the means of achieving that objective and a corner stone legislation to reach the goal of a 55% reduction of carbon emissions by 2030 compared to the 1990 emissions.[9]

When introduced, the CBAM will require economic operators in the European Union to declare the CO2-emissions embedded in the imports and buy certificates from a yet to be established CBAM Authority in the EU to

---

[5] . "Commission Staff Working Document, Impact Assessment Report - Accompanying the document, Proposal for a regulation of the European Parliament and of the Council establishing a carbon border adjustment mechanism", European Commission, July 14, 2021, 5, https://eur-lex.europa.eu/resource.html?uri=cellar:be5a8c64-e558-11eb-a1a5-01aa75ed71a1.0001.02/DOC_1&format=PDF.

[6] . "European Parliament resolution of 10 March 2021 towards a WTO-compatible EU carbon border adjustment mechanism", European Parliament, March 10, 2021, https://www.europarl.europa.eu/doceo/document/TA-9-2021-0071_EN.html.

[7] . European Parliament Resolution, Art. 7.

[8] . Ibid.

[9] . "Communication From The Commission to the European Parliament, the Council, the European Economic and Social Committee and the Committee of The Regions, 'Fit For 55': Delivering the EU's 2030 Climate Target on the Way to Climate Neutrality", European Commission, July 14, 2021, 1, https://eur-lex.europa.eu/legal-content/EN/TXT/PDF/?uri=CELEX:52021DC0550&from=EN.

pay for the carbon content of the goods that are imported into the EU.[10] This means that covered products from non-EU countries with a environmentally less advanced production method would become more expensive upon their import into the EU. Given that countries from the Global South have specifically requested a slower pace of climate policies within the Paris Agreement, this could mean that exactly these countries could be hit first by the introduction of the CBAM.

b. Scope

· Products and Countries

The CBAM is to be created as a so called notional Emission Trading System (ETS) for imported products into the EU.[11] This means that the CBAM would function as an ETS but for non-EU goods imported into the EU.[12] The real difference with the EU ETS is that the certificates in the CBAM, contrary to the allowances under the EU ETS, would not be tradeable among the businesses to which the regulation applies. However, just as the EU ETS, the CBAM would be determined by a price linked to the carbon content that is embedded in imported products. Currently the CBAM proposal is limited to five types of goods: cement, electricity, fertilizers, aluminum, and iron and steel.[13] However, during the discussions in the European Parliament and in the Council of the European Union (Council) there were indications that lawmakers would prefer to expand the scope, for instance to copper and cooling gasses among others. It is therefore likely that, at the first opportunity, the product scope of the CBAM will be expanded. Annex I of the CBAM Regulation clarifies that also processed products from the above-mentioned goods are considered in the scope of the CBAM when they originate in third countries. The EFTA countries, i.e. Iceland, Liechtenstein, and Norway, would be exempt since these countries already have their own ETS, which functions on the same basis as the

---

10 . Proposal for a Regulation of the European Parliament and of the Council establishing a carbon border adjustment mechanism, European Commission, July 14, 2021, 1, https://eur-lex.europa.eu/resource.html?uri=cellar:a95a4441-e558-11eb-a1a5-01aa75ed71a1.0001.02/DOC_1&format=PDF
11 . Giulia Bedini, "EU's carbon border levy should resemble a 'notional' ETS, Dombrovskis says,"Mlex February 18, 2021, https://mlexmarketinsight.com/news/insight/eu-s-carbon-border-levy-should-resemble-a-notional-ets-dombrovskis-says .
12 . The EU ETS is further explained under title 3.1. of this chapter.
13 . "Annexes to the Regulation of the European Parliament and of the Council establishing a carbon border adjustment mechanism," European Commission, July 14, 2021, 1 – 3. https://eur-lex.europa.eu/resource.html?uri=cellar:a95a4441-e558-11eb-a1a5-01aa75ed71a1.0001.02/DOC_2&format=PDF.

EU ETS or are even connected to it.[14] Unless there is a well-established carbon price paid in the country of origin, recognized by the European Commission, a carbon measure will be applied to covered products coming from non-EU countries. Least-developed countries as well as emerging markets will therefore be the focus of this measure as they have negotiated a slower process towards climate neutrality and objected to a global price on carbon content.

- *Emissions*

The CBAM would cover, after a certain time of implementation, both direct and indirect carbon emissions. Direct emissions are the carbon emissions which result from the industrial process of a product or good and over which the manufacturer has direct control, such as, for instance, the CO2 that is emitted to produce a ton of aluminum. Indirect emissions relate to the production of goods, such as the CO2 emitted by the method of electricity generation used to produce that ton of aluminum.[15] Indeed, a megawatt of electricity coming from an offshore wind farm does not produce the same amount of CO2 as a megawatt of electricity produced by the burning of coal. This means that the CO2 that is released during the production of a CBAM-covered good as well as the CO2 that comes from the raw materials, parts, and other inputs that are used in the manufacturing process will be covered under the CBAM. However, as this is a very complex endeavor, which will likely require cooperation from non-EU partners, the CBAM would, at its entry into force, only cover direct emissions and start with using default emissions. Default emissions are emissions that the EU will determine per country and will reflect an average carbon emission to produce a covered product in that country. For instance, Morocco's aluminum production, in the absence of an EU recognized CBAM mechanism, will be given a default emission by the EU, based on the carbon content of all the inputs for the aluminum produced in Morocco. The EU will thus look at Morocco's facilities and determine how much CO2 is emitted by all these facilities and then determine what the default emission is for aluminum in Morocco. However, this means that Moroccan aluminum produced with electricity coming from a solar field will pay as much CBAM Certificates as Moroccan aluminum produced next to a coal plant.

---

14 . "Annexes to the Regulation on the Carbon Border Adjustment Mechanism (CBAM)", Annex I, 4.
15 . "Proposal for a Regulation of the European Parliament and of the Council establishing a carbon border adjustment mechanism, European Commission," July 14, 2021, 4, https://eur-lex.europa.eu/resource.html?uri=cellar:a95a4441-e558-11eb-a1a5-01aa75ed71a1.0001.02/DOC_1&format=PDF

c. CBAM Administration

The introduction of the CBAM requires a serious administrative effort from both economic operators and the EU institutions. In order to properly govern the necessary filings of reports, the buying and selling procedure as well as the issuing and surrendering process of CBAM certificates, a CBAM Authority is to be created. The actual importation of the goods, covered under the CBAM, would have to be declared by an 'authorized declarant' to the national customs authority of the EU Member State where the goods are declared for entry into the EU. The customs authority would then communicate with the CBAM Authority which would further govern the mechanism. The CBAM Authority would be financed by the income generated from the trade in CBAM Certificates. Therefore, the authorized declarant would have to submit a CBAM declaration.[16] In this declaration, the authorized declarant should declare the total amount of imported goods during the previous year.[17] The declarant will be required to report the emissions embedded in the goods imported into the EU.[18] The declarant should also surrender the number of CBAM certificates that corresponds with that total amount of embedded emissions.[19] In the case where the authorized declarant has paid a carbon price "*in the country of origin for the declared emissions*", the number of CBAM certificates that should be surrendered in the EU can be reduced.[20] However, the authorized declarant is responsible for ensuring that the declared CO2-emissions are verified by an independent verifier that is accredited by the CBAM Authority. This means that the CBAM Authority will keep a register of independent verifiers as well as a register of controlled production facilities in third countries. If the authorized declarant would fail to comply with the assignments mentioned above, or the declarant would provide false information, he or she could be held liable and face criminal prosecution.

Since the CBAM is a legal innovation, the European Commission decided that it was better to introduce the measure by using default emissions.[21] This means that the EU would set emission levels per country. It would be up to companies to prove they are below these default levels, which would then have to be verified, in order to be able to qualify for fewer CBAM certificates.

---

16 . "Proposal for a Regulation establishing the Carbon Border Adjustment Mechanism," Art.6, 30.
17 . Ibid.
18 . Ibid.
19 . Ibid.
20 . Ibid., Art. 9.
21 . Ibid., Art. 7.2.

However, this practice has been heavily criticized by both the European business sector, which is not keen on such a heavy burden of proof, and by trade partners of the EU, which do not appreciate that industry using electricity from a hydro power plant is treated equally than industry that uses electricity coming from a coal burning plant in the same country. These default emissions are especially negative for developing countries.

2. The Framework In Which the CBAM Was Conceived

As set out under title two of this chapter, the Carbon Border Adjustment Measure is a complex and innovative legislative proposal that combines environmental law with trade law. It is also created at a time when politics have moved away from unrestricted free trade towards industrial autonomy. It is for these reasons that it is relevant to understand the broader framework in which the CBAM was conceived and why, consequently, it is a recipe for disaster.

a. The EU's Emission Trading System

It is important to understand that there is an inherent link between the CBAM and the EU's ETS. The EU's ETS finds its origins in the 1997 Kyoto Protocol, which built on the 1992 UNFCCC in which 192 countries agreed that man made carbon emission is driving climate change.[22] The Kyoto Protocol led to an international commitment to cut carbon dioxide (CO_2), hydro-fluorocarbons (HFCs), Methane (CH_4), Nitrogen trifluoride (NF_3), nitrous oxide (N_2O), per-fluorocarbons (PFCs), and sulphur hexafluoride (SF_6), also called Green House Gasses or GHGs.[23] The Kyoto Protocol has led to the use of different, more environmentally friendly gasses in sprays and the replacement of cooling gasses, called F-gasses, in fridges and air-conditioning units by substitutes that are friendlier to our planet. The same Protocol has also led to national legislation, pushing industry to reduce CO_2 and NOx emissions of road vehicles.[24] Parties to the Kyoto Protocol have previously discussed the idea of a global emission trading system but no

---

22 . "Kyoto Protocol to the United Nations Framework Convention on Climate Change", UNFCC, 1998, https://unfccc.int/resource/docs/convkp/kpeng.pdf.
23 . Ibid., Annex A, 19.
24 . "Proposal for a Regulation of the European Parliament and of the Council setting emission performance standards for new passenger cars as part of the Community's integrated approach to reduce CO2 emissions from light-duty vehicles," European Commission, December 19, 2007, 3, https://eur-lex.europa.eu/LexUriServ/LexUriServ.do?uri=COM:20 07:0856:FIN:EN:PDF.

consensus could be found.[25] Thus, even though signatory countries to the Kyoto Protocol discussed an ETS, they failed to agree on a global ETS by the entry into force of the Protocol in 2005. The EU, along with some other nations, meanwhile, moved forward with the idea. By the Kyoto Protocol's entry into force in 2005 the EU started with its own ETS on the EU market.

The EU ETS is a cap-and-trade system, which provides for an amount of CO2 allowances that can be traded between in-scope companies and in which CO2-intensive industries are allocated free emissions in order to remain competitive internationally.[26] However, at each revision of the ETS, the amount of the 'accepted maximum' of CO2-emissions has been reduced, and the price of carbon allowances has increased as a consequence. Before the start of the war in Ukraine, which temporarily lead to plummeting CO2-prices, a ton of CO2 emissions cost €98.[27] In this context, it is important to clarify that in-scope companies with less CO2-emission can trade their excess allocation of CO2-emissions with other EU ETS-covered businesses that lack CO2-emission rights so as to allow them to produce at a normal level.[28] However, the European Commission does not foresee free allowances nor trade in Certificates between in-scope companies under the CBAM. Certificates are bought from and surrendered directly to the CBAM Authority. This discrepancy between the ETS and CBAM is the reason why non-EU countries are accusing the EU of protectionism and discrimination.

b. From Subsidy for Domestic Producers to Cost at The Border for Importers

In its Fit for 55 legislative package, the European Commission also proposes to overhaul the ETS.[29] The Commission determined that if the EU wishes to achieve its 55% CO2-reduction target by 2030, the EU would have to get rid of free allowances in its ETS since these allowances enable

---

25 . Kyoto protocol, Art. 17.
26 . "EU Emissions Trading System (EU ETS) – 'A cap and trade' system, European Commission, https://climate.ec.europa.eu/eu-action/eu-emissions-trading-system-eu-ets_en#a-cap-and-trade-system.
27 . "EU Carbon Permits," section : Summary, Trading Economics, https://tradingeconomics.com/commodity/carbon.
28 . "EU Emissions Trading System (EU ETS) – 'A cap and trade' system, European Commission, https://climate.ec.europa.eu/eu-action/eu-emissions-trading-system-eu-ets_en#a-cap-and-trade-system.
29 . "Proposal for a Directive of the European Parliament and of the Council amending Directive 2003/87/EC establishing a system for greenhouse gas emission allowance trading within the Union, Decision (EU) 2015/1814 concerning the establishment and operation of a market stability reserve for the Union greenhouse gas emission trading scheme and Regulation (EU) 2015/757", European Commission, July 14, 2021, 9, https://ec.europa.eu/info/sites/default/files/revision-eu-ets_with-annex_en_0.pdf.

industries in Europe to take a slower pace in 'greening' their CO_2-intensive production.[30] EU Member States are on the same page with the European Commission since free allowances are *de-facto* subsidies that have to be provided from EU Member States' budgets. Therefore, eliminating free allowances alleviates budgetary pressure on EU Member States.

A surging CO_2-price in the EU's ETS combined with a significant reduction in CO_2-emission allowances puts heavy pressure on EU industry. Indeed, business will be pushed to increase efforts to de-carbonize European production. Given the EU's wish to increase the pace of de-carbonization, it is argued by business that, without compensation, European industry could become uncompetitive, even on the domestic market, against environmentally less friendly – and therefore cheaper – competition from non-domestic producers.[31] In order to limit carbon leakage, without adding new budgetary pressure on governments through subsidies, the EU has opted for a notional ETS for non-EU goods in the form of the Carbon Border Adjustment Measure. This way, importers of non-EU products into the EU which are in the scope of the CBAM, are paying a price for their respective carbon content. The EU and its Member States believe that in this way, a level playing field can be created between environmentally friendly produced European products and non-European products that are produced outside the EU in an environmentally less friendly way. However, this only covers the issue inside the European internal market. Business is also requesting a solution for exports. After all, European business does not only produce goods in Europe for the European consumer. It exports these products to the rest of the world. To remain competitive internationally, the levy on carbon must be arranged in a way which safeguards competitiveness towards non-EU goods that did not incur the costs (or at least much less) in their countries of origin for the direct and indirect carbon emissions during production. An electric vehicle (EV) produced in the EU with European alloyed steel would have to pay, not just for the environmentally friendlier produced European alloyed steel but also for the environmentally friendlier generated electricity with which the alloyed steel was produced. If the same EV was produced with imported Chinese alloyed steel, the EV manufacturer in the EU would have to pay a CBAM. However, the Chinese competitor does not need to pay for the direct and indirect carbon content in the Chinese alloyed steel. This would mean that, even before considering all tariff and

---

30 . Ibid., 18.
31 . "Carbon Border Adjustment Mechanism (CBAM) Proposal", Eurometaux, October 6, 2021,
11 . https://eurometaux.eu/media/lpeo0it1/eurometaux-cbam-position-paper-06-10-2021-final.pdf.

non-tariff barriers in place, European EV's would become substantially more expensive in non-domestic markets compared to their Chinese competition. Without a solution for exports, carbon leakage for the part of production that is currently done in the EU but destined for non-EU markets could occur. European lawmakers have understood this risk and have been looking into a form of export rebate. However, any export rebate risks being incompliant with the rules of the WTO multilateral trading system as it would be considered an export subsidy, which is prohibited under the above-mentioned rules.

c. A WTO Compliant CBAM That Works for Trading Partners of the EU

It is important to underline in the discussion about the EU's commitment to introduce a CBAM that the European Commission does not envisage to provide exemptions for the Least Developed Countries (LDC's). As a consequence, concerns have arisen about the unfair burden that could be placed on many countries in the Global South, and on LDC's in particular, if they are not exempted.[32] In its CBAM resolution, the European Parliament suggests that LDCs could possibly become beneficiaries of the revenues generated from the CBAM.[33] One option the European Parliament is considering is an increase in the EU's contributions to international climate finance.[34] Nonetheless, even though some members of the European Parliament have suggested to exclude LDCs from the CBAM, the Commission is of the opinion that excluding these countries, or other countries with a carbon price in place, from the scope of application of the CBAM, would also make the CBAM incompatible with the rules of the MTS. WTO rules provide for preferential tariff treatment for goods imported from LDCs. These rules even explicitly permit what is called *"special and differential treatment"* (SDT) for WTO Members with developing country status. The European Commission argues that, since LDCs have a different or no ETS in place, it is impossible to exclude them from the scope of the CBAM. LDCs are therefore very concerned about what the impact on them will imply and whether the CBAM will not disproportionally harm their much-needed preferential access to the EU market. However, the EU does not only face a serious diplomatic pickle with LDCs over the CBAM. Other countries, from

---

32 . "LDCs and the proposed EU Carbon Border Adjustment Mechanism", UN, May 4, 2021, https://www.un.org/ldcportal/news/ldcs-and-proposed-eu-carbon-border-adjustment-mechanism.
33 . European Parliament Resolution, Art.33.
34 . "LDCs and the proposed EU Carbon Border Adjustment Mechanism".

the Global South and beyond, have called CBAM a tool for protectionism. India, one of the world's biggest emerging markets, perceives CBAM as discriminatory for emerging economies.[35] Australia, a fully industrialized economy, called CBAM protectionist and discriminatory.[36]

d. A WTO-Compliant CBAM That Works for European Industry

From the above it is clear that there are some important external legal issues for the EU to tackle with regard to its trading partners. In spite of external these issues, within the EU there are also a few legal issues to sort out still since the European business community genuinely fears losing global competitiveness when CBAM is introduced without a compensation for exports. Some therefore call for the introduction of export rebates. Export rebates define as *"the refund of value-added tax and consumption tax already paid on exported goods during production, circulation and sales"*.[37] The European Commission has been skeptical about any type of rebate system linked to the CBAM since it cannot see a way in which a rebate would be compatible with the rules of the multilateral trading system (MTS) as governed within the framework of the World Trade Organization. However, the European Commission stated that it was ready to investigate options to compensate for the loss in competitiveness in non-EU markets. One of the suggestions is to grant funds from the EU Innovation Fund in a more flexible manner to those sectors that fall under the scope of the CBAM.[38] In this way, the direct link between the levy of the CBAM and the compensation for exports would be avoided. This is necessary since export rebates would only be considered WTO compatible when these are linked to taxes on goods, such as value-added taxes. However, since the CBAM is not a tax but a notional carbon measure in the form of a levy, the rebates could be considered as a trade distorting measure that violates the principles of the WTO Agreement on Subsidies and Countervailing Measures.

---

35 . Anna-Loreen Mondorf, "An ever greener Union: The EU, carbon pricing and India", Polis Blog, December 6, 2021, https://polis180.org/polisblog/2021/12/06/an-ever-greener-union-the-eu-carbon-pricing-and-india/.
36 . Trisha Huang and Kevin Adler, "Australia labels possible EU carbon border tax "discriminatory", S&P Global, August 4, 2021, https://cleanenergynews.ihsmarkit.com/research-analysis/australia-labels-possible-eu-carbon-border-tax-discriminatory.html.
37 . "Annex II to the Agreement on Subsidies and Countervailing Measures", WTO Analytical Index, December 2021, I.1, https://www.wto.org/english/res_e/publications_e/ai17_e/subsidies_annii_oth.pdf.
38 . "Directive 2003/87/EC of the European Parliament and of the Council,", October 25, 2003, Art. 10a(8), https://eur-lex.europa.eu/legal-content/EN/TXT/PDF/?uri=CELEX:02003L0087-20200101&from=EN.

The reason why the CBAM is not created as a tax is because the introduction of this environmental policy is not uncontroversial within the European institutions. Given that certain EU Member States are opposed to increasing taxes at European level in general, the European Commission determined it was 'safer' to suggest a Carbon Border Adjustment Measure rather than a tax. A measure can follow the ordinary legislative procedure, in which the proposal of the European Commission is approved by a 50% plus one vote in the European Parliament and a qualified majority vote in the Council.[39] The introduction of a tax, on the other hand, would require unanimity in the Council.[40] The European Commission is of the belief that unanimity is unachievable and has therefore determined that it is better to propose a measure instead of a tax.

Even though options are being explored to address the decreasing global competitiveness of European industry due to CBAM, especially for those goods covered under the measure, the problem of circumvention persists. It is perfectly plausible that in non-EU markets producers organize their environmentally friendlier production for the European market in order to avoid paying CBAM whereas a less environmentally friendly production is employed for non-EU markets. It is therefore questionable whether money from the Innovation Fund would suffice to compensate for the lack in global competitiveness. Equally questionable is whether a more flexible allocation for in-scope good producers is sufficient for compensating the loss in global competitiveness of the European downstream industry, i.e. companies that use the in-scope goods in their production.

e. Textbook example of EU legislation hitting the Global South

The consequence of all the above is that the CBAM is far from easy to establish in a way for it to be effective on the one hand, meaning that it manages to limit carbon leakage, and WTO compliant on the other hand, i.e. that it does not discriminate between members of the WTO nor between domestically produced goods and imported 'like goods' after they have passed the border. This confronts the European Union with a political conundrum. Even though the European Commission claims that it has squared that circle and that it has delivered a proposal that is both effective and WTO compliant, reactions from non-EU countries indicate that

---

[39] . "Consolidated Versions of the Treaty on European Union and the Treaty on the Functioning of the European Union," OJ C 326/1, October 26, 2012, Art. 294, https://eur-lex.europa.eu/legal-content/EN/TXT/PDF/?uri=OJ:C:2012:326:FULL&from=EN.

[40] . "Treaty on European Union and the Treaty on the Functioning of the European Union," Art. 113.

such a claim is certainly not uncontested. In a time in which the MTS has been undermined by years of damaging trade policies of its members, it is worrying that the most powerful union of WTO members, with an intrinsic interest in a world order based on the rule of law, is going ahead with a proposal without providing convincing arguments for business inside and partners outside the EU.

CBAM is not an isolated example of complex legislative proposals hitting the Global South disproportionally in a negative way. As mentioned before, the objectives that the European Union pursues are commendable and uncontested. However, the legal instruments created to pursue these objectives reek of hastiness and ambiguity. In its attempts to reach its climate objectives, the EU is continuously confronted with the burden of alleviating its companies from the economic and competitive disadvantages created by these instruments, and to which its competitors do not have to abide by outside the EU. This is where the EU environmental policy links up to the EU's industrial policy, in which the bloc pursues an 'open strategic autonomy'.[41] The EU wishes to remain open for business but tries to block non-EU competition that does not live up to the same requirements elsewhere. In addition, the EU constantly tries to impose its policy objectives onto other countries and regions in the world by taking unilateral initiatives for multilateral problems. Other examples of recent EU initiatives that display the same hastiness and ambiguity are the Land Use and Land Use Change and Forestry (LULUCF) Regulation, the Renewable Energy Directive (RED), the Conflict Minerals Regulation (CMR), the Forced Labour Regulation (FLR), or the Corporate Sustainability Due Diligence Directive (CS3D) among others. These regulations and directives all pursue the goal of a more sustainable world but contain elements of protectionism in them at the same time. LULUCF and the RED, for instance, could have serious negative consequences for palm oil producers whereas palm oil arguably needs less land use and provides more energy when compared to rape- and flaxseed grown in the EU. The CMR, already implemented for some time, still has not led to the establishment of a list of risk countries. The establishment of such a list would lead to a retraction of European activities in certain countries, especially in the Global South. The same goes for the FLR and CS3D. If poorly implemented, these will guide European business away from countries mainly in the Global South, leaving space for other dominant economies with less ambitions when it comes to sustainability

---

41 . Eric Van den Abeele, "Towards a New Paradigm in Open Strategic Autonomy?", - Working Paper 2021.03, (Brussels: European Trade Union Institute, 2021), https://ssrn.com/abstract=3873798 or http://dx.doi.org/10.2139/ssrn.3873798.

and the respect for human rights. This would not only lower the economic output for countries in the Global South, but would also not be helpful when it comes to improving human rights, health, labor, and environmental standards in these countries.

3. Climate and Protectionism

In normal circumstances, the above-mentioned reactions and comments about such a ground-breaking legislative proposal would lead to reflection and conciliation. However, under the pressure of the French Presidency of the Council and with the French Presidential elections of April 2022 in mind, the Council did not explain or clarify the instrument with business inside the EU nor with its trading partners. It seems that preference was given to first start the measure and solve problems along the way of implementation. Some would argue that this is a very poor way of regulating. Others argue that, in a complex world, with little time to save the planet, this is the only way forward. What is certainly true is that the CBAM is a polarizing piece of legislation. However, in these extremely volatile times of international tensions, why is it that the European Union seems to be in such a rush with implementing the CBAM? There are arguably few benefits for the EU to pursue the CBAM in the state in which it is proposed.

One could argue that the climate crisis urges the EU to take the lead and implement drastic measures to achieve much-needed policy goals, such as a 55% reduction in CO_2-emission by 2030 and climate neutrality by 2050, as set out in the European Green Deal. The CBAM, with all its pros and cons, is deemed so essential to achieve the objective that there is simply no time left to wait. In this regard, business, and trading partners alike, must—just as the EU does—adapt along the way during implementation. This said, this argument is clearly contested by business and international partners of the EU. First, the CBAM is not the only legislative proposal made by the EU to achieve its climate objectives. A hasty adoption of the CBAM for that reason only should make European lawmakers wonder how strong - or weak - the other tools to fight climate change are. Secondly, pushing for the adoption of CBAM seems to provoke negative reactions from all kinds of partners. The European Union fails to convince partners of the real reasons behind the introduction of many of its climate policies. They seem to be under the impression that proposals such as the CBAM are used for protectionist rather than for climate reasons. In this light it did not help that France was presiding in the Council and pushed the CBAM through the European legislative process amidst the French presidential election campaign with

Emmanuel Macron as incumbent, who favors an *"open France within a Europe that protects"*.[42]

It is worrying for the EU that so many partners experience the EU as protectionist. Yet, the Union presses on even though the European Commission itself has stated that the EU is more vulnerable when the 'rule of might' prevails over the 'rule of law'. The European Union, which is much more than a customs union, but far less than a (con)federation of nations, has an intrinsic interest in a world order based on the rule of law. Even though it can use its socio-economic strength in its international relations, the Union has proven itself unable to force others to adhere to what the Union considers the right path forward. Many European lawmakers understand this. Many of the same European lawmakers also understand that when an economy uses its socio-economic powers to force other economies into submission, this backfires for the powerful economy since it requires, in this case, the EU to undermine the only strength it has: its economy. A good illustration for this is the sanction not to import Russian steel into the EU. Russian steel is now being sold in other countries of the world and processed in products that compete on the European market. The EU had to introduce additional sanctions in order to keep those goods out of the European market but it does not solve the competitive disadvantage on non-EU markets if those markets do not follow the same sanction, namely blocking processed steel products with Russian steel content from their markets.[43] It is for that reason that the European Commission has stated from the start of the CBAM discussions, that whichever measure comes out of the democratic process, the CBAM should be compliant with the rules and regulations that govern the MTS. This implies that a CBAM must respect the fundamental principles of international trade law, i.e. the Most Favored Nation (or MFN) principle of Article I of the General Agreement on Tariffs and Trade (GATT), and the national treatment principle of Article III of the GATT. Therefore, the CBAM should not discriminate between members of the WTO, nor should it discriminate products from non-EU WTO members once they have passed the borders of the EU. In essence, it should not be, nor should it be perceived as being a tool for protectionism rather than a tool to counter carbon leakage. Failing to convince partners in the legislative

---

42 . Solenn de Royer and Cécile Ducourtieux, "Comment Emmanuel Macron entend s'imposer à Bruxelles", Le Monde, June 22, 2017, https://www.lemonde.fr/europe/article/2017/06/22/comment-emmanuel-macron-entend-s-imposer-a-bruxelles_5149128_3214.html.

43 . Council Regulation (EU) 2022/1904 of 6 October 2022 amending Regulation (EU) No 833/2014 concerning restrictive measures in view of Russia's actions destabilising the situation in Ukraine, OJ L 259 I/7, October 6, 2022, Art. 1,4, https://eur-lex.europa.eu/legal-content/EN/TXT/PDF/?uri=OJ:L:2022:259I:FULL&from=EN.

process could lead to more problems throughout the implementation, either through countermeasures or through copied CBAMs all working on a similar but different basis and, with that, leading to even more disruption for intra-depending global value chains.

4. Local-for-Local Is the New Normal

The European Union has an undeniable problem in explaining the Carbon Border Adjustment Measure to its international partners. But the Union also seems to underestimate the magnitude of the effect of the CBAM as a fire accelerator for global economic disintegration. Many politicians in favor of the measure see this legal innovation as an instrument to de-carbonize Europe. However, others warn that it could also lead to a de-industrialization process in Europe.[44]

Economic sanctions against Russia have isolated the country and require Russia to reinvent its domestic industrial base to be self-sufficient. "Made in India" is a program of the Indian government that aims to improve the industrial autonomy of India.[45] China pursues its Made in China 2025 policy, with which Beijing wishes to make China technologically independent from the rest of the world by 2025.[46] The EU itself pursues in its newest industrial strategy an "*open strategic autonomy*", in which the bloc wishes to become less dependent on other regions of the world in so-called strategic sectors.[47] The USA, in turn, is arguably on an inward trajectory since the terrorist attacks of 9/11. It is in this framework that an important industrial evolution is taking place on a global scale, i.e. 'local-for-local' manufacturing.

With local-for-local manufacturing, business sources locally to sustain local production. This local production is compliant with all local legislation, which is needed in order to supply the local consumer in accordance with its local values. However, the result is that the business sector is in a process of decoupling its global value chains. Rather than sourcing steel from China

---

[44] . Andreas Rogal, "Carbon Border Adjustment Mechanism (CBAM) will stem 'carbon leakage', European Commission tax and customs chief tells MEPs", The Parliament Magazine, September 13, 2021, https://www.theparliamentmagazine.eu/news/article/carbon-border-adjustment-mechanism-cbam-will-stem-carbon-leakage-european-commission-tax-and-customs-chief-tells-meps.

[45] . "Major Initiatives", PMINDIA, https://www.pmindia.gov.in/en/major_initiatives/make-in-india/.

[46] . Elisa B. Kania, "Made in China 2025, Explained", The Diplomat, February 1, 2019, https://thediplomat.com/2019/02/made-in-china-2025-explained/.

[47] . Cristiano Cagnin, et al., "Shaping and securing the EU's Open Strategic Autonomy by 2040 and beyond", EUR 30802 EN, (Luxembourg: Publications Office of the European Union, 2021), https://publications.jrc.ec.europa.eu/repository/handle/JRC125994.

to produce one type of vehicle in Europe for the world, the Chinese steel is sourced to produce a Chinese car for the Chinese consumer.

At first sight, this change could be perceived as a welcome evolution, as short chain supply tends to have a weaker impact on the climate. However, for the European economy, in which a lot of employment is created, especially in small and medium sized enterprises, due to their integration in global value chains, local-for-local manufacturing should raise serious concerns with both employers and labor unions.

The industries most integrated into global value chains are the chemical, pharmaceutical, technological and food processing industries. They also require a big and multi-modal logistical sector in which many millions find employment. These industries are at the same time the biggest employers of the European labor force. If the process of decoupling global value chains is pursued, mergers and acquisitions in the coming decade will not happen with the aim to benefit from economies of scale, but rather to guarantee local-for-local production. Instead of specialization and cutting costs based on comparative and absolute cost advantages of one region compared to the other, manufacturing will be organized in less competitive forms, often sustained by substantial subsidies from governments in order to preserve certain production that would otherwise be economically unprofitable.

A clear example of this is the Imported Project of Common European Interest for Microelectronics II.[48] Even though a lot of knowledge about semiconductors is available in the EU thanks to its world-renowned universities and research and development facilities, the bloc lacks most of the necessary inputs to sustain significant production and is dependent on other countries for the supply of raw materials. In an MTS, based on the rule of law, in which the intra-dependency between countries is regulated, there would be no reason for concern. However, in a more decoupled global economy, this requires vast amounts of public funding to produce those same semiconductors in an economically viable way in Europe. Taxpayers' money spent in the IPCEI Microelectronics II is money that cannot be spent for other policies. Furthermore, the question remains what the impact on the quality of those products will be and how prices will evolve when public funding runs out or essential raw material suppliers decide to limit or ban the exports of these raw materials to guarantee strategic production of semiconductors in their own country. The consequence of that is that there is less funding available for other governmental activities.

---

48 . "About the IPCEI", IPCEI, https://www.ipcei-me.eu/what-is/.

Even though some would argue that the Global South could attract more industry in this scenario, there are serious reasons of concern for the Global South. In the context of local-for-local manufacturing, business will favor the biggest markets compared to smaller, less significant ones. A global disintegration of the economy will lead to less supply, arguably less-environmentally friendly supply, and supply of lower quality in the Global South. At the same time, it will reduce the Global South's integration in more local value chains. This local for local strategy will increase the global divide rather than reducing it.

The CBAM, perceived by many trading partners of the EU as a protectionist tool, will lead to the creation of similar CBAMs around the world. Others, from this perception of protectionism, will either sue the EU in the WTO or, given the dire state of affairs in the organization, will instantly retaliate by imposing tariffs or reducing strategic resource supplies to the EU. The fact that business is aware of such possibilities will favor local-for-local manufacturing and will lead to a continuation of the global economic disintegration, which in turn will result in political competition between countries and regions in which the Rule of Might takes over from the Rule of Law.

5. Conclusion

Early in the new millennium, the world failed to create a global emission trading system. It also failed to put a global price on carbon. Nonetheless, the EU, along with a few other countries, pursued their own Emission Trading System in which business must pay a price for the carbon emissions that follow from their industrial processes. However, to avoid carbon leakage, carbon intensive industries were subsidized through free emission allowances. Now, in order to meet the new and more stringent climate objectives, these allowances must disappear, and the EU wishes them to disappear sooner than originally scheduled. This puts a heavy burden on carbon intensive industries and their downstream users in the EU since they must improve their production methods faster than originally planned. The required investments are only economically justifiable if European business remains competitive. However, it risks becoming uncompetitive, both internationally as well as domestically, if it has to compete with cheaper imports from countries where less or no such price is put on carbon emissions. Hence, the creation of the CBAM.

The CBAM is a complex legal innovation and is seen as an instrument to create revenue from imported goods based on their direct and, at a later stage, indirect carbon content. As such it should create a level playing field on the European market between 'green' EU goods and 'grey' imported like products. Even two months before the intended introduction of the CBAM, discussions between European legislators were ongoing about the destination of that revenue. Some want to use the revenue for making the CBAM self-sufficient. Others wish to use the revenue to increase the EU Innovation Fund, a fund that is used to assist business in introducing production methods with a smaller carbon footprint. And some lawmakers suggest providing funds for LDCs with the same objective of introducing production methods with a smaller carbon footprint in these countries.

The CBAM is also vastly complex and requires authorized declarants, heavy reporting duties, and a heavy burden of proof with independent verifiers that will inspect production facilities around the world. The CBAM, for it to be effective in fighting carbon leakage, will have to find solutions for European industries that depend heavily on exports. However, such effective solutions seem to make the CBAM WTO incompatible. Even though the EU claims it has proposed a WTO compatible and effective instrument, actions from European business and reactions from trade partners suggest that the EU has failed to convince both EU and non-EU stakeholders of that claim. The fact that the EU was seemingly rushed in adopting the measure, thereby omitting to clarify many open questions, does not help when trying to explain to the business sector and to trade partners the intentions behind the CBAM.

The CBAM therefore seems to be a recipe for disaster. It is good in its ambition, but the CBAM arguably works as a fire accelerant to global economic disintegration. Even though some will argue that this is a positive evolution, as it would bring jobs back from other regions and provide for shorter and therefore more climate friendly supply chains, the fact is that such disintegration is detrimental to the European industrial base and also disproportionately and negatively impacts the Global South. The Global South is also committed to its objectives, as determined in the Paris Agreement, but it is a trajectory that is slower than the European. Given that the EU plans on introducing default emissions per country, even green producers in countries of the Global South will be hit hard by the more polluting production facilities. CBAM could therefore seriously harm access to the European market, displace or destroy value chains and thereby negatively impact revenue and labor in the Global South. The fact that the EU is somewhat aware but seemingly unwilling to address these issues before introducing the CBAM demonstrates that the European Union is currently detached from economic and diplomatic realities, and is most likely going to understand the consequences of that detachment the hard way.

Biographies

Abdelaaziz Aït Ali

Abdelaaziz Ait Ali is a principal Economist and head of the Research Department at the Policy Center for the New South. He joined the Center in 2014 after five years of experience at the Central Bank of Morocco. He worked as an economist in the International Studies and Relations Department and was analyzing the real estate price index and financial asset prices for monetary policy and financial stability purposes. Since then, Abdelaaziz has focused on cyclical and structural issues of the Moroccan economy, including macroeconomic management and industrial policy design. He has published articles on the reform of the exchange rate regime in the Moroccan economy and its implications for macroeconomic regulation, as well as on the evolution of the macroeconomic framework over the last two decades. A. Ait Ali has examined the implications of the recent health crisis and published articles on the macro, social and regional impacts of the pandemic on the Moroccan economy. He has also contributed to the evaluation of industrial policy in light of the challenges facing the Moroccan economy and the new global context. He published an article on the role of the manufacturing sector in growth and made recommendations for a better design and implementation of industrial policy. Abdelaaziz A. Ali holds a Master's degree in econometrics from Hassan II University in Casablanca.

Christian Bachheimer

Christian spent 30 years in Southeast Asia working as a CEO and Group Director in the largest Indonesian conglomerate. As a keen observer of contemporary events of historical importance, he had 'one-in-a-life-time' chance to witness the resurgence of Asia, from the so-called Asian Tigers era to the aftermath of the 1997 financial crisis that resulted in this unprecedented economic and political dynamism across the region.

Christian completed his Master of Arts in International Relations at Fletcher School of Law & Diplomacy, in September 2017, as a capstone in his Asian life. His thesis dealt with China's Foreign Policy impact on Southeast Asia ('Old Wine' in New Bottle: China's Trade, Guns and Ports' The Impact of China's International Trade & Investment Policy on ASEAN countries' foreign policy autonomy) under supervisor Dr. Robert L. Pfaltzgraff.

He presented a paper at the University of Louvain during a conference in December 2018, updated under the title 'China as a Regional Power: A new Tianxia'. Another essay followed in May 2019 titled 'China in an Evolving World: Between Westphalia and Tianxia' that endeavoured to understand China's state of mind as a polity. Christian is also a contributor to East Asia Forum, with "Global Value Chains aren't going anywhere" in 2020, and "China's mercantilist threat to ASEAN is exaggerated" in 2021, both debunking widely held beliefs.

Christian holds a Doctorate in Business Administration (Southern Cross University, 2003, Australia – Thesis "A Strategic Model for Global Capital Intensive Industries"), a Sloan Master of Science (London Business School, 2008, UK, Thesis 'Industry structure Evolution: A Case study of the Ophthalmic Lens Ecosystems') and an MBA (Edinburgh Business School, UK, 1998).

Currently a Doctoral researcher at SOAS, London; under Dr. Tat Yan Kong and Dr. Michael Buehler, https://www.soas.ac.uk/staff/staff150430.php, Christian is working on unpacking hedging strategies and domestic factors in Maritime Southeast Asia

Rim Berahab

Rim Berahab is Senior Economist at the Policy Center for the New South, which she joined in 2014. She is currently working on themes related to energy issues and their impacts on economic growth and long-term development. Her research areas also cover trade and regional integration challenges in Africa. Previously, she has also worked on questions related to gender inequalities in the labor market of North African countries. Rim spent three months at the International Monetary Fund (IMF), in 2016, in the Commodities Unit of the Research Department. She holds a State Engineering degree from the National Institute of Statistics and Applied Economics (INSEA).

Otaviano Canuto

Senior Fellow at the Policy Center for the New South, principal at Center for Macroeconomics and Development and non-resident fellow at Brookings Institute. Former Vice President and Executive Director at the World Bank, Executive Director at the International Monetary Fund (IMF) and Vice President at the Inter-American Development Bank. He was also Deputy Minister for international affairs at Brazil's Ministry of Finance, as well as professor of economics at University of São Paulo (USP) and University of Campinas (UNICAMP).

Serhat S. Çubukçuoğlu

Dr. Serhat S. Çubukçuoğlu is a senior consultant working at the intersection of international affairs, policy, and media. With 20 years of experience across four continents, his expertise is in policy analysis, strategic planning, and research focusing on the Middle East. He earned his doctorate degree in international affairs from Johns Hopkins University SAIS in Washington DC, and his master's degree from The Fletcher School of Law and Diplomacy at Tufts University. Earlier in his academic career, he received a bachelor's degree in Computer Science and an MBA degree, both from The University of Edinburgh.

Dr. Çubukçuoğlu frequently appears on regional media networks both as a commentator and a moderator, reflecting on the ongoing politico-economic developments and strategic discussions. Also, as a participant to the editorial board of Energy Policy Turkey journal, his publications appeared on a wide range of international outlets including Trends Research and Advisory, The Atlantic Council, Cambridge University's MENAF Manara Magazine, The Fletcher Forum of World Affairs, OnFrontiers, Turkish Heritage Organization, and Koç University's Maritime Forum. Dr. Çubukçuoğlu will join Trends Research and Advisory in Abu Dhabi, UAE as a Senior Fellow for Strategic Studies in January 2023.

In his previous roles, Dr. Çubukçuoğlu executed technology consulting and partnership strategy roles blending a singular mix of broad cross-industry expertise. He combined end-to-end project management and negotiation skills necessary to prioritize, execute, and consistently surpass annual strategic business targets. With expertise in consultancy, research, and policy analysis, his growing interests are in geo-economics and energy security in emerging markets.

Marcus Vinicius De Freitas

Marcus Vinicius De Freitas is Senior Fellow at Policy Center for the New South, focusing on International Law, International Relations and Brazil, and is currently a Visiting Professor of International Law and International Relations at China Foreign Affairs University in Beijing, China. Previously, he was a Professor of The Armando Alvares Penteado Foundation in Sao Paulo, where he served as the coordinator of their International Relations Program from December 2012 until December 2013. He was president of the Sao Paulo Directorate of the Progressive Party, having run for vice governor of the State of Sao Paulo in 2010, where his party polled in third place with more than 1.2 million votes. He also served as the Administrative Director of the Sao Paulo Metropolitan Housing Company until December 2015. Early in 2017, Mr. De Freitas, was a Visiting Fellow of Practice at the Blavatnik School of Government at the University of Oxford. Prior to his current appointment, he was advisor to several investment companies investing in Brazil and Latin America, with particular emphasis on export financing, crypto- assets, crypto-currencies and Blockchain technology. Mr. De Freitas holds an LL.B. (Bachelor of Laws) degree from the University of Sao Paulo, a master of laws from Cornell University and a master of arts in economics and international relations from The Johns Hopkins University School of Advanced International Studies (SAIS).

Amine Ghoulidi

Amine Ghoulidi is a researcher at King's College London currently focusing on geopolitics and security. A career political risk consultant, Amine advises leading multinational corporations on reputational risks and security threats particularly linked to their operations in Africa and the Middle East. He was previously part of a Big Four company's Strategic Threat Management practice based in Washington, DC, where he assisted Fortune 500 companies in assessing business risks across various industries and jurisdictions. Amine is a Fulbright Scholar and has two Master's degrees in geopolitics and conflict analysis from King's College London and the American University in Washington, DC, respectively.

Len Ishmael

Ambassador, Dr. Len Ishmael is a Senior Fellow of the Policy Center for the New South and a Senior Fellow and Distinguished Visiting Scholar of the German Marshall Fund of the United States. She is the Global Affairs Advisor of the Brussels Diplomatic Academy and visiting Professor of the Vrije Universiteit Brussel (VUB) and the Mohammed 6 University, Morocco. Dr. Ishmael is a Commissioner on the Lancet Commission on COVID-19's Regional Task Force for Latin America. She is the former Ambassador of the Eastern Caribbean States to the Kingdom of Belgium and European Union, and past President of the 79-member African, Caribbean & Pacific (ACP) Committee of Ambassadors in Brussels. She is a former Director & Head of the Regional Headquarters of the United Nations Economic Commission for Latin America & the Caribbean; Director General for the Organization of Eastern Caribbean States, Alternate Governor of the World Bank and Director for the Foundation Leadership for Environment & Development (New York) of the Rockefeller Foundation. She is The Fletcher School Tufts University GMAP Endowment Fellow and member of The Fletcher School GMAP Advisory Council. She is the author of several publications and books on the Global South, Geopolitics, Africa-EU relations, China, and the Trans-Atlantic relationship. Her most recent publication as Editor and co-author: Aftermath of War in Europe: The West versus The Global South? will be released in December 2022. Dr. Ishmael was conferred a Doctoral Degree in Development Economics from the University of Pennsylvania, and Global Master of Arts in International Relations and Diplomacy from the Fletcher School of Law and Diplomacy, Tufts University. She received a Master of Arts in Urban Planning from the City University of New York and a Bachelor of Arts in Economics and Geography from the University of the West Indies. She was recognized by King Carlos with the Order of Merit of the Kingdom of Spain in March 2010 for her contributions to the Spanish-Caribbean relationship.

Rida Lyammouri

Rida Lyammouri is a Senior Fellow at the Policy Center for the New South. His research activities focus on geopolitics and international relations in the West African Sahel, a region he has worked on for about a decade. He has extensive experience supporting both governmental and non-governmental organizations in the areas of international aid, development, and security. Some of the topics he covers include countering violent extremism (CVE), conflict prevention and conflict sensitivity, humanitarian access, and migration. Mr. Lyammouri has contributed to numerous in-depth research and analysis reports aiming at building deeper understanding of regional and domestic challenges. He is often solicited by various stakeholders to provide policy recommendations on how to address various security, economic and political challenges related to West African Sahel. Mr. Lyammouri has also been presented as an expert at various conferences in the US, Europe, and Africa and holds a Master's degree in Public Policy with an emphasis on National Security from the School of Policy, Government, and International Affairs at George Mason University.

Badr Mandri

Badr Mandri is an Economist who joined Policy Center for the New South after two years' experience at the Moroccan national statistics office (HCP, High Commission for Planning). His research activities focus on development macroeconomics especially on fiscal policy and development financing. Badr Mandri holds a master's degree in applied economics and is currently a PhD student at Mohamed V University in Rabat.

Rahul Sharma

Rahul Sharma is a former newspaper editor who now advises corporates and governments on policy and business and communication strategies.

A keen world-watcher, he is deeply interested in international affairs, global diplomacy and global economy since they all impact businesses and companies. He is co-founder and former president of the Public Affairs Forum of India, an organization for public and corporate affairs professionals in the country. Sharma is an alumni of the Fletcher School of Law and Diplomacy and curates a foreign policy blog in his free time. He writes and comments on foreign affairs and is the co-editor of the book A New Cold War -- Henry Kissinger and the Rise of China.

He studied journalism in India before starting his career in media in the 1980s. Sharma later lived in Hong Kong when it was still a British colony, Sri Lanka, Singapore and the UAE in his various roles as a correspondent and editor before shifting to consulting a decade ago. As a strategic policy and communication consultant, he has advised governments, industries, and businesses across sectors – helping them build reputation and manage crisis issues. He is a keen traveler, an amateur photographer and a student of history, technology and politics and believes strongly in the power of books.

Isabelle Tsakok

Isabelle Tsakok, development practitioner, policy analyst, researcher, and teacher, is a Senior Fellow at the Policy Center for the New South. She grew up in the Republic of Mauritius, a multi- lingual, multi-ethnic and multi-cultural society. She holds a PHD in Economics from Harvard University, and a BA in Phil/Econ from the London School of Economics. As World Bank staff and consultant, she has focused on agricultural and rural development including on issues of agricultural transformation, food security, and poverty reduction. She has worked in most regions of the developing world, including Africa –North and South of the Sahara; Asia - South, Southeast and East; and Latin America. She has taught courses on agricultural policies and institutions at the World Bank; the School of Agricultural and Rural Department, Renmin University of China; the School of International and Public Affairs (SIPA), Columbia University; and the Université Polytechnique Mohamed VI, Morocco. Her publications address issues of methodology of partial equilibrium analysis for assessing agricultural policies and distortions; and of agricultural transformation from smallholder, subsistence to demand-driven commercial farming. Her latest book publication is Success in Agricultural Transformation: What it Means and What Makes it Happen (Cambridge Univ. Press, 2011).

Kevin Verbelen

Kevin Verbelen is company lawyer and senior expert international trade at Agoria, the Belgian association of technologically inspired companies. Kevin Verbelen provides technical legal advice on international trade and investment as well as on customs law. He is head of the Agoria Academy Customs & Trade, a certified course for customs representatives. He is member of the Steering Committee of the National Customs Forum of Belgium and Chair of the Digital Trade Policy Group at DIGITALEUROPE. Prior to joining Agoria, he worked as International Trade and Investment Policy Advisor at the Department of Foreign Affairs of the regional Government of Flanders. As policy advisor, he assisted in negotiating the Belgian compromise for the trade agreement between the EU and Canada (CETA). He also assisted the Minister-President of Flanders during his annual missions to the World Economic Forum. Kevin Verbelen is also Head of the International Organisations Expert Group of the Brussels Diplomatic Academy, where he teaches Foreign Trade and Investment Policy of the EU, US, and China. Kevin Verbelen holds a Master of Law from the Vrije Universiteit Brussel, specialising in European and International Law. He holds a LL.M

International Trade and Business Law from the University of Arizona, where he was awarded for his excellence in International Environmental Law. He studied WTO-law during his Erasmus exchange at the University of Copenhagen and interned at the Belgian Representation to the WTO in Geneva and at the Belgian Embassy in Nairobi.

Copyright © 2022 by Policy Center for the New South
All rights reserved.

Printed in Poland
by Amazon Fulfillment
Poland Sp. z o.o., Wrocław